THE MARVELOUS HAIRY GIRLS

MERRY WIESNER-HANKS

THE MARVELOUS

Hairy Girls

THE GONZALES SISTERS
AND THEIR WORLDS

YALE UNIVERSITY PRESS
NEW HAVEN AND LONDON

For information about this and other Yale University Press publications, please contact:
U.S. Office: sales.press@yale.edu   www.yalebooks.com
Europe Office: sales@yaleup.co.uk   www.yaleup.co.uk

Set in Bembo by IDSUK (DataConnection) Ltd.
Printed in Great Britain by TJ International, Padstow, Cornwall

Library of Congress Cataloging-in-Publication Data

Wiesner, Merry E., 1952–
    The marvelous hairy girls : the Gonzales sisters and their worlds / Merry Wiesner–Hanks.
        p. cm.
    Includes bibliographical references and index.
ISBN 978-0-300-12733-1 (ci : alk. paper)
    1. Sex role—Europe—History. 2.   Abnormalities, Human—Europe—History.
3. Women—Europe—History.   I. Title.
    HQ1075.5.E85W54 2009
    305.4087'094—dc22

                                                                    2008044089

A catalogue record for this book is available from the British Library.

10 9 8 7 6 5 4 3 2 1

Contents

ঔ৺৹

Illustrations

Cast of Characters

The Gonzales family

PETRUS (c. 1537–c. 1618): born on Tenerife

CATHERINE (?–1623): his wife, probably born in Paris

MADDALENA (c. 1575–c. 1644): daughter of Petrus and Catherine, married and had children

PAULO (c. 1577–?): non-hairy son of Petrus and Catherine, married and had children

ENRICO (c. 1580–1656): son of Petrus and Catherine, married four times and had children

FRANCESCA (c. 1582–1629): daughter of Petrus and Catherine, never married

ANTONIETTA (c. 1588–?): daughter of Petrus and Catherine, probably died young

ORAZIO (1592–1628): son of Petrus and Catherine, married and had children

ERCOLE (1595–?): son of Petrus and Catherine, probably died as an infant

The French royal family

KING HENRY II (1519–59): ruled 1547–59, raised Petrus Gonzales at his court

CATHERINE DE MEDICI (1519–89): wife of Henry II and powerful queen mother

FRANCIS II (1544–60): son of Henry and Catherine, ruled 1559–60, married Mary Stuart, Queen of Scotland

ELIZABETH (1545–68): daughter of Henry and Catherine, married Philip II, King of Spain

CLAUDE (1547–75): daughter of Henry and Catherine, married Charles, Duke of Lorraine

LOUIS (1549): son of Henry and Catherine, died as an infant
CHARLES IX (1550–74): son of Henry and Catherine, ruled 1568–74, married Elizabeth of Austria
HENRY III (1551–89): son of Henry and Catherine, ruled 1574–89, married Louise of Lorraine
MARGARET (1553–1615): daughter of Henry and Catherine, married Henry of Navarre (who was later King Henry IV of France)
FRANCIS (1555–84): son of Henry and Catherine
JOAN and VICTORIA (1556): twin daughters of Henry and Catherine, died as infants

The Farnese family

OTTAVIO FARNESE (1521–86): Duke of Parma, grandson of Pope Paul III
MARGARET OF PARMA (1522–86): illegitimate daughter of Emperor Charles V, governor of the Spanish Netherlands, wife of Ottavio Farnese

ALLESANDRO FARNESE (1545–92): son of Ottavio and Margaret, Duke of Parma 1586–92, general of the Catholic forces in the Dutch wars of religion, married Maria of Portugal
RANUCCIO I FARNESE (1569–1622): son of Allesandro and Maria, Duke of Parma 1592–1622, supported Gonzales family at his court
ODOARDO FARNESE (1573–1626): son of Allesandro and Maria, cardinal in the Catholic Church, provided positions for Enrico and Orazio Gonzales at his palace in Rome

The Wittelsbach rulers of Munich

ALBERT V (1528–79): Duke of Bavaria 1550–79, ardent Catholic, collector of rare objects
ANNE OF AUSTRIA (1528–90): wife of Albert, sister to Archduke Ferdinand II Hapsburg
WILLIAM V (1548–1626): son of Albert and Anne, Duke of Bavaria 1579–97, ardent Catholic, owner of several paintings of the Gonzales family
MARIA ANNA (1551–1608): William's sister, aunt to Emperor Rudolf II

The Hapsburg collectors

FERDINAND II (1529–95): Archduke of Tirol 1564–95, owner of Ambras castle and the Gonzales portraits in it
RUDOLF II (1552–1612): Ferdinand II's nephew, emperor 1576–1612, owner of the largest cabinet of curiosities in Europe

The artists

JORIS HOEFNAGEL (1542–1601): Flemish illustrator, court artist to William V of Bavaria, painter of the emblem book with the Gonzales family in it

JACOB HOEFNAGEL (1575–1630): Joris's son, court artist to Rudolf II, painter of the Gonzales family group portrait

LAVINIA FONTANA (1552–1614): Italian artist, painted the oil portrait of Antonietta Gonzales and made the sketch of a Gonzales sister in pencil

AGUSTINO CARRACCI (1557–1602): Italian artist, painted the group portrait of humans and animals for the Farneses that included Enrico Gonzales

ANNIBALE CARRACCI (1560–1609): Italian artist, Augustino's brother, painted many portraits of gods and heroes for the Farnese palace in Rome

The physicians and scientists

AMBROISE PARÉ (1510–90): French surgeon, author of *On Monsters and Marvels*

ULISSE ALDROVANDI (1522–1605): Italian scientist and collector, author of *Monstrorum historia*, examined Antonietta Gonzales in Bologna

FELIX PLATTER (1536–1615): Swiss doctor and scientist, examined two Gonzales children in Basel

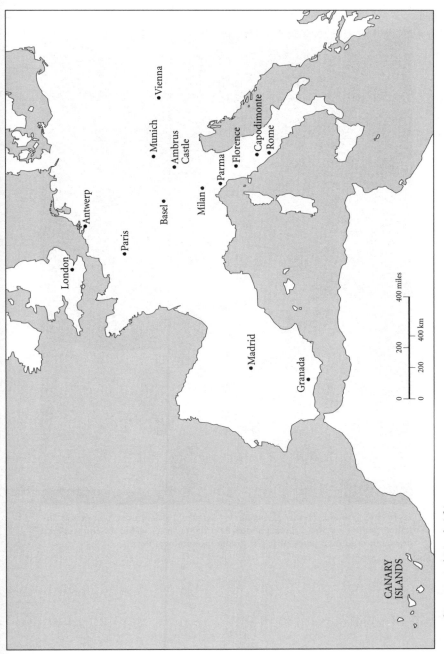

Map of Europe and North Africa

1. Lavinia Fontana, *Portrait of Antonietta Gonzales*, 1590s. In this oil portrait, the Italian painter Lavinia Fontana shows Antonietta in an elaborate embroidered dress and holding a piece of paper giving biographical details.

Preface

THE GONZALES SISTERS AND
THEIR WORLDS

One afternoon in 1594, the scientist Ulisse Aldrovandi visited the home of a wealthy friend in Bologna in Italy. Among other visitors at the elegant home was Isabella Pallavicina, whose noble title was marchesa of Soragna, or wife of the marquis of Soragna, a city near Bologna. With the marchesa was Antonietta Gonzales, the young daughter of Petrus Gonzales. Like her father and like most of her sisters and brothers, Antonietta Gonzales suffered from a genetic abnormality now known as *hypertrichosis universalis*, which meant much of her body was covered with hair. Aldrovandi studied the little girl carefully, and later noted that "The girl's face was entirely hairy on the front, except for the nostrils and her lips around the mouth. The hairs on her forehead were longer and rougher in comparison with those which covered her cheeks, although these are softer to touch than the rest of her body, and she was hairy on the foremost part of her back, and bristling with yellow hair up to the beginning of her loins."[1] This report, along with woodcuts of Antonietta and other hairy members of her family, were included in *Monstrorum historia*, an enormous catalog of human and animal abnormalities mostly written by Aldrovandi, though not published until 1642, long after his death. Aldrovandi also ordered portraits of Petrus Gonzales and one of his daughters for his country villa, to be hung alongside portraits of himself and his wife.

Aldrovandi's friend Lavinia Fontana, a painter from Bologna known for her portraits of nobles and children, may have been at the house that day as well, for she later painted Antonietta's portrait in oils, which now hangs in the castle of Blois in France. In the painting, Antonietta holds a paper that gives details about her life: "Don Pietro, a wild man discovered in the Canary Islands, was conveyed to his most serene highness Henry the king of France, and from there came to his excellency the Duke of Parma. From whom [came] I, Antonietta, and now I can be found nearby at the court of the Lady

2. Lavinia Fontana, *Portrait of a Gonzales Sister*. Done in red pencil, this sketch captures the personality of the little girl better than the more formal oil portrait. Her hair is arranged very differently than in the oil painting, and this portrait may have been of Antonietta's older sister Francesca.

Isabella Pallavicina, the honorable marchesa of Soragna." Lavinia Fontana also drew a sketch in pencil of a little hairy girl, perhaps Antonietta, or perhaps her older sister Francesca, for she looks quite different than the girl in the oil painting. Two hairy girls are shown in the *Monstrorum historia*, described there as age eight and age twelve, and these may be the same as those in Lavinia Fontana's portraits.

Some years before Aldrovandi and Fontana portrayed the young Gonzales sisters, other scholars and artists focused on their older sister Maddalena and their older brother Enrico. An unknown artist at the court of William V of Bavaria painted life-size portraits of Petrus, his non-hairy wife, and their two hairy children, a girl of about seven and a boy of about three. William apparently gave these huge paintings to his uncle Ferdinand II, archduke of Tyrol, who installed them in a portrait gallery at his summer palace, Schloss Ambras, near Innsbruck in the Alps. Ferdinand ordered copies of the paintings—and of hundreds of other portraits in his collection—made in miniature, storing them in several trunks. Here they can still be found, and the palace has given its name to the genetic condition, which is also known as "Ambras syndome." The Flemish painter Joris Hoefnagel saw the paintings while he was William's court painter in Munich, and made his own portraits in watercolor, which he eventually included as the only humans in a four-volume set of miniatures of animals. The Gonzaleses traveled to Basel, where the physician and anatomist Felix Platter examined two of the children, ordered pictures made of them, and later discussed them in a book of medical observations.

Gazing down from the walls of Austrian or French palaces, or up from the pages of illustrated books of the world's unusual creatures, the portraits of the Gonzales family are dramatic and arresting. The father and children are what later came to be exhibited at sideshows as freaks of nature—"dog-faced girls" or "lion-men"—but they are also courtiers and court ladies of the Renaissance, in ruffs and doublets and expensive gowns. This double identity made them intriguing, both in their own day and in ours.

Their genetic condition, though extremely rare—fewer than fifty cases have been documented world-wide since the sixteenth

3. *Portrait of Maddalena Gonzales* by an unknown artist, 1580s. This life-size painting of the oldest Gonzales sister, dressed in a golden gown decorated with pearls and jewels, hung on the walls of Ambras castle in the Alps, alongside portraits of her father, mother, and brother.

century—continues to be a source of fascination. In September 2006 Supatra Sasuphan, a young girl in Thailand with Ambras syndrome who is just about the age of Antonietta when she was examined by Aldrovandi, was featured on news reports around the globe. Two brothers in Mexico have appeared on cable television programs about the wonders of the world. Fictional individuals with Ambras syndrome appear as well—as the main character in the 2001 film *Blood Moon*, as a supporting character in the 2006 biopic *Fur* about the legendary photographer Diane Arbus, and as a plot device in a recent episode of the police drama *CSI*, which featured a young woman with Ambras syndrome who hid herself away in the Nevada desert.

I first saw one of the portraits of Antonietta when I was looking for something else, and like others who saw her or her portrait, I could not forget that face. I knew I had to find out more about her, and as I did, I came to learn more about the rest of her family as well. The Gonzales family left traces in many kinds of record from sixteenth- and seventeenth-century Europe: scientific treatises, medical case histories, letters, diplomats' reports, baptismal and death registers, and account books. From these sources, we can sketch an outline of their lives. We learn that Petrus Gonzales was born on the Canary Islands off the coast of Africa. He came to the French court of Henry II and Catherine de Medici in 1547 as a boy, where the king had him educated in Latin, and gave him a minor position among his hundreds of courtiers. In Paris, Petrus married a woman named Catherine, and the couple had a number of children, most of whom were hairy. The hairy children eventually included three daughters, Maddalena, Francesca, and Antonietta, and two sons, Enrico and Orazio; a third son, Paulo, was not hairy, and a fourth, Ercole, died so soon after he was born that no mention was made of his condition.

Around 1590, the Gonzales family made a slow journey south-ward and ended up in northern Italy, in the city of Parma, ruled by the powerful Farnese family, whose members included popes, cardinals, and generals. They were dependent on the Farnese family for their support, so although they were not exactly slaves, they were not completely free either. The ruling duke of Parma, Ranuccio Farnese, gave Enrico Gonzales to his brother Odoardo, who was a cardinal in the Catholic Church and very interested in the exotic and the unusual. Enrico moved to the Farnese palace in Rome, and later his younger brother Orazio lived there as well. As the paper she holds in the oil portrait indicates, Antonietta Gonzales was also given as a gift by Ranuccio Farnese—to an Italian noblewoman, Isabélla Pallavicina, the marchesa of Soragna, whose daughter was married to a Farnese cousin. In 1602 Enrico Gonzales left Rome and settled in the small village of Capodimonte, which was under the authority of the Farnese family. Here he married and had children. Eventually the other surviving members of the family left Parma and joined him.

The story of the Gonzales family can be told in a few pages, for none of the sources concerning them is very long. By taking a few steps backward and widening our scope, however, we can see and hear a great many things about the times in which they lived. These were times when, to many observers, marvelous things were growing ever more common. "And if there ever was an age when one sees varied and wondrous things," wrote the Italian poet and story writer Matteo Bandello in 1554, "I believe ours is one, for it is an age in which, more than any other, things happen that are worthy of astonishment, compassion, and reproach."[2] The hairy Gonzales family, at once human and monstrous, was among those "varied and wondrous things," but there were many more, which is why Bandello makes his comment. The story of this unusual family connects with many of these, and through them we can see the age of astonishment in a fresh light. We can listen to the voices of people who encountered them or their pictures, look at the pictures themselves and others which were placed near them in books and collections and consider the often tumultuous events that swirled around them. By doing so, we see a different sixteenth century emerging.

The family's story connects with every important change in the era. First among these are European overseas conquests. The Canary Islands where Petrus Gonzales was born was one of the first Spanish colonies and later a stopping-off point to the Americas. He may have been a Guanche, one of the indigenous inhabitants of the Canaries whose defeat by the Spanish in the fifteenth century was a prelude to (and model for) Spanish conquests in the New World. Then there are the religious wars resulting from the Protestant and Catholic Reformations which tore Europe apart. The Gonzales family lived in Paris during a particularly bloody series of these, when preachers and pamphlet-writers damned their religious opponents and angry mobs responded with massacres. The cultural changes we usually call the Renaissance, including new artistic forms and innovative styles of learning, were important for the Gonzales. The French royal court was one center of these, as was the Farnese court in Parma where the Gonzales family spent much of its life. The pictures through which we know the Gonzales family are portraits, the quintessential Renaissance artistic form, made by painters trained in the latest styles. Finally, there were the major changes in science and medicine that proved to be a prelude to the "Scientific Revolution" of the seventeenth century. Those who examined the Gonzales family or wrote about them included physicians trained in Europe's best medical schools and scientists who established museums, botanical gardens, and university departments. The study of abnormal people and animals was a key way that learned men examined the world around them and developed theories about how that world worked.

Not everything was changing, though, and aspects of their lives were very much part of a continuum from an earlier world as well. The Gonzales family spent most of their lives at royal and noble courts, which remained centers of wealth, power, and display just as they had been in the Middle Ages. Petrus married in a Catholic ceremony that had not changed much for centuries, and his children were born with the aid of a midwife, just as children had been in European cities for hundreds of years. The advice his wife got while she was pregnant was of ancient origin, and was accepted and passed on by the physicians and scientists who on other matters were so innovative.

So, the Gonzales family as a whole are a reflection of their own "varied and wondrous" times. The lives of the hairy members of the family were not all alike, however. Petrus Gonzales and his two hairy sons held minor official positions from time to time, so their names show up in royal and noble account books and in official reports. From one of the sons, Enrico, a few letters survive, and the archives of the tiny Italian village where the family ended up provide further information about his business activities and relations with the community.

The three Gonzales sisters, Antonietta, Francesca, and Maddalena, never held an official position or received a salary. They wrote no letters, or at least none that were saved. They thus left a fainter trace in the sources than did their father and brothers. In this they were not very different from other girls and women of their day, however, whose lives have also come down to us largely as whispers. Their fates paralleled those of sisters in many other families—Maddalena married and had at least one child, Francesca remained unmarried until she died as a middle-aged woman, and Antonietta probably died young.

When people looked at the Gonzales sisters, or their pictures, they saw beasts or monsters as well as young women, but this was also true when they looked at most women. The ancient Greek philosopher Aristotle, whose ideas were still powerful in the sixteenth century, had described women as monsters because they were not as perfect as men. Medieval and Renaissance theologians and philosophers placed women between men and animals in the hierarchy of creation, for women, in their view, had less reason than men and were therefore more like animals. The lives of the Gonzales sisters highlight this complex relationship between beastliness, monstrosity, and sex. The story of the Gonzales sisters cannot be told apart from the story of the male members of their family, but much of this book will focus more intently on the girls. This lens brings the world of all women in the sixteenth century into sharper focus, for even among marvels the lives of women and men were very different.

4. Tilman Riemenschneider, *Hairy Mary Magdalene Being Carried to Heaven by Angels*, 1490–2. The German sculptor shows the saint with long flowing hair and covered with fur, details that were added to the ever-expanding story of Mary's life in the Middle Ages. Mary Magdalene was only one of many hairy women whom people had heard about, and whose stories shaped their reactions to the Gonzales sisters.

1

Wonders, Beasts, and Wild Folk

INNER AND OUTER WORLDS IN RENAISSANCE EUROPE

In his descriptions of Antonietta Gonzales, Ulisse Aldrovandi focused on the exact nature of her hair, and on the paper that is part of her portrait of the little girl, Lavinia Fontana described her father as a "wild man." "Hairy" and "wild" were the most common terms used to describe the members of the family, but other words were sometimes used as well—monsters, marvels, beasts. Each of these words carried with it a tradition of stories and associations.

So, just how did people see the extraordinary family? The Gonzales family brought to mind many things at once. Their hybrid nature was what made them fascinating, and what caused them, like other marvelous things of their era, to provoke "astonishment, compassion, and reproach." Confronting any member of the family, or seeing their pictures, people thought about wonders and prodigies, marvelous species, exotic foreign peoples, animals and animal hybrids, and wild folk. When people encountered the Gonzales sisters, they brought with them not only Aristotle's ideas of women as monsters and medieval theologians' ideas of women as irrational animals, but also traditions about hairy women, both saintly and vengeful.

Prodigies and wonders

Most people's first reaction to the Gonzales family was to think that they were weird, which made them want to look at them again. Just as now, sixteenth-century Europeans were fascinated by anything that departed markedly from the norm and the expected. News of a cow born with unusual growths on its body or conjoined human twins or multiple stalks of wheat growing from one seed spread quickly from village to village, and people came to see. When such rumors reached a town, the town council might immediately send out an artist to sketch it and describe it, knowing that the animal or the child wouldn't live very long or that the wheat would soon fall off the stalk. The artist's drawing was turned into a woodcut or engraving, and given to local printers eager to produce things that would sell widely and quickly. Hundreds of copies of this one-page broadside were sold from the printer's shop or on the street. Printers in towns far from where the marvel appeared didn't want to miss out on the action, and so took an engraving from their shelves of something that sounded similar, added a new headline, and sold these too. One deformed calf or set of conjoined twins or miraculous wheat stalk was not that different from another.

Sometimes broadsides simply showed a picture, but often they included a description and interpretation. What did the birth of a misshapen calf or a deformed child or a multiple wheat stalk mean? The German reformer Martin Luther thought that a calf born in 1522 with an unusual flap of skin around its neck was a "monk-calf," for the flap looked like the cowl of a monk's clothing. He had just written a harsh condemnation of monks as part of his call to reform the Christian Church, and was certain that God agreed with him:

> God has given the calf the dress of clergy and a holy cowl. In this, he has undoubtedly put great meaning. It will soon become completely evident that all of monkery and nunnery is only false pretext and lies, just external appearance of a holy, godly life. For until now we poor people have thought that the Holy Spirit was under the cowl, and that such a garment did not cover a frivolous spirit. But God shows with this that it only covers a calf, as if he was saying: It is a scoundrel's cap. . . . If you look at this monk-calf, you see that the cowl is the whole clerical way of life with all of the church services that

5. Lucas Cranach, Woodcut of "monk-calf," 1523. The monk-calf, first shown in a pamphlet written by Martin Luther and his associate Philip Melanchthon, was interpreted as a sign of God's displeasure with the monastic way of life. Catholics later used images of the creature as well, reading it as a sign of God's condemnation of Luther.

they regard so highly with prayers, masses, singing, fasting, etc. But who are they doing these services for? Who is honored with these? What do they hang on? On a calf. For the cowl decorates and clothes a calf, as you see. What is this calf? It is their false idol in their hearts full of lies.[1]

Hans Zimmermann, an Augsburg printer who specialized in broadsides of "true and wondrous" events, was just as certain of the meaning of seventy-three stalks of wheat growing out of one seed as Luther was about the monk-calf. "Every day there are miracles from God," wrote Zimmermann on a broadside displaying the fruitful stalks, "that show how he feeds the whole world with little." The wheat demonstrated the value of sharing the harvest, and was evidence that God would provide "better and larger harvests" for those who lived "good and penitent lives." The birth of conjoined twins was more problematic. The parents of a pair born in 1565 were "pious people who earned their daily bread with hard work,"

6. Hans Zimmermann, Broadside showing conjoined twins, 1565. Conjoined twins were an especially common subject for single-sheet broadsides of marvels and monsters, sold cheaply as sensational "news," and copied by other printers. Such children, if they really existed at all and were not just stories, would have died quickly.

wrote Zimmermann, so "no one can be sure what such a wondrous birth means, for God alone knows." There was no doubt that it was a warning, however, directed especially to "pregnant women and their devoted husbands" who were to live morally and pray to God that he would send them "fruit of the body with a natural appearance and proper limbs."[2]

Zimmermann's comment about God being the only one who really knew what such events meant was widely relevant because pretty much all marvels and wonders were open to different interpretations. Those who thought that monks lived godly lives and performed important tasks viewed the "monk-calf" as a sign of God's displeasure with Luther, who had recently been a monk himself, not with monks as a whole. But most people assumed that whatever they meant, such messages came from beyond the natural world. Even the words used suggested this. "A *monstrum*," wrote St Augustine in the fourth century, which comes "from *monstrare*, to point to, means a marvel that points to some meaning. So *ostentum* ["sign" in English] (from *ostendere*, to show) and *portentum* (from *portendere* or *praeostendere*, to show a long way off) and *prodigium* (from *porro dicere*, to declare things a long way off) all mean a marvel that is a prediction of things to come."[3] Augustine's opinion was shared by many in the Middle Ages, and by both Catholics and Protestants in the sixteenth century. People who stared at the members of the Gonzales family, or saw their pictures on castle walls or in books, sometimes wondered what God had been trying to point to in creating them.

Marvelous species

Marvels that were close to home were usually single individuals, wondrous because they differed so much from what was expected. People were also fascinated by whole species of unusual animals or people that lived in far-away foreign lands. The stories that were told about the Gonzales family always included their origins in the exotic Canary Islands, which hinted at the species of extraordinary beings that had long been read or heard about.

People learned about remarkable species not from broadsides, which focused on what was new and nearby, but from longer written works, including huge encyclopedias of the natural world. The grandfather of these encyclopedias was written by the first-century Roman official and writer Pliny the Elder. His *Natural History*—an enormous collection of geographical features, peoples, animals, objects, and phenomena that Pliny had seen or read about—was copied and recopied in many Latin versions throughout the Middle Ages. Among the numerous things Pliny covers were races of people whose behavior or form made them monstrous:

> Some Sythian tribes, and in fact a good many, feed on human bodies . . . to the north [are those] who drink out of human skulls and use the scalps with the hair on as napkins hung round their necks. . . . On the mountain named Nulus there are people with their feet turned backwards and with eight toes on each foot, while on many of the mountains there is a tribe of human beings with dogs' heads who wear a covering of wild beasts' skins, whose speech is a bark and who live on the produce of hunting and fowling, for which they use their nails as weapons . . . . [There is] a tribe of men called the Monocoli who have only one leg, and who move in jumps with surprising speed; the same are called the Umbrella-foot tribe, because in the hotter weather they lie on their backs on the ground and protect themselves with the shadow of their feet . . . and again westward from these some people without necks, having their eyes in their shoulders . . . the Choromandae [are] a forest tribe that has no speech but a horrible scream, hairy bodies, keen grey eyes, and the teeth of a dog . . . [and] the Astomi tribe, that has no mouth and a body hairy all over; they dress in cottonwool and live only on the air they breathe and the scent they inhale through their nostrils.[4]

The monstrous species were generally found, according to Pliny, beyond the world he knew directly, which meant in Africa or India. Medieval world maps confirmed this idea, placing unicorns, centaurs, manticores, and umbrella-footed people in Africa or Asia.

7. Hartmann Schedel, *Liber chronicarum* (World Chronicle), 1493. Schedel's history of the world includes woodcuts of many of Pliny's monstrous species, including the one-legged Monocoli who used their foot as an umbrella. These illustrations were often copied by mapmakers.

"Africa," wrote the Italian natural historian Pietro Scarabelli, "merits having been dubbed a Theater of Marvels, because she is the fertile mother of monsters."[5]

Scandinavia and Ireland, the other edges of Europe, were also filled with unusual things. "Just as the countries of the East are remarkable and distinguished for certain prodigies peculiar and native to themselves," wrote the twelfth-century clergyman Gerald of Wales in his description of Ireland, "so the boundaries of the West also are made remarkable by their own wonders of Nature. For sometimes tired, as it were, of the true and the serious, Nature draws aside and goes away, and in these remote parts indulges herself in these shy and hidden excesses."[6]

Some monstrous species seemed so fantastic that they could not be placed in any specific location, and mapmakers drew them in the margins of the map, as far away from the Mediterranean (the center of most medieval world maps) as possible. "At the furthest reaches of the world often occur new marvels and wonders," wrote the fourteenth-century English monk Ranulph Higden in his history of the world, "as though Nature plays with greater freedom secretly at the edges of the world than she does openly and nearer us in the middle of it."[7] Borders were where creatures that themselves blurred boundaries—human/animal, animal/bird, species/species—were more likely to be found. Borders were also places of danger, where normal rules did not apply.

Medieval writers as well as mapmakers incorporated Pliny's stories into their own works, describing giants who could turn into animals, dog-headed people, and other wonders. Today, copying the words of another author without attributing them is regarded as plagiarism, a form of intellectual dishonesty. Things were very different in the manuscript culture of medieval Europe, where the only way to get another copy of a work you thought important was to make the copy yourself, or hire someone to do it. Copying was thus essential in the transmission of ideas. More importantly, the writings of ancient authors were viewed as authoritative, not outmoded. Taking stories from Pliny (or concepts from Aristotle or St Augustine) gave your work weight and convinced readers that you knew what you were talking about. Today we praise writers and scholars for the newest ideas, but in medieval Europe the more ancient authorities you could quote, the better. Pliny's monstrous species therefore appear in many types of work, sometimes given a moral meaning—as were the individual wonders found close to home—and sometimes simply viewed as a sign of nature's quirkiness.

This emphasis on the wisdom of the ancients was enhanced, not diminished, by the Renaissance. In the sixteenth century, the Italian artist, architect, and author Giorgio Vasari coined the word "Renaissance" (rebirth) to describe new types of art made by Michelangelo—whom he described as a "genius universal in each art"—and other painters and sculptors. This art looked back to the classical past for its inspiration, and soon Vasari's term was also used to describe literature, education, and other aspects of culture that similarly looked to the ancient Greeks and Romans for models. Artists and writers hoped to recapture the glories of the classical world, so spent long hours wandering around Roman ruins, closely studied ancient statues, and modeled their poetry and epics on those of first-century Roman authors, especially the orator Cicero. Scholars established schools and academies in Italian courts and cities that mainly taught classical literature and history, calling their new curriculum the *studia humanitatis*, or humanism. This self-conscious cultural movement emphasized a break with the immediate past, which proponents of the new styles saw as a "dark," "Gothic," or at best "middle" age—a deep trough between two peaks of civilization, the classical era and their own.

The invention of the printing press with movable metal type, around 1450 in Germany, enhanced the influence of ancient authors. Pliny's *Natural History* was widely printed, and his stories showed up in the works of even more authors than they had before. Pliny was translated into the major spoken languages, including Italian, French, German, and English.[8] People who could not read Latin could still read Pliny's work, and he became the standard authority on certain topics. So, stories about monstrous species were told in cottages as well as scholars' houses, and were never very far from people's minds.

Travelers' tales

Pliny and the many authors who copied him were one source of stories about marvelous beings beyond the borders of Europe, but actual travelers increasingly told tales that were just as fantastic. Thus when people encountered the Gonzales family or their pictures, they recalled other exotic encounters, stretching back over the previous several centuries.

Stories told by the Venetian merchant Marco Polo were among the most stupendous. During the thirteenth century, the Mongols under Genghis Khan and then Kublai Khan controlled an enormous empire stretching from eastern Europe to the Pacific. They welcomed trade and established enough order for travelers generally to proceed safely, and large numbers of merchants, missionaries, and ambassadors crossed the Mongol Empire regularly. One of these merchants was Marco Polo, who apparently spent twenty years in Asia and acted as a representative for Kublai Khan. Shortly after he returned to Europe at the very end of the thirteenth century, he became a prisoner of war during one of the many wars between Italian cities. While in prison, he told tales of his travels to a writer of romance stories, who wrote them up in French. These *Travels of Marco Polo*, as they came to be known, made great reading, so they were translated into other languages, copied many times, and later published. Marco Polo's stories were so amazing that some people who read them doubted whether they could be true, and the book was nicknamed Il Milione – the millions – because the author so frequently described everything as occurring in large numbers. Many people today also wonder about how much of what he reported actually happened, and a few even dispute whether Marco Polo ever went to the Mongol Empire at all, although most people think that he did.

Marco Polo is today the most famous medieval European traveler to the East, but in the fifteenth century the most popular book about the wonders of the East was not Polo, but *The Travels of Sir John Mandeville*. This account of fabulous riches, powerful rulers, and strange species describes the travels of an English knight to Africa and Asia in the mid-fourteenth century, where he was employed by the sultan of Egypt and the Mongol khan. It was translated from the French in which it was originally written into nearly every European language, and printed in multiple editions soon after the invention of the printing press. There are doubts about Marco Polo's exploits, but not about his existence. By contrast, no one today thinks that John Mandeville was a real person, though in the sixteenth century they did. Whoever wrote *The Travels of Sir John Mandeville*— we don't know the exact identity of the author—based it on Polo's reports, stories that dated back to Alexander the Great's eastern conquests, and Pliny's *Natural History*. Pliny's monstrous races make their appearance, as do the Amazons, "noble and wise" female warriors who live without men, elect their queen, and cut off one of their breasts "so that it will not hinder them in shooting."[9]

Marco Polo and Mandeville became essential reading for anyone interested in the strange and exotic, and their stories gradually became part of oral traditions as well. Most people in the sixteenth century could not read, but learned about the world through stories told while they were working or sitting in the evenings in a tavern or at home around a fire. When they got together, people talked about the day's events, friends and acquaintances, and other aspects of village life, but they also told stories, recited poems, and sang ballads about famous folk, unusual creatures, and amazing heroes. Those stories included ones about wondrous beings that originated with Pliny, and about distant lands that originated with Polo or Mandeville. By the sixteenth century, story-telling might involve someone reading from a printed book, or at least showing the pictures in a book bought on a trip to town. Thus stories that appeared in books were familiar even to people who could not read. The flow of information between learned and popular culture went both ways—ordinary people came to know the stories that were in books, and stories told by villagers were included as evidence in books alongside stories that came from Aristotle or Pliny or Polo.

By the time the Gonzales family was living in Paris and Parma, travelers' tales read silently or aloud included those of sixteenth-century voyagers as well as medieval merchants and knights. Among these were the letters of Columbus, which began with one to Queen Isabella and King Ferdinand of Spain after his first voyage in 1492. This was quickly published, first in Spanish and then in many other languages. Letters and reports describing his subsequent voyages flew off the presses, as did those of other mariners and adventurers. The Florentine trader and captain Amerigo Vespucci wrote particularly vivid and extensive descriptions of his various voyages, through which his name became permanently attached to newly discovered lands to the west. Antonio Pigafetta, a Venetian diplomat who traveled with Ferdinand Magellan on his voyage westward in 1521, kept a journal, parts of which were published later in the century. (The publication of Pigafetta's journal, in fact, clinched Magellan's fame as the first to circumnavigate the world, even though Magellan was killed half-way around in the Philippines, and another captain actually achieved this.) Enterprising publishers frequently gathered into single books the most exciting stories from explorers. The Venetian publisher Giovanni Battista Ramusio, for example, included accounts of many journeys in *Navigations and Voyages*, published in 1550 in Italian and eventually growing into three huge volumes. Along with Columbus' journal, Ramusio's volumes contained accounts of the exploits of Vasco da Gama, Hernan Cortés, Francisco Pizarro, and Jacques Cartier, among many others, with Marco Polo thrown in for good measure. His books were pilfered for stories by publishers putting out books in other languages, who often included only the most bizarre and exciting accounts, titling the book "Strange Tales from Foreign Lands" or something similar.

Columbus, Vespucci, and other sixteenth-century explorers found no people with umbrella feet or eyes in their shoulders, but they did find others who seemed nearly as strange. In his letter to Ferdinand and Isabella, Columbus reports that people on the islands where he landed were naked, and treated him and his men with affection and kindness. So as not to disappoint his royal backers, he did note that neighboring islands were said to contain ferocious cannibals, people with tails, and women who fought with bows and javelins. (We are free to imagine how he learned this from people whose language he could not understand.) Vespucci, too, comments on the naked- ness of the indigenous people, and also on their skin color: "their flesh is of a colour that verges into red like a lion's mane; and I believe that if they went clothed, they would be as white as we." He was more fortunate than Columbus in actually finding some of the monstrous races mentioned in Pliny and Mandeville. No cannibals or umbrella-footed people, but there were women whose strength approached that of the Amazons: "a woman reckons nothing of running a league or two, as many times we saw them do; and herein they have a very great advantage over us Christians: they swim (with an expertness) beyond all belief, and the women better than the men: for we have many times found and seen them swimming two leagues out at sea without anything to rest upon."[10]

Although travelers to the New World did not find many of Pliny's monstrous species, what they did find was so amazing that they changed their minds about earlier writers. After traveling in Brazil in the 1550s, the French Protestant explorer Jean de Léry commented, "I have revised the opinion that I formerly had of Pliny and others when they describe foreign lands, because I have seen things as fantastic and prodigious as any of those—once thought incredible— that they mention."[11] The English poet and explorer Sir Walter Raleigh agreed, noting that even the stories in Mandeville that "were held as fables for many years" seemed more believable after the voyages of discovery: "we find his relations true of such things as heretofore were held incredible."[12]

Incredible was not necessarily good, however. Discussing native people in Brazil—where he tried to found a colony in the 1550s— the French adventurer Nicolas Durand de Villegaignon wrote: "they were wild and savage people: remote from all courtesy and humanity, utterly different from us in their way of doing things and in their upbringing: without religion, nor any knowledge of honesty and virtue, or of what is just or unjust; so it seemed to me that we had fallen among beasts bearing a human countenance."[13] Villegaignon's opinion was widely shared among European explorers and colonists all over the Americas, who regularly used terms like brutish and beastly to describe indigenous peoples. Commenting on the indigenous inhabitants of Peru, the Spanish official Juan de Matienzo noted that they were "participants in reason so as to sense it, but not to possess it or follow it. In this they are no different from the animals for they are ruled by the passions."[14] Such judgments were only partially amended by Pope Paul III's declaration in 1537 that the "Indians of the West and the South" were not "dumb brutes," but "truly men," and thus "capable of understanding the Catholic Faith."[15] Most Europeans who did not travel beyond the seas agreed with Villegaignon more than with Pope Paul. Those who knew the origins of the Gonzales family in one of Europe's first colonies, then, could see them as living examples of "beasts bearing a human countenance," and only slightly more brutish than their less hairy kin.

Strange and familiar beasts

Opinions about the wild and animal-like nature of indigenous peoples shaped reactions to the Gonzales family, and ideas about real animals did as well. Members of the family were, in fact, often compared with animals. Aldrovandi describes the young Petrus as a boy "not less hairy than a dog," and Antonietta as a girl "whose face resembles that of a monkey." Ideas about animals were influenced by fables and stories, artwork, sermons, songs, and much else besides. Information about animals came from different sources, but was often gathered together in books called bestiaries, favorite reading for adults and children alike. Handwritten medieval bestiaries described local animals such as horses and hedgehogs, exotic animals such as lions and tigers, and fantastic creatures such as phoenixes (which set themselves on fire and were reborn from the ashes) and manticores (which had the head of a man, the body of a lion, and the tail of a scorpion). The most elaborate manuscript bestiaries, produced for wealthy kings and noblemen, included hand-painted illustrations on nearly every page, but there were smaller ones as well.

8. Manticore, from Edward Topsell's *Historie of Foure-Footed Beastes*, published in London in 1607. Topsell takes the story of the manticore from ancient authors, and notes that it is "bred among the Indians." Renaissance books of animals included exotic monsters and domestic livestock, and their illustrations were sometimes printed separately and hung on walls.

The development of printing brought mass-produced bestiaries, ranging from huge learned tomes in Latin to paper-covered booklets you could carry in your pocket. Smaller bestiaries focused especially on the weird and wondrous, while larger works were more inclusive and scholarly. The sixteenth-century Swiss naturalist Conrad Gesner, for example, includes more than a hundred pages on the horse alone in his massive *Historia animalium*, basing his account on his reading of many authors along with his own observations of live animals, skins, and skeletons. Like Pliny, Gesner's descriptions and illustrations were to be found in translations in many languages, sometimes attributed to him and sometimes not. Joris Hoefnagel copied Gesner in many of the paintings of animals that appear in his volumes of miniatures that begin with the Gonzales family. The English clergyman Edward Topsell published his own *Historie of Foure-Footed Beastes* in 1607, which he claimed was taken from many authors, but was almost all just translations from Gesner.[16] Enterprising printers then pulled words and images from Topsell to produce smaller illustrated bestiaries on cheap paper that sold briskly.

The colorful depictions of the manticore, dragon, and phoenix in bestiaries incorporate information from long-ago times and far-way lands, while descriptions of familiar animals mix exotic stories with everyday observations. Topsell's long description of the cat, for example, begins with a Greek myth about Venus turning a cat into a beautiful woman and then back into a cat when she proved *too* beautiful. He cites ancient scientists on why cats can see in the dark and how they hunt apes in Egypt. Then Topsell includes story after story about how cats behave that would be familiar to anyone who owned a cat, then or now:

> Having taken a Mouse, she first plays with it, and then devours it, but her watchful eye is most strange. . . . [I]t is needless to spend any time about her loving nature to man, how she flatters by rubbing her skin against one's legs, how she wurls with her voice, for she has one voice to beg and to complain, another to testify her delight and pleasure, another among her own kind by flattering, by hissing, by puffing, by spitting, insomuch as

some have thought that they have a peculiar intelligible language among themselves.[17]

Cats could bring illness and death, according to Topsell, particularly to children. "I have heard," he writes, "that when a child has gotten the hair of a cat into his mouth, it has so cloven and stuck to the place that it could not be gotten off again," and the child died. His source for this idea was his neighbors, not ancient authorities—"I have heard," he writes, not "as Aristotle reports"—for the notion that cats can steal away the breath of infants was widely held. (And has not disappeared today.)

Bestiaries shaped what people thought about animals, from strange foreign creatures to household pets, and also about the proper sources of authoritative information. They confirmed that ancient philosophers, medieval scholars, observers in distant lands, and one's own experience all taught largely the same thing. The best-known bestiaries were compiled by university-trained men, often clergymen, physicians, or natural scientists. Such illustrious authors gave the books a further stamp of authority. Stories from broadsheets, encyclopedias, and bestiaries were sometimes mixed together with other material into almanacs or what were termed "books of wonders." Although they relied on oral descriptions from ordinary people for many of the things they contained, their pages also incorporated ancient wisdom and the most up-to-date ideas of highly educated men.

Aldrovandi's *Monstrorum historia* is a perfect example of just this sort of learned book of wonders. Written in Latin for a scholarly audience—as was Gesner's *Historia animalium*—it contains hundreds of pages of accounts and illustrations of human and animal wonders. These include the familiar stories that originated with Pliny and Mandeville, and others based on Aldrovandi's collection of tens of thousands of natural objects, drawings, and paintings. Aldrovandi himself did not publish *Monstrorum historia*, but the former student of his who put it together and published it in 1642 made sure Aldrovandi's name was on it, because his reputation gave the book greater authority. The Gonzales family makes its first appearance in the book—with their portraits—near the beginning, and shows up several more times as well, surrounded by pictures and discussion of other fabulous creatures. Like the cat in Topsell's bestiary, the Gonzales sisters are described in the *Monstrorum historia* in a narrative that blends ancient authorities, direct observations, and neighborhood tales.

Petrus Gonzales and his children reminded people of animals, and Antonietta in particular seems to have been kept as a sort of pet by the marchesa of Soragna. Yet they were clearly *not* animals, and in their hybrid nature they challenged the distinction between humans and animals. In the ancient Greek and Germanic worlds, the boundaries were fluid. In myths and stories, animal–human hybrids such as centaurs and fauns provide wise advice or foolish diversions, and animals teach humans lessons. Gods and heroes change into animals, often having sex with human women while they are in animal form.

Early Christianity sharply separated humans and animals, viewing animals primarily as property or food rather than exemplars, and introducing laws prohibiting bestiality. By the twelfth century, this Christian paradigm of a sharp split between humans and animals began to break down, and people seemed less sure of the distinction. Animals that seemed close to humans, such as monkeys and apes, and human/animal hybrids, appeared more often in art and stories, reflecting concerns that there might be intermediate categories rather than one clear line. The thirteenth-century philosopher Albertus Magnus, in fact, proposed three categories of beings in creation— humans, animals, and "man-like creatures," a category in which he placed apes and Pygmies, both of whose existence he knew about not directly, but from reading ancient authors. The "monstrous races" described in Pliny might be in this third category as well, he speculated. As often happens in such situations, the laws that set humans apart from animals actually became *more* stringent, as people attempted to shore up a boundary line that they thought should be firm but feared was not. Bestiality moved from a minor sin to the worst of all sexual sins, and trials and punishments increased. Stories about animal/human hybrids in the Middle Ages were not tales of wise centaurs as they had been in ancient Greece, but of "unnatural" and "abominable" intercourse between humans and animals that resulted in monstrous creatures. They were thus a visible sign of an invisible sin.

The line between humans and animals could also be crossed by shape-shifting, which appeared in stories and illustrations more often after the twelfth century. Animals turned into humans, usually with the assistance of demonic powers, or demons appeared in the shape of animals. Such demon-animals, called "familiars," became an element in accusations of witchcraft, which grew into a flood in the fifteenth century. Humans might also degenerate into animals through their actions, as the "beast within" overcame their human qualities, of which the most important was reason. Unusually powerful or seemingly crafty animals might thus actually be demons or humans.

Of these shape-shifters, werewolves were the most feared. The early medieval Church forbade people to believe in werewolves, much as it forbade them to believe in the power of witches, for both of these attributed to other beings powers that belonged only to God. Such prohibitions were never effective, and official church opinion changed. By the fifteenth century church officials were regularly trying people as witches and occasionally as werewolves. The *Malleus maleficarum*, an influential handbook of demonology published in 1484, describes werewolves who devoured children and raped women. Demonologists and others solemnly debated what exactly werewolves were. The *Malleus* views werewolves as demons in disguise, but other demonologists and officials thought they were shape-shifting humans. Some doubted whether werewolves could really exist. Henri Boguet, for example, a French official and author of demonologies and legal guides, argued that there were no werewolves, because when a human transformed into a wolf, the skull had to shrink because wolves' skulls were smaller than those of humans. An entire human brain couldn't fit into the new skull, which meant that the person would lose his or her human reason and possibly soul. This loss God would never allow, so werewolves could not exist, according to Boguet's logic.

Boguet's argument remained a minority opinion, and most people believed firmly in the reality of humans that changed into wolves, just as they believed that witches flew through the night to wild orgies and killed children and animals with a glance. Chroniclers and

9. Lucas Cranach the Elder, *The Werewolf*, 1512. The ferocious and deranged werewolf drags a helpless infant off into the woods, while the bodies of his other victims sprawl on the ground and the child's mother shrieks in the background. Cranach's woodcut captures standard elements in most stories about werewolves.

travel writers reported werewolf attacks in forests and wild areas, and illustrated pamphlets spread stories of lycanthropy, of humans changing into super-powerful wolves. While Petrus Gonzales was in Paris, the case of Gilles Garnier, the so-called "Werewolf of Dôle," became a sensation. According to trial testimony, Garnier stalked and killed several children, eating parts of them. He claimed to have made a pact with the devil, who gave him an ointment that turned him into a wolf, and to have hunted and eaten the children while in wolf form. Garnier was burnt at the stake for both witchcraft and lycanthropy. Gilles Garnier cannot have been far from the minds of those who saw Petrus, despite his courtier's clothing. The Gonzales family provoked fear and anxiety as well as wonder, reactions shaped in part by beliefs about werewolves.

Wild folk

Werewolves were not the only hairy creatures that Europeans worried about, for among the stories told by ancient and more recent authors were tales of hairy wild folk. Unlike most monstrous species, wild folk were not limited to far-away places. Europeans (and people in many other parts of the world) thought that wild men and wild women also lived in forests and mountains closer to home. Those who met the Gonzales family, or saw their portraits, had a long tradition of wild man stories on which to draw. "Wild" is one of the words most commonly used to describe Petrus Gonzales, and when people used this they were thinking not only of animals or New World natives, but of wild and savage people who, they feared, lived nearby.

According to the stories, wild men slept in caves or hollows in trees, and ate food they had gathered or animals they had hunted, devouring this raw. Sometimes these wild folk had begun life as normal people, but had left civilization, growing progressively hairier the longer they were away. Most wild men were thought to be violent and fearsome, attacking travelers with clubs or uprooted trees, snatching children, and howling with rage. In medieval chivalric romances, bold knights rescue fair maidens from their clutches, just as they save them from the claws of dragons. In their actions and hairiness wild men were similar to werewolves, although these were two different types of being in people's minds.

St Augustine had declared that wild folk, like all people whose bodily forms were unusual, were human, and children of Adam and Eve: "What is true for a Christian beyond a shadow of a doubt is that every real man, that is, every mortal animal that is rational, however unusual to us may be the shape of his body, or the color of his skin, or the way he walks, or the sound of his voice, and whatever strength, portion or quality of his natural endowments, is descended from the single first-created man."[18] Most medieval writers, especially those learned in theology as Augustine was, agreed, though many more ordinary people did not. They saw wild folk as something distinct, a midway stage between humans and animals, or even creatures of the devil. The fifteenth-century preacher and theologian Geiler von

Kaysersberg tried to make people less fearful of wild men in one of his sermons, and divided them into categories to help people understand them. Yet even the highly educated Geiler wondered whether some wild folk were so evil that they might be the work of the devil.

Not all wild folk were dangerous for medieval Christians. Some were revered as saints, such as John the Baptist, who lived in the wilderness, dressed in skins, and grew his hair and beard long. Wild men included solitary hermits who had dedicated themselves to God, their hair a covering against the elements provided by divine power as a blessing. St Onuphrius, for example, was thought to have been a king's son from the fourth century who spent most of his life

10. Jean Bourdichon, *Wild Folk, c.* 1505–10. This manuscript illumination by a French court artist shows a peaceful family scene, and was part of a group of four miniatures usually called "The Four Conditions of Society." The other paintings showed a richly dressed noble family, an artisan's family hard at work, and a very poor couple, sickly and in rags. With these, Bourdichon presented wild folk in a positive way, more healthy and content in their cave than the poor in their squalid hovel.

in a cave. He lived on dates and bread that appeared miraculously, and as his clothes wore away, shaggy hair grew to replace them.

Both terrifying and saintly wild folk were described in stories told to children, epics and romances recited at court and read by the fireside, and books of saints' lives. They were shown in sculpture, paintings, stained glass, tapestries, and on dishes, chests, drain downspouts, and playing cards. They were in the margins of books, on choir stalls in churches, and on cathedral doors. Everywhere people looked, they saw hairy wild people. Images of wild men became even more common in the fifteenth and sixteenth centuries, when Europeans were coming into contact with people they regarded as "wild" in Africa and the Americas.

Sometimes these shaggy folk were alive. Village festivals and city carnivals included wild men in costumes made of hair or rope, who terrified the crowds by roaring and beating at them with sticks. In Nuremberg, this carnival, called the *Schembartlauf*, grew so raucous that the city council banned it in 1524. An attempt to bring it back a decade later saw it become even more unruly and destructive, with costumed wild men shooting off fireworks toward the houses of city leaders. That was the end of the *Schembartlauf*, although other towns have maintained their festivals, complete with wild men, until today. In England, a leaf-clad figure representing human links with nature, sometimes dubbed the "Green Man," walked in city processions and fought men costumed as knights. (He has been resurrected in recent years for a variety of purposes: as a figure of pre-Christian paganism, a link to Merry Olde Englande for tourists, a name for pubs, and a symbol of environmental awareness.) In Germany, Archduke Ferdinand of Tyrol—in whose castle were several paintings of the Gonzales family—rode into the city of Vienna accompanied by a very large courtier dressed in animal skins, swinging a club, and yelling that he was a giant.

The wild man was such a common part of festivals that Europeans even took him across the sea. In 1538, the Spanish conquerors of Mexico decided to hold a festival celebrating a peace treaty between Spain and France. They built a forest in the main square of Mexico City (where the Aztec temples had been earlier), stocked it with animals, and staged a battle between two groups of wild men, one armed with sticks and one with bows and arrows. The chronicler Bernal Díaz del Castillo reported that the trees seemed "so natural that they might have grown there from seed . . . with weeds that seemed to grow out of them" and that the Spanish inhabitants of the city were amazed at the spectacle.[19] We can only imagine what the Aztecs who were watching might have thought.

Although living depictions of wild men were sometimes judged a threat to orderly city life, artistic images grew increasingly positive in the sixteenth century. Noble families and urban groups began to celebrate wild men and women not for their holiness, but for their physical strength, endurance, and freedom from the rules of society. Wild men with clubs were incorporated in the coats of arms of more than two hundred families in Europe, mostly in German-speaking areas. Inns and taverns were named The Wild Man, and their painted signs showed the common scene of a hairy man with a club. In the Swiss city of Basel, men from various occupations formed a special men's club *Zur Haaren*—literally "to hairiness!"—and decorated their meeting place with paintings of wild men. The club numbered among its members many prominent men, including associates of the city doctor Felix Platter, who examined the Gonzales children. The artist Hans Holbein, later famous for his portraits of kings and queens, was working in Basel at the time. Holbein was a friend of the members of *Zur Haaren*, and designed a wild man emblem for them. Holbein's wild man exhibits standard features—mountains in the background and a club in his hand—but he is framed by classical pillars, and his body hair is not long enough to hide his well-defined muscles. The wild man has become a Renaissance ideal.

Beast, saint, or hero? The wild man was all three.

Hair and manliness

For centuries people in Europe had seen and heard about hairy wild folk, in nearby woods and also in far-away lands. There were Pliny's Choromandae with their hairy bodies and speech like a scream, and hairy mouthless Astomi who lived by breathing in smells.

11. Hans Holbein the Younger, *A wild man brandishing an uprooted tree trunk*,
1528. This drawing was probably a design for a window painting in the Basel
men's club *Zur Haaren*, whose members included Holbein's friends. Basel still
celebrates an annual festival in which a man dresses in skins, twirling around
and threatening the crowd with an uprooted tree.

Mandeville's *Travels* told of "people who walk on their hands and their
feet like four-footed beasts: they are hairy and climb up trees as readily
as apes." Further on his voyage was "another isle, where the people are
covered in feathers and rough hair, except for the face and the palm of
the hand."[20] Not surprisingly, when Europeans actually traveled to the
lands Mandeville claimed to have visited, the stories continued. On his
voyage with Magellan, Pigafetta never saw a hairy human, but on the
island of Mindanao a captive told him about "hairy men who are
exceedingly great fighters and archers. They use swords one span in
width, and eat only raw human hearts with the juice of oranges and
lemons. Those people are called 'Benaian, the hairy.' "[21]

Sadly (in the eyes of European explorers), such hairy people
remained rumors, not realities. With their bristling beards and often

extensive body hair, European men were actually far more hairy than most of the people they encountered on their voyages. Both Columbus and Vespucci mention the lack of body hair among indigenous residents of the Americas, and Vespucci notes further that "they hold hairiness to be a filthy thing." In fact, hairiness (along with smelling bad and a lack of manners) became part of the stereotype of Europeans in East Asia, part of what made them, to Chinese and Japanese eyes, "barbarians."

When confronted with the paradox of their own hairiness, European men reinterpreted the meaning of male body and facial hair. Instead of judging Asians and Native Americans to be less animalistic because they had less hair, they judged them to be less masculine. "To hairiness!" was in some ways the motto of sixteenth-century European masculinity more broadly and not simply of one men's club in Basel. Most adult men who are not members of the clergy have facial hair of some type in sixteenth-century portraits, usually beards of various shapes and lengths. This marked them as distinct from adolescents, and so as mature members of society. It also marked them, of course, as distinct from women.

The Italian cleric and scholar Piero Valeriano Bolzani even argued in a short work that this sign of masculinity should be allowed to male members of the clergy. "Nature," Bolzani argued, "has made women with smooth faces, and men rough and full of hair. . . . Therefore whosoever, by any craft of business, goes about to make a man beardless, it may be said to his charge that he has done against the laws of Nature . . . it beseems men to have long beards, for chiefly by that token (as I have often said) the vigorous strength of manhood is discerned from the tenderness of women."[22] The English physician and natural philosopher John Bulwer agreed, commenting that "the beard is the sign of man . . . by which he appears a man. . . . Shaving the chin is justly to be accounted a note of Effeminacy," and those "who expose themselves to be shaved are called, in reproach, women."[23] His comment appeared in a long work, *Anthropometamorphosis: Man Transform'd, or the Artificiall Changeling*, attacking, as its full title noted, the "mad and cruel Gallantry, foolish Bravery, ridiculous Beauty, filthy Fineness, and loathesome Loveliness of most Nations" for "fashioning and altering their Bodies from the Mould intended by Nature." We cannot know if any of the Gonzales men ever shaved, or if they followed Bolzani and Bulwer's advice and left themselves as nature made them.

Shortly after the family moved to Italy, the learned physician Marcus Antonius Ulmus published *Physiologia barbae humanae* (1602) in Bologna, a 300-page book providing the opinions of "illustrious doctors and philosophers" from many centuries on beards. As did other medical authors at the time, Ulmus linked the growth of facial hair with sexual potency. Neither he, Bolzani, nor Bulmer would have been surprised that Petrus and Enrico fathered a number of children.

Wild women

People thought of many things when they looked at any member of the Gonzales family—monsters and prodigies, marvelous species, exotic foreign peoples, amazing animals, wild men—but the Gonzales sisters brought still more things to mind. Petrus Gonzales and his sons were remarkably hairy, but most adult men in Europe in the sixteenth century had visible body hair and wore beards, so the hairiness of the Gonzales men was a matter of degree. Most women, however, whether from nearby or beyond the sea, did not have extensive facial or body hair, so the hairiness of the Gonzales sisters was striking. Here as well, though, there were myths and traditions on which people could draw.

Everyone knew stories of hairy female saints, beginning with Mary Magdalene. In a tale that was first told in the tenth century, Mary and some companions, set adrift by heartless non-believers in a boat without a rudder, landed in southern France. (That she was pregnant with Jesus' baby at the time is a story that is much newer than the tenth century.) She preached to the local people, winning many converts, and then lived alone in a cave, doing penance for her formerly sinful life. The barren surroundings offered no food, but Mary was miraculously taken up to heaven seven times a day by angels, an experience that replaced her need for earthly food. Details taken from the stories of other hermit-saints were gradually added to her life. Like

Onuphrius, Mary's body became covered with hair, sometimes shown as beautiful flowing strands and sometimes as rough fur. The hair transformed her into a saintly wild woman, and she became a model for legends of other women whose hair helped protect their honor, making them unattractive to any would-be attacker.

One of these was a female saint, whose life was first described in the fourteenth century, usually called St Wilgefortis or St Uncumber. As the story goes, Wilgefortis was the Christian daughter of a pagan king of Portugal who wanted to escape an arranged marriage. She prayed for a miracle, and God caused hair to grow all over her face. This made her fiancé reject the marriage, and her father had her crucified; depictions of St Wilgefortis usually show a bearded figure with long hair on a cross wearing an ankle-length tunic. Where did the legend of St Wilgefortis come from? The official Catholic position, shared by many art historians, is that it arose from a misunderstanding about a famous crucifix in the Italian city of Lucca. This crucifix, known as the Holy Face, was an important object of veneration in the Middle Ages, and had its own legend of origin. According to that tradition, the crucifix was carved by Nicodemus, one of the men who helped bury Christ, and its features were exactly those of Jesus. The crucifix was buried for centuries, and was then transported to Italy in a boat with no sails and to Lucca in an ox-cart with no driver, arriving there in 742. The historical record of the Holy Face crucifix begins in about 1100, when the cathedral that housed it became an increasingly popular center of pilgrimage. Pilgrims chipped off pieces of the crucifix in order to gain a bit of its power and have holy relics; they hacked off so much that a new one had to be carved in the thirteenth century. Large and small copies were made, and some of these became associated with miracles as well. As these images were carried around Europe, people were confused by the long dress of the figure on the crucifix, and invented their own stories to explain what this was: not Christ, but Wilgefortis, a bearded woman on a cross.

Whether this is the actual origin of the Wilgefortis legend or not, by the fifteenth century it had spread around Europe, and she became a popular saint, especially with women. She was known by different names in different parts of Europe: Uncumber in England,

Kümmernis in Germany, Ontkommer in the Netherlands, Liberata in Italy, and many more. Many of these names come from words referring to "freeing" something, and she was an especially favorite saint of women who wished to free themselves of abusive husbands. ("Uncumber" in English is an old form of "disencumber.") Learned opinion was often dismissive of her cult, and charged that women prayed to her when they wished to be rid of *any* husband, not just a violent one. The English scholar and government official Thomas More commented in 1529 that "women hath therefore changed her name, and instead of Saint Wilgefortis call her Saint Uncumber, because they think that she will not fail to uncumber them of their husbands."[24] With the Reformation in England, icons of St Uncumber were smashed and burnt, but she remained popular on

12. Hans Burgkmair, *St Kümmernis* (St Wilgefortis), 1507. In this single sheet woodcut, Burgkmair tells the story of St Wilgefortis' miraculous beard and crucifixion. He also describes a later miracle attributed to her, in which she gave a poor violin player one of her golden shoes, which sits here on the altar.

the continent and was included in the official list of Roman Catholic saints in 1583. (She was removed from this list, along with many saints whose historical existence is doubtful, such as St Valentine, in 1969.) Devotion to St Wilgefortis was especially strong in southern Germany, Austria, and Switzerland, where many of the pictures of the Gonzales family were made and Felix Platter examined the children. Thus when people saw the girls, and particularly when women saw them, they may have been reminded of the images of St Wilgefortis that were in their churches or that they carried in their pockets. Devotion to the hairy Magdalene was also widespread in these areas, so people may have been reminded of her as well. No woman in France or Germany recorded what she thought about the Gonzales sisters, or at least no women's comments have survived. What the sisters thought about the women they saw— selling vegetables, spinning wool, tending the sick, nursing children, delivering messages, making candles, carrying firewood, or peddling meat—has not left a trace in the sources either, of course.

There were other tales of hairy women besides those about saints. From Greek mythology came the story of the Gorgons, fierce female monsters with writhing snakes as hair who turned anyone who looked at them into stone. The Gorgons were thought to live somewhere in the west, and so when Pliny told about hairy women living on Atlantic islands, he called these women "Gorgades," which means Gorgon-like ones. Pierre d'Ailly repeats Pliny's story in his *Imago mundi*, an encyclopedic account of the inhabitants of the world written in the fifteenth century: "The Gorgodes Islands of the ocean . . . are inhabited by the Gorgades, women of destructiveness, with coarse and hairy bodies."[25] (Columbus had d'Ailly's book as well as Pliny's in his sea chest on his first voyage, but he does not seem to be as keen on finding Gorgades as he is on finding cannibals. Columbus *was* interested in finding those muscular women of Greek mythology, the Amazons, but they were not thought to be hairy.)

Northern Europe was also home to hairy women. In his *Description of Wales*, the medieval chronicler Gerald of Wales told a story about one of these:

> One evening . . . he happened to meet a girl whom he had loved for a long time. . . . He was enjoying himself in her arms and tasting her delights, when suddenly, instead of the beautiful girl, he found in his embrace a hairy creature, rough and shaggy, and indeed, repulsive beyond words. As he stared at the monster his wits deserted him and he became quite mad.[26]

Sometimes the transformation went the other way. In the medieval German epic *Wolfdietrich*, the hero—who had earlier been saved by a pack of wolves from being killed at the order of his father—encounters Raue Else, a wild woman who runs on all fours toward his fire. She "had a body covered with a thick hairy pelt, slimy and wet like the bride of the devil" and demands that Wolfdietrich love her. He refuses, she turns him into a wild man, he promises to marry her if she will become a Christian, she does, and *poof!* she turns back into her former self, a smooth-skinned princess.

Like those of wild men, depictions of wild women became more positive during the sixteenth century, even those who did not magically turn into princesses. On stained-glass windows and drinking cups, wild women held up shields with coats of arms, often nursing a baby at the same time. Their hair did not interfere with their motherly nurturing as they offered protection and strength to the noble family whose shield they displayed.

Destructive hairy women did not disappear from the sixteenth-century imagination, but emerged in a new form: as witches. In the Spanish play *La Celestina*, and in Shakespeare's *Macbeth*, women who are witches are described as bearded. In the opening scene of *Macbeth*, the Scottish general Banquo first meets three witches, whose beards cause him to be uncertain about their gender: "You should be women, and yet your beards forbid me to interpret, that you are so." Most woodcuts and engravings of witches do not show them with facial hair, but a few do. In these there is no doubt about the witches' gender, however, as their breasts often hang out of their clothing, or they wear no clothing at all. Witches did not need facial hair to make them seem evil, for the long, unruly hair on their heads was enough. Respectable married women always covered their hair with some kind of hat or

Elß zů Wolffdietßerichen in den wald. do sy lagen bey dem feüre. Vnnd betzaubert jn mit jrem zů gan. vnnd fürt jn mit jr. vnnd bitt jn das er bey jr schlaffe. sy wölte jm ein gantz künigkreich geben.

13. *Wolfdietrich and Raue Else*, from a collection of epic stories published in Strasbourg, 1509. In this woodcut by an anonymous artist, the hairy but still sexy wild Else appears before the hero Wolfdietrich. He transforms her back into a princess not by kissing her—the standard method of transformation in later fairy stories—but by converting her to Christianity.

kerchief, and prostitutes were routinely forbidden to wear head coverings that might disguise their dishonorable occupation. Witches' uncovered hair was a sign of their uncontrolled sexuality, and hinted at their demonic lovers, even if the devil did not appear in the picture. Witches are often shown with animal companions, and their hair blends into that of the animal as they ride goats through the darkness or nuzzle cats. According to the demonology that underlay beliefs about witchcraft, these animals might be demons in disguise. Even if they were not, showing naked witches in close contact with animals

14. Martin Schongauer, *Wild Woman and Heraldic Shield, c.* 1490. The hairy wild woman suckling her child is here an emblem of fertility, suggesting the promise of an enduring family line for the noble family whose shield she holds. This engraving may have been a model for a goldsmith or glassmaker, who would fill in the appropriate family crest of the person who ordered it.

suggested sexual relations between them, and placed witches within the realm of the beasts.

Witches were not the only women in the realm of beasts. In sermons, poetry, and many other texts, women were often compared to animals. Women were like horses, for both needed to be made obedient with a whip, went a common saying. A virtuous wife is like a snail, for she never leaves her house. A wicked wife is a venomous snake. The medieval French author Richard de Fournival created a whole bestiary along these lines, *The Bestiary of Love*, in which women are compared to wolves, crocodiles, monkeys, crows, vipers, and many other animals. *The Bestiary of Love* began with a quotation from Aristotle, "One may learn the nature of one animal from the nature of another," a line which Richard de Fournival included to demonstrate that the equating of women with animals had a long history.

Comparisons of women to animals are so common that they show up as proof when authors are trying to make a point about something else. In a debate held in the Spanish city of Valladolid in 1550–1 about whether Native Americans could legitimately be enslaved, the Spanish scholar and theologian Juan de Sepúlveda asserted that the Indians were "as inferior to the Spaniards as children are to adults, women are to men, the savage and ferocious to the gentle, the grossly intemperate to the continent and temperate, and finally, almost as monkeys are to men."[27] In this argument, Sepúlveda also draws on Aristotle, who argued in the *Politics* that women had less reason than men, as did those whom Aristotle referred to as "natural slaves."

Aristotle's *Generation of Animals* was clear on women's inferiority. There Aristotle described women as imperfect men, the result of something wrong with the conception that created them—their parents were too young or too old, or too diverse in age, or one of them was not healthy. Nature always aimed at perfection, and Aristotle termed anything less than perfect "monstrous"; a woman was thus "a deformity, but one which occurs in the ordinary course of nature."[28] While scholars debate what exactly Aristotle meant by this, medieval and Renaissance thinkers had few doubts and simply noted that Aristotle thought women were monsters. Although by the sixteenth century Aristotle's ideas about some things were being questioned and challenged, he remained the most influential non-Christian source in many fields.

Aristotle's conclusion that all women were at least somewhat monstrous cannot have been far from the minds of many of those who saw the Gonzales sisters, for they spent much of their lives in circles where knowledge of the teachings of ancient philosophers was commonplace. Sepúlveda's argument was made just about the time their father was brought to the French court, and contained a whole series of binaries that structured people's thinking about many issues. In each of these binaries, the Gonzales sisters were the inferior of the pair: they were children, they were female, their background was colonial and "savage," and their faces looked, to some observers, like those of monkeys.

The Gonzales sisters had hair all over their bodies, but most people saw them in long dresses, so that their facial hair was what was most readily apparent. People may have thought they were bearded rather than hairy, but facial hair alone was enough to hint at the monstrous. Bolzani's treatise arguing that male clergy should be allowed to wear beards also contains a few comments about beards on women: "Nature has made women with smooth faces . . . [so] it has ever been a monstrous thing to see a woman with a beard, [even] though it is very little," he wrote.[29] John Bulwer agreed, commenting that "woman is by nature smooth and delicate; and if she have many hairs she is a monster."[30]

Whether at home or in distant lands, most sixteenth-century Europeans expected to see an occasional wonder, meet a wild man, or cross paths with a witch. Though their excited expectations about wild folk and monsters were generally not met, such preconceptions shaped Europeans' response to real people they did encounter. This included the Gonzales family, beginning with Petrus. Here was an actual hairy person, not just a story, found in a wild western island, a place where monsters had long been thought to live.

15. Agostino Carracci, *Hairy Arrigo, Crazy Peter, the Dwarf Amon and Other Beasts*, 1599. The artist gathers together oddities and exotics housed in the Farnese palace, with Enrico Gonzales as the focal point of the painting.

2
Myths and Histories

Several years after Lavinia Fontana painted Antonietta Gonzales' portrait in Bologna, another Bolognese painter, Agostino Carracci, painted a group portrait of people and animals that lived in the sumptuous Farnese palace in Rome. This painting was later described in an inventory of the huge Farnese collection of art and objects as a picture of "hairy Arrigo, crazy Peter, the dwarf Amon and other beasts." The "other beasts" include two dogs, two monkeys, and a parrot that clamber on the humans and eat fruit out of their hands. Hairy Arrigo, who appears to be naked except for a skin cape tied over his shoulders, looks at crazy Peter and points toward the dwarf, both of whom are dressed in courtly clothing. "Arrigo" was an Italian version of the Spanish "Enrico," and the name the Farneses generally used for a man who is himself listed on the inventory: Enrico Gonzales, the oldest hairy Gonzales brother.

Odoardo Farnese, the cardinal who owned both the painting and its subjects, was fascinated by the exotic, and was also an avid collector of Greek and Roman antiquities. The gardens of the Farnese palace were filled with classical statuary as well as animals, and Odoardo sought to add to the collection. These could only be the best, in keeping with the palace itself, for which Michelangelo had designed the courtyard and some of the windows. In came New World animals, including the parrot in the picture, and then Odoardo heard that his brother Ranuccio had acquired something even more exotic: an entire hairy family. He pestered Ranuccio, the duke of Parma, to send him the teenaged son. Ranuccio obliged.

Enrico Gonzales' arrival in Rome in the summer of 1595 was described in a report about events in the papal city by a representative of the duke of Urbino. Like any ruler, the duke of Urbino, a small state in northern Italy, wanted to know everything that was happening in Rome, so that he did not miss out on any political developments, cultural trends, or scandals. "The Duke of Parma gave the Cardinal Farnese an eighteen-year-old wild man as a present," the report read. "This person is completely hairy in his face; he has long blond hair on his forehead."[1]

Wild man and classical hero

In the painting, Carracci places the exotic animals in a way that emphasizes Enrico's own exotic nature, for the parrot eats cherries out of his hand and the monkeys perch on his shoulder and climb onto his lap. This connects Enrico with what people understood about his origins: that his father had been born on Tenerife, one of the Canary Islands whose "uncivilized" inhabitants had been conquered by the Spanish in what became a model for later Spanish conquests in the Americas. Enrico's lack of clothing also suggests his wild nature, and the skin cape that he wears makes this more specific. The cape is Carracci's best idea of what a goatskin *tamarco*, the traditional garment of the original residents of the Canary Islands, looks like. Carracci suggests visually what contemporary commentators on any member of the Gonzales family suggested in words: that Petrus Gonzales was a Guanche, one of the indigenous people of the Canary Island of Tenerife.

Alonso de Espinosa, a Dominican friar who wrote the earliest account of the Canary Islands in the 1580s, described *tamarcos* as

> Lambs' skins, or of the skins of sheep, of the colour of chamois hair, worn like a shirt without folds, collar, or sleeves, and sewn with thongs of the same skin. They are sewn with such skill that

there is no skinner who could dress the skins so well, nor who
could sew them together with such excellence, so that the seams
can scarcely be seen; and this without needles or awls, other than
fish bones or thorns from trees. The dress was fastened with
thorns in front and at the sides, leaving room for the arms.[2]

Carracci's dressing Enrico in a *tamarco* for the painting was not
an accident, and it did not represent his normal way of dressing.
The report of Enrico's coming to Rome in the cardinal's coach
described him as "splendidly dressed," and he generally wore
clothing like that of the dwarf and the madman in the painting. In
Aldrovandi's *Monstrorum historia*, he is shown in a ruff and velvet
jacket, as is his father. With the *tamarco*, however, Carracci portrays
Enrico as a Guanche, "wild" not only because of his hairy face
and body, but also because of his origins in one of the lands to the
west where, as Gerald of Wales had said centuries earlier, "Nature
indulges herself" with wonders.

Enrico's hairy body was the main reason the Farneses wanted
him in their collection, but his reputation as a Guanche made him
even more exotic and valuable. In this second aspect of his wildness
he was akin, in European eyes, to the Native Americans occasionally shown off at European courts in the sixteenth century. In fact,
Europeans sometimes confused the two. When the Spanish king
sent an American Indian slave to Venice in 1497, people assumed
he was a Canary Islander. Conversely, when Petrus first arrived at
the French court, many people thought he had been born in the
Americas. Columbus knew Canary Islanders were different from
the people he encountered in the Caribbean, but thought there
might be links between the two. They looked somewhat alike, he
wrote, commenting in the journal of his first voyage that the indigenous people he had met in the Caribbean "were not black, but
the color of the inhabitants of the Canaries, which is a very natural
circumstance, they being in the same latitude with the island
of Ferro in the Canaries."[3] Both Native Americans and Canary
Islanders died quickly when enslaved, he noted. This would probably change with time for Native Americans, he speculated, for

Canary Islanders taken as slaves during his lifetime did not die as readily as had those taken earlier. Unfortunately Columbus proved to be wrong.

Enrico's ethnic background as a Guanche was a central part of his identity, and later accounts of any member of the Gonzales family invariably mention this feature of their personal history. But were the Gonzaleses really Guanches? Twelve years before Enrico's celebrated arrival in Rome, William V of Bavaria, the German nobleman who owned portraits of Enrico and his sister Maddalena as children, as well as portraits of their parents, also commented on the family's background. He had written to someone in France asking for details of the family, and learned that "the mother and father of the man [that is, of Petrus] were not wild, but like other people, and, if I have it right, they were Spanish." As William himself admits, he might not have the story straight; in addition, his use of the word "wild" here might simply mean hairy, not native to an uncivilized place. But his words raise doubts about Enrico and the *tamarco*. The sixteenth century was a time when many people told stories about themselves that were not completely accurate. For a variety of reasons, some people obscured their actual backgrounds or created new personal histories. Might the Gonzaleses' ethnicity have been one of these invented stories?

Carracci's painting portrays Enrico as a wild Guanche, but not simply that. With his nakedness and skin cape, he is also a god, or at least a hero. The Farneses owned hundreds of paintings and statues of nude or nearly nude figures, depictions of ancient gods, goddesses, and mythological heroes. As Carracci painted him, with well-developed musculature and a long straight nose, Enrico fits right in. He is a living blend of the interests of those who owned him, a mixture of the exotic and the classical.

The Farneses were attracted to anything ancient, but were particular fans of the Greek hero Hercules. They had acquired a huge Greco-Roman statue of Hercules found in the ancient Roman Baths of Caracalla, and placed it in a special room of the palace. Annibale Carracci, Agostino's brother, painted stories of Hercules' exploits on the walls and ceiling of the room. He and his brother and other artists from their workshop then began an enormous fresco, *The Loves of the Gods*, on the ceiling of the palace's grand salon. In these frescos, the male gods are generally naked, just like Hercules in the statue that stood in the center of the room, and just like Enrico in Agostino Carracci's painting.

Many things in the painting suggest myths about Hercules. Enrico holds fruit, just as the statue does—in Hercules' case, these are apples stolen from the garden of the Hesperides, beautiful nymphs who guard an island far to the west with an orchard sacred to the goddess Hera. Stealing the apples of the Hesperides was one of the last of the twelve labors of Hercules, a group of nearly impossible tasks given to the mythical hero as a penance after he had killed his wife and

16. Farnese Hercules, probably made in the third century CE as a copy of a fourth-century BCE original. The massively muscled Hercules rests on his club, with the apples of the Hesperides held behind his back. The statue was recovered from the ruins of the Baths of Caracalla in Rome in the middle of the sixteenth century and moved to the Farnese palace, where it served as a model for paintings and sculptures of the gods for centuries.

children in a fit of madness. The first of those tasks was killing and skinning the Nemean lion, a beast with extraordinary powers that Hercules killed with his bare hands after a long battle. The skin of the Nemean lion, complete with its head, then became Hercules' standard garment, providing him with protection because it was impenetrable. Hercules wears his lion skin when stealing the apples of the Hesperides, and in some versions of the story the skin itself plays a part in his success at this task. In most paintings and statues, Hercules wears the skin, although in the Farnese statue it is at his side, draped over his club. Enrico, too, wears a skin cape in Carracci's painting, draped around his shoulders just as Hercules' lion skin usually was. With his skin cape and club, his strength and endurance, the heavily muscled Hercules was the perfect model of the Renaissance version of the wild man, protective rather than dangerous. Enrico, too, exhibits this blend of qualities: exotic wild man, classical hero, protector of those less powerful, in this case the animals that interact peacefully around him. As with every painting of any member of the Gonzales family, Carracci's painting of Enrico suggests a hybrid nature, a mixture that was both fascinating and frightening.

If Enrico represents a stereotypical western wild man in the painting, and also a classical hero, is there anything about the painting that is really him? Can we consider this a portrait of an individual at all? These questions can be asked about any of the Gonzales portraits. Many of them were done by artists looking at other paintings, not at the members of the family themselves, and they seem somewhat generic, almost ideal types of hairy people rather than real individuals. In this, they contrast with what is often described as a key element of art in the Renaissance, and of Renaissance culture in general: that it put more emphasis on the individual, both the invidual artist as a genius of creation and the individual subject. Artists began to sign their works, and patrons ordered stand-alone portraits of themselves or their family members, or had themselves inserted as recognizable faces in biblical and classical scenes.

The paintings of the Gonzales family might not deviate from this pattern quite as much as they seem to at first, however. Many portraits from this era are actually less individualized than they appear at first to be, showing graceful noblewomen who fit with idealized standards of feminine beauty (red-blond hair, high forehead, sloping shoulders) or powerful noblemen who fit with idealized standards of masculine strength (elaborate armor, fierce gaze, piercing eyes). The portrait painters most in demand, such as Raphael and Titian, painted their subjects just as the subjects themselves wanted to be seen. One of Titian's most famous portraits shows the Italian noblewoman Isabella d'Este in a magnificent ermine wrap and brocade dress, gazing out with an unlined and exquisite face from under a jeweled headdress. Isabella herself ordered the painting and by all accounts was very pleased with it, particularly because it showed her forty years younger than she actually was. Like many of those who painted the Gonzales family, Titian based his portrait on an earlier painting, not on a study of its subject. In portraits, as in stories that people told about themselves, the mythical and the real were combined, with the line between the two blurry and difficult to see at a distance.

By itself, then, Carracci's painting cannot tell us if the Gonzaleses were actually descendants of the Guanches, or allow us to judge the extent to which the story of Petrus and his children connects with that of European colonial conquests. Perhaps the history of the Canaries and other islands in the Atlantic can help answer the question of their identity, though that story, too, is one in which myths and reality intertwine.

Islands fortunate and frightening

When Gerald of Wales wrote in the twelfth century, Ireland was the western edge of the world known to Europeans, but by the fourteenth century Portuguese ships were inching further and further down the African coast, searching for better and more direct supplies of gold and slaves. Prevailing winds in the Atlantic meant that though ships could stick close to land when sailing south, they had to cut far to the west when sailing home to Portugal. Such travel patterns led to the Portuguese discovery in the late 1300s of the uninhabited Azores, Cape Verdes, and Madeira Islands, all far to the west of Ireland. In the 1450s, a Genoese merchant under the sponsorship of

Prince Henry the Navigator of Portugal made direct contact with the Mali Empire of West Africa; trade in gold and slaves expanded dramatically. Henry also encouraged colonization and farming in the Atlantic islands, which were soon exporting wheat and sugar.

Word of Portuguese voyages drew all sorts of people to Lisbon, including Christopher Columbus. He had joined the crew of a merchant ship as a teenager, and while in his twenties settled in Lisbon with his brother, making maps to support himself. He married a woman whose father was one of Henry the Navigator's captains and a governor of the Portuguese colony of Madeira. The couple lived on Madeira for a while, and Columbus visited many other islands and the Portuguese trading posts on the west coast of Africa. Here he saw at first hand the possibilities that overseas colonies could offer.

Most of the Atlantic islands had no people living on them when the Portuguese arrived, but they were not unknown. Greek and Celtic stories tell of islands far to the west. There were the Fortunate Islands or Isles of the Blessed, where Greek heroes went after they died. The sixth-century Irish monk Brendan the Navigator reached their shores as well, according to legend, traveling in a skin boat. Their location was vague in Greek mythology and Irish saints' lore, but the second-century Greek geographer Ptolemy put them on the map that he drew of the known world. In fact, Ptolemy set the prime meridian, the line of longitude from which everything is measured, at the Fortunate Islands, off the coast of Africa in the Atlantic Ocean. When Portuguese ships reached various Atlantic islands, first one group and then another was dubbed the Fortunate Islands, although the name didn't stick with any of them.

Many of the western islands were thought to be home to unusual women, who were marked by extraordinary hair. There were the beautiful and gentle Hesperides, usually shown with long flowing locks, who tended the gardens and orchards of Hera. There were the Gorgons, with claw-like hands and snaky hair, whose glance turned people into stone.

To ancient readers, and those in the sixteenth century, the Gorgons had apparently bequeathed some of their qualities, slightly altered, to later inhabitants of the island. Pliny reports that the fifth-century BCE Carthaginian navigator Hanno made it to these islands from North Africa, where he found a race of people Pliny—in honor of the Gorgons—calls the Gorgades. They no longer had snaky hair, but the "women had hair all over their bodies" while the "men were so swift of foot that they got away." The men were lucky, for Hanno caught several of the women, skinned them, and, according to Pliny, "deposited the skins of two of the female natives in the Temple of Juno [or actually of Tanit, the Carthaginian equivalent of the Roman goddess Juno] as proof of the truth of his story and as curiosities, where they were on show until Carthage was taken by Rome."[4]

Pliny had read about Hanno's expedition and the hairy women in various ancient authors, but Hanno himself may have written a report about the trip. A Greek manuscript known as the "Periplus of Hanno" claimed to be a translation of an earlier inscription written in Punic, the language spoken in Carthage. Like Pliny, Hanno described a violent encounter:

> This [island] was full of savages; by far the greater number were women with hairy bodies, called by our interpreters "gorillas." We gave chase to the men but could not catch any for they climbed up steep rocks and pelted us with stones. However we captured three women who bit and scratched their captors. We killed and flayed them and brought their skins back to Carthage.[5]

The men may have been hairy, too, although neither Pliny nor Hanno mentions this, but then hairy men would not have been as worthy of note as were hairy women. Travelers' reports (from any century) generally highlight only what the traveler finds new or unusual. To Hanno, the fact that the men ran away while the women fought back seems especially strange, for it went against his expectations of proper feminine and masculine behavior.

Pliny probably heard Hanno's story at second hand, but in the sixteenth century people could read the "Periplus of Hanno" itself. A manuscript copy of the Greek text surfaced in Basel in Switzerland, probably brought from Constantinople after that city was taken over by the Turks in 1453. (Greek scholars and Christian officials took—we might say "stole"—many manuscripts as they left the city.) There it came to the attention of the Froben family, prominent publishers known for their classical religious and philosophical books. Froben's assistant Sigismund Gelen put the "Periplus of Hanno" together with a few other texts of ancient geographers, and published them in 1533 in Greek. By the time Petrus Gonzales showed up at the French court in 1547, then, highly educated readers could have read Hanno's story about hairy people on islands off West Africa directly, as well as in Pliny. They could also have seen pictures of Pliny's Gorgades in various histories of the world, although they were generally shown as peaceful rather than threatening, perhaps taking on some aspects of the gentle Hesperides.

17. Gorgades in Hartmann Schedel's *Liber chronicarum* (World Chronicle), 1493. The Gorgades here look more like the Hesperides, with beautiful long flowing hair, than like the vicious, snake-haired Gorgons. Illustrations such as this one were widely reprinted, and shaped people's ideas about women of the Americas as well as those from the islands of the Atlantic.

In the 1540s, knowledge about African islands was fairly vague, however, and many at the French court thought the little boy had come instead from the Americas. Several decades later, when people encountered Petrus' daughters or their pictures, they had a better sense of Atlantic geography. They were also more likely to have read Hanno, for it was too great a story to be limited to people who could read Greek. The Venetian publisher Giovanni Ramusio had it translated into Italian, and included it in his *Navigations and Voyages*, published in 1550. In 1556, it appeared in French translation, and English travel writers began to include it in their collections of travels to distant lands.

One of those who no doubt read Ramusio's books was Conrad Gesner, the Swiss naturalist busy compiling his huge work on animals that was pirated by so many people. Gesner took time out from his other work to translate Hanno's story into Latin, publishing this in 1559. The Basel doctor Felix Platter does not mention the Gorgades or the "gorilla" women from Hanno in his brief description of a Gonzales sister, but they could not have been far from the learned physician's mind as he examined the hairy little girl.

In the ancient text, Hanno brought skins as well as stories back to Carthage. Sixteenth-century European travelers also collected skins, so people could see actual skins, as well as read about them in Hanno. "On a Spanish island there is an almost boundless number of wild men," reports the *Monstrorum historia*, "who wish to enter into no kind of contact with those who live beside the sea." The editor then adds, "A certain man brought part of a wild man's pelt to the most excellent Ulysses Aldrovandi, which is still kept in the museum of the most illustrious Bolognese Senate."[6] Who exactly this wild man was, or where his "pelt" had been collected, is unknown.

It is just as unclear who the hairy people were that Hanno encountered. Pliny thought that Hanno was talking about hairy human women, and most sixteenth-century retellers of the story agreed. Illustrations of his story in travel books, or in editions of Pliny, sometimes use illustrations of the Gorgons that a printer happened to have on his shelf to suggest to readers what the "women with hairy bodies" looked like. These books shaped people's encounters with apes. The English merchant Richard Jobson, who traveled in western Africa in 1620, reported on what he called "baboons" along the Gambia River (they may actually have been chimpanzees), but decided that they were "a race and kind of people." He based this judgment about their humanity on his observation that they obeyed their leaders and worked together, but he certainly knew Hanno's story, and this shaped his point of view. By the nineteenth century, however, commentators on Hanno—and there continued to be many—thought that the ancient Carthaginian captain was talking about some sort of ape, a being clearly distinct from humans. Thomas Savage, an American missionary doctor with a solid classical education, was working in Gabon in the 1840s and discovered the largest of the great apes. In honor of Hanno, he named these "gorillas," and the name stuck.

What Hanno encountered, and where he was exactly, we will probably never know. Scholars continue to debate every aspect of his voyage, including whether there was a Hanno and whether he actually wrote anything. Given Renaissance respect for ancient authorities, however, few people in the sixteenth century doubted that hairy women (and speedy men) had existed on an island somewhere off the African coast in ancient times, and might still be there. Knowing Hanno's story, people could view the Gonzales sisters not only as monsters or wild folk, but also as living examples of the hairy women the Carthaginian captain had met (and skinned) so long ago.

The settling and conquest of the Canaries

Stories told about ancient voyages to any of the islands in the west formed people's reactions to the Gonzales family, although most of these islands had no people, hairy or otherwise, living on them when Europeans arrived. The Canary Islands, by contrast, much closer to the African coast, *were* inhabited—with a population somewhere between 50,000 and 100,000—when Portuguese, Genoese, and Spanish ships began landing on them in the fourteenth century. At first they were one of the places called the Fortunate Isles, "fortunate because of the abundance of their fruitage" and their "promising grape vines," according to Pierre d'Ailly in his 1410 account of inhabitants of the world. This name was given in error, though, d'Ailly comments, by pagans who "regarded the islands as Paradise because of the fecundity of the soil."[7] To a pious Christian official such as d'Ailly, no earthly place could be truly blessed. A better name, he thought, was Insula Canaria, or Island of the Dogs, a name given because one of the islands was "abounding in dogs of immense size." Mapmakers and mariners came to agree with d'Ailly, and that was the name that stuck: Insula Canaria, which was later mistranslated into English as the Canary Islands. (The bird gets its name from the islands, where it was native, not the other way around.)

These were the islands where Petrus Gonzales was born, the only Atlantic islands where his parents could have come from a group that did not arrive in European ships. Those ships dramatically altered the lives of the people already living in the Canaries, bringing destruction and disease. In the process of conquering and colonizing the Canaries, Europeans enslaved many of the original inhabitants, taking some of them off to Europe to display and sell. Was the little hairy boy later named Petrus one of these? Answering that question requires a closer look at the history of the Canaries, which can also provide clues to other elements of the Gonzaleses' story that at first seem unrelated to their origins on Tenerife.

The original settlers reached the Canaries from North Africa some time before 1000 BC. There were probably several waves of migration afterward, as the languages and religious practices of the islands differed, and people on the islands varied in their skin color and other physical attributes. They lived primarily by raising sheep, pigs, and goats, which they had brought with them from Africa, along with the dogs that herded them. Canary Islanders did not weave cloth, but dressed in the animal skin *tamarcos* that Carracci paints and Espinosa describes. They also raised barley in fields watered through irrigation, and lived in houses surrounded by their flocks, or sometimes, reports Espinosa, "in a cave formed by nature." These Canarian caves may have inspired King Henry II to have a cave constructed later for Petrus in the gardens of one of the royal palaces, and certainly influenced the many paintings of the family that place them in cave-like settings.

Espinosa describes rulers and "general assemblies" where decisions were made, and where "each person showed off his valor, making a parade of his accomplishments in leaping, running, and dancing what is called the *Canario*, with much agility and movement." "Things are recounted of their strength and agility," continues Espinosa, "which seem almost incredible." As a demonstration of strength, men lifted a stone so large that "now there is not a man, however strong he may be, who can lift it off the ground. Their agility was such that at ten paces they could hurl a lance or a stone and never miss, for they aimed with much dexterity. In running, even over steep or rocky ground, which others could not get over walking, they could overtake a goat and catch it by the legs."[8] The original Canary Islanders were already the stuff of legend by the time Espinosa writes in the 1580s—"things are recounted," he says, not "I saw"—and they sound more like Hercules than mere mortals, or like the speedy island men described by Hanno, whose story Espinosa probably knew. Even Espinosa will not pass on all the stories he has heard, however, commenting that it was said "there were giants among them of incredible size; but that it may not appear fabulous, I will not repeat what is said on the subject."

The Canaries were not cut off from the rest of the world after they were initially settled. Hanno and other Phoenician captains probably landed on the islands, as did a few Roman and Arabic traders. In the fourteenth century, Spanish, Italian, and Portuguese ships took animals, crops, and a few native people back to Europe. In 1402, Jean de Béthencourt, a French adventurer supported by the Spanish king, decided to conquer the islands. He set off with a small group of men—made even smaller by desertions along the way—including several native men who had earlier been taken to Europe, whom he planned to use as translators. Béthencourt was met peacefully by local dignitaries, who hoped they could ally with him against the other Europeans who regularly plundered their villages. He built a fortress as a defense against marauders, but after recruiting more men from Spain, captured a ruler of one of the smaller islands and forced a military surrender. The king agreed to be baptized as a Christian, and soon afterward most of the local residents did as well. This had been a very common pattern in the spread of Christianity into new areas of Europe centuries earlier—first a ruler was baptized, then the people under his power, and then there might be some instruction in what Christianity was all about. Several Franciscan friars did accompany Béthencourt, and his translators had been baptized earlier in Europe, so there may have been some attempt to communicate basic Christian teachings.

Béthencourt extended his authority to a few of the smaller islands, but the people living on Gran Canaria, Tenerife, and the other large islands resisted Spanish takeover for nearly a century. The Spanish monarchs—especially the ambitious Ferdinand and Isabella, who assumed the throne in 1474—sent military expeditions of Spanish soldiers and mercenaries with horses, cannons, and hand-held arquebuses, an early type of musket. They often lost to the Canary Islanders, who had well-organized battle tactics though they were armed only with javelins and rocks, but Spanish forces gradually took over more of the islands.

After they conquered an area, the Spanish took captives back to Europe, exhibiting them as savage wild men in their skin garments. Here the Canary Islanders were expected to show off their legendary strength and agility as a public spectacle; the name of one captured leader, Adargoma, means "shoulders of rock." Other captives were sold as slaves in Cádiz, Valencia, and Seville. A German traveler, seeing a group of adults and children for sale in fifteeenth-century Valencia, described them as "wild beasts." Putting European clothing on them, however, "made these beasts in human bodies into tame human beings."[9]

When Petrus Gonzales was taken from Tenerife, he most likely ended up first in one of these Spanish cities, owned by slave traders. By that point, Canary Islanders had been sold as slaves in Spain for more than a century. When he arrived at the French court, the little boy was apparently given the name Petrus (Pierre in French), a relatively common name, but one also linked, in Latin, to the word for rock. Out of all possible names, did whoever named the "wild" boy choose this one because of its suggestions of the Canarians' great strength? Had he seen Canarians display such strength? Like so much else about the Gonzales family, Petrus' given name offers tantalizing hints, but nothing definitive.

Canary Islanders who rebelled against Spanish overlordship were hanged or sent to Spain as slaves, and their children distributed among the Spanish conquistadores. In theory, Christians were not supposed to enslave other Christians, and there were protests by a few missionaries, which led to a ruling by the pope against slave-taking in the Canaries. Prisoners of war could always legitimately be enslaved, however, so revolts were classified as "just wars" (*buena guerra* in Spanish) for those concerned with legal niceties. In any case, the pope was far away.

In 1491, Ferdinand and Isabella were engaged in expansion of their territory on multiple fronts. Spanish troops, including some soldiers who had earlier fought in the Canaries, were besieging the Moorish kingdom of Granada, the last Muslim territory in the Iberian Peninsula. Columbus was preparing his first voyage. A young nobleman experienced in the long siege of Granada, Alonso Luis Fernández de Lugo caught the attention of the monarchs long enough to gain their permission to conquer the last two Canary Islands. He obtained financial backing from Italian merchants and recruited men by promising slaves, land, and booty. His expedition reached the Canaries in late 1492, shortly after Columbus' three boats had stopped there on their way west and the Moors had surrendered to Spanish forces in Granada. Over the next several years, Lugo's forces, assisted by native people from other islands and a series of agreements made and broken, defeated local forces on Palma and Tenerife.

Their conquest of Tenerife, the largest and most heavily populated of the Canaries, was made much easier by the outbreak of some kind of plague. Chroniclers with the Spanish troops, who usually concentrated on battlefield exploits, report the bodies of plague victims everywhere they went. The indigenous people of Tenerife, the original Guanches, had no resistance to disease from the European mainland, and died by the hundreds each week. Gradually the Guanches who were still resisting Lugo's forces surrendered. Lugo ordered them baptized, a church built, and celebratory masses sung.

He took a group of Guanche leaders to Spain and presented them at the court of Ferdinand and Isabella. A painting from the time shows the royal couple seated on their thrones, surrounded by courtiers dressed in somber black, with *tamarco*-clad Canary Islanders in front of them. The artist chose to add fleece-fringed leather knee-socks to their outfits, though no shoes.

Sugar, slavery, and Spanish rule on Tenerife

With the surrender of the last Guanche forces on Christmas Day, 1495, Lugo was appointed governor of Tenerife and Palma. He began distributing land, almost all of it to soldiers who had been part of the conquering forces or to wealthy absentee landlords who lived in Spain, Portugal, or Italy. As more and more native people died of disease and famine, or were deported into slavery, immigrants from Europe came to the islands. They included nobles and merchants who hoped to acquire land and make large profits, but especially peasants and laborers brought in to work the land and process agricultural goods. The Europeans built towns centered on a public square in the style of those in Spain and Portugal, with government buildings, churches, monasteries, and convents.

Some estates raised sheep and goats, just as the native people had before European conquest; indigenous people continued their work as herders, but now as slaves or servants to European landholders. On Tenerife, all free Guanches were ordered to put themselves in the employ of a European and stop living in isolated hilly areas. They were not to follow their traditional way of life, and were supposed to wear woven clothing, not a *tamarco*. Lugo ordered European immigrants to hunt down those who resisted, and transport them off the island. Despite his promises of money to all who did, this was a difficult process. The governing council complained, "as they are native, and know the land, they can't be caught . . . and they say that the land and animals were their grandparents. . . . They follow their old customs and go about in tamarcos. . . . They hide and feed each other in the mountains . . . and would die rather than reveal their secrets . . . to find them out by torture is impossible even if they are cut to pieces."[10]

Although some of the new landholders raised stock, more turned to new crops, especially sugar cane. Producing sugar takes expensive refining machinery and many workers to chop and transport heavy cane, burn fields, and tend vats of cooking cane juice. This means that it is difficult for small growers to produce sugar economically, and what developed instead were large estates, often owned by distant merchants or investors.

Shipping and slavery made sugar an increasingly affordable luxury. European ships carried raw sugar and molasses made from sugar cane juice to Europe. Raw sugar was refined into white sugar in the Netherlands and used to make sweet wine in Portugal. Sugar and wine were shipped to England and other parts of Europe in exchange for cloth, manufactured goods, and machinery. Ships took flour and lumber from North America to tropical plantations, and carried molasses on the way back, which was processed into rum. Rum and wine were on every European ship crossing any ocean, for they could be sold at a profit almost anywhere and were part of the crews' daily rations. West Africa, Europe, and the Caribbean formed three points in what is often called the "triangle trade" of the Atlantic.

On their trips from West Africa, those ships also carried slaves. Slave traders from West African coastal areas went further and further inland to capture, buy, or trade for more and more slaves. Some rulers tried to limit the slave trade in their areas, but others profited from it, and raiders paid little attention to regulations anyway. They encouraged warfare to provide captives, or just grabbed people from their houses and fields. The slave trade grew steadily, and first thousands and then tens of thousands of people a year, the majority of them men and boys, were taken from Africa to work on sugar plantations. For 350 years after Columbus' voyage, more Africans crossed the Atlantic than did Europeans. The slave trade by itself did not bring spectacular profits, but the plantation system was an essential part of a business network that provided steadily increasing wealth for European merchants and investors.

Alonso de Lugo quickly recognized the great profits that could be made in sugar. He ordered that sugar be planted on his vast properties, and erected sugar mills on many of the islands. Only those who promised to plant cane and build sugar mills received land grants from Lugo. By the time mills were in operation in the Canaries, however, there were too few native people left to do the back-breaking work sugar requires. The mills relied on slaves, captured on the coast of Africa and brought to the islands. Extra slaves were sent on to Spain, for slave-trading combined easily with sugar production, and enhanced profits. Most of the actual sugar farming was carried out by poor immigrants from Europe, especially Portuguese, who received a share of the harvest for their labors. Guanches and other Canary Islanders served on some of the ships that raided for slaves on the African coast—generally as slaves themselves—and they worked as slaves in Europe, but they did not work crops or in sugar mills in their homeland.

Church officials wanted to make sure that all who lived on the Canary Islands—immigrants from Europe, African slaves, the few Canary Islanders that remained, and the growing number of people with a mixed ethnic background—were good Catholics. They obtained grants of land for the building of monasteries and churches, and in 1499 brought in the Spanish Inquisition to enforce religious uniformity. The efforts of the Inquisition ran counter to the need for workers in the Canaries, however. Slaves from West Africa were often Muslim, and arresting them for religious crimes meant that they could not work. European immigrants included a number of Jews, especially after 1492, when Ferdinand and Isabella ordered all Jews living in Spain to convert or leave. The political leaders in the Canaries (somewhat quietly) allowed Jews to immigrate, and later they allowed in Spanish Muslims from Granada when royal edicts made their lives increasingly difficult. The situation of non-Christians in the Canaries was still precarious, however. Immigrants were scrutinized for Jewish and Muslim practices, and native peoples, particularly those who lived on their own in the hills, were denounced, investigated, and sometimes punished for not performing Christian rituals or failing to go to Mass.

By the middle of the sixteenth century, there were very few native Canary Islanders for the Inquisition or anyone else to worry about. In 1513, the government counted only 600 Guanches on

Tenerife, down from tens of thousands twenty years earlier. By mid-century the number was even lower. Espinosa notes many times that his descriptions, written in the 1580s, are of "the people who *formerly* inhabited the island," obtained by talking with "old Guanches," not direct observation. Those who survived often inter-married with slaves from Africa, or with immigrant peasants and workers from Portugal, Spain, and Italy.

This was the world, then, into which Petrus Gonzales was born. He came to the French court in 1547 as a boy, so he was probably born in the late 1530s. Sugar production on Tenerife was in full swing, with thousands of European settlers and African slaves coming to the island each year to work and to replace earlier immi-grants and slaves who had died in the harsh fields and processing facilities. La Laguna, the largest city on Tenerife, had a population of about 5,000, most of them Portuguese immigrants. Those who became wealthy on sugar built beautiful houses and dressed in imported silks, but most people living on Tenerife were ordinary workers and farmers and slaves, dressed in wool and linen cloth. Did anyone still wear the *tamarco*? Probably not. Even before Lugo tried to Europeanize (or exterminate) Guanches who lived away from settlements, Canary Islanders had adopted European clothing. It was cheaper, especially as the wool did not have to be imported, but came from local sheep. It was easier to make, as it could be sewn with an ordinary needle and thread, and did not have to be punched to allow pieces to be fastened together.

The Guanche Gonzaleses

Petrus Gonzales came from Tenerife, but did this mean he was a Guanche? By the seventeenth century, Lugo's desire to exterminate Guanche culture had been replaced by a fascination on the part of many Europeans with the original inhabitants of the Canaries. The reports of their physical strength and bravery in battle made them seem a perfect example of the wild man celebrated by noble fami-lies and city artisans. Travelers and tourists reported finding "living Guanches" in more isolated parts of the islands, judging people's ethnicity by their physical appearance, customs, housing styles, food, tools, names, and work patterns. More recently anthropologists have used high-tech analysis of blood types and other anatomical features in their search for surviving native Canary Islanders. Some scholars think that there might be a few, especially in villages in the south of Tenerife, where in the late fifteenth century the Guanches made their last stand against Spanish forces. Most anthropologists and historians are not so sure. Living in "Guanche-style" houses or participating in "traditional" wrestling matches does not make one a Guanche. Although visitors with romantic notions about the survival of an ancient culture might choose to think so, contemporary rural people on Tenerife do not. They view the Guanches with sympathy and admiration, and continue to follow some of their traditions. But they refer to them as "them," not "us." Blood tests indicate that many people are related to the Berbers of North Africa, as were the Guanches in the generally accepted view of their origins. Immigration from North Africa—of both slaves and free people—continued long after Spanish colonization, however, so this evidence is not conclusive.

It is difficult to tell today whether a person is a "real" Guanche, and it is impossible to decide this for someone in the sixteenth century. By the time Petrus was born, forty years after Lugo's conquest of the island, there were only a few hundred Guanches left on Tenerife. Immigrants included people who were native to other islands of the Canaries (so not technically Guanches, though by this time the word was used for the original inhabitants of all the islands), but they were already intermarrying with Europeans and Africans.

Petrus Gonzales is described in several sources—including the painting of his daughter Antonietta by Lavinia Fontana—as "Don Pedro," that is, with the title of respect, "Don," used by Spanish nobles. Spanish officials sometimes used the title "Don" in the Americas to describe men of high rank, the chiefs and leaders of indigenous groups. Was Petrus a descendant of a ruling family in the Canaries? And did he relate this detail of his background to Henry II in France? Or did someone at the French court just add this to the story to make Petrus even more sensational, in the same way that Europeans transformed so many indigenous American women into "Indian princesses" when they told stories about them? The surviving evidence does not tell us whether Petrus described himself as a Guanche lord, or whether those who observed him and his family added this detail to their story, knowing he had been born on Tenerife. Enrico, however, *did* talk about himself as a Guanche to the men who owned him, painted him, and gave him as a gift. It was Enrico who most likely told Agostino Carracci about *tamarcos*, and, if there was an actual skin cape and not just talk of one, perhaps made it himself. Enrico's knowledge of these garments probably came only from speaking with his father, for it is doubtful whether he had ever seen a real *tamarco*. This might be why the *tamarco* in Carracci's painting looks so much more like Hercules' cape than like the garment described by Espinosa. Travelers' reports published in Italy in the sixteenth century mention *tamarcos* briefly, but only Espinosa gives a full description, and his report was in Spanish and not widely available in Italy. Like Enrico himself, the *tamarco* in Carracci's painting reflects stories about the Guanches as much as their history. Those stories lived on even after he died. When the Italian printmaker Stefano della Bella made an engraving of Enrico's younger brother Orazio after his death, he showed him in a *tamarco*, or at least in what had been Carracci's idea of what a *tamarco* looked like.

Real and created selves

Enrico probably thought he *was* a Guanche, but even if he knew otherwise, his adopting an identity different from his original one put him in good company. In the sixteenth century, many people fashioned selves different from their "real" ones or obscured their background for a variety of reasons, including money, social prestige, honor, and staying alive. With their hairy faces, the Gonzales family could not fully transform themselves, but the contrast between those faces and their courtly clothing reminded people that fancy clothes could always hide secrets. As we are today, people were both worried and fascinated by what we now often term "passing," pretending to belong to a group different from what one

18. Stefano della Bella, *Engraving of Orazio Gonzales, c. 1630.* As the engraving itself notes, this was an effigy portrait of Orazio (Horatio in Latin) Gonzales, done after his death for Mercurio Ferrari, who served with Orazio at the Farnese court in Rome. As was common in effigy portraits, the engraver includes a short verse about the deceased and his connections to the person who ordered the portrait. In the verse, the relationship between the two men is described as love ("amore"). Whether this love might have included sex is not clear, for passionate language was often used for same-sex friendships in this era.

Gonzalus gleams here, well-known in the Roman court
Animal hair bristles from his human face
And to you, Ferrarius, who once was joined in love [with him]
He lived, and lives breathing still, in fidelity.

actually is. Might certain behavior, manners, and clothing just be a disguise, adopted for deceit or betrayal?

Fictional identities masked people at the highest levels of society, including many with connections to the Gonzales family. The first Farnese to own the Gonzaleses was Odoardo and Ranuccio's father Alessandro Farnese, the son of Margaret of Parma and her second husband Ottavio Farnese. Margaret was the illegitimate daughter of the Holy Roman Emperor and king of Spain Charles V, born to a servant in a house where he was staying. There was no attempt to hide her parentage, and Margaret served, as had her aunt and great-aunt before her, as governor of the Netherlands, an important position. The parentage of Margaret's first husband was another story. Margaret had been married at fourteen to Alessandro Medici, the first duke of Florence. Alessandro was regarded as the half-brother of Queen Catherine de Medici, for they were both recognized as children of Lorenzo de Piero de Medici. Catherine was born to Lorenzo's wife, although her father was dead from syphilis by the time she was born. Alessandro's mother was a servant in the Medici household—of this there is no doubt—and, judging by the features for which he received the nickname "Il Moro" ("the Moor"), probably of African background. She may have been a slave, for many wealthy households in Italian cities had female slaves from Africa and other areas at the time. Alessandro Medici's maternal parentage was never officially recognized, however, and his identity as what we would term a "mixed-race" person is often still overlooked or downplayed.[11] In fact, Alessandro's maternal parentage was not the only thing about his identity that was hidden. Although Lorenzo de Piero de Medici was officially regarded as his father, many historians think that Alessandro was actually the son of Lorenzo's brother Giulio, who later became Pope Clement VII. This made him cousin to Catherine de Medici instead of half-brother. Thus everything about Alessandro was not what it seemed, although his position as a member of the powerful Medici family trumped everything, and his descendants later married into most of the ruling houses of Europe.

Other high-ranking families with links to the Gonzales family also had members whose public identity did not match their parentage. The best-known portraits of the hairy family were owned by Ferdinand II, archduke of Tyrol, who was Margaret of Parma's cousin. Ferdinand had married Philippine Welser, a commoner, and in doing so had given up his chance to become emperor. Their marriage was kept secret on the order of Ferdinand's father, and their children were officially viewed as adopted orphans. We can only wonder if these children saw any parallels between their situation and that of the hairy children whose portraits were on the walls above them.

Middle-class people also made themselves into something different from what they were. Scholars Latinized their names, and lawyers and government officials bought or were granted noble titles, transforming themselves and their families into aristocrats. The English scholar Thomas More, for example, the son of a lawyer, rose through a series of ever more powerful positions to become Lord Chancellor of England, second only to the king. The Farnese family had been nobles for centuries when they first encountered the Gonzaleses, but Catherine de Medici, who was queen of France when Petrus first came to Paris, had ancestors who were wool traders. Such social mobility was praised by some, but old noble families often sniffed at these newcomers, whom they saw as not really worthy of their titles. The male members of the Gonzales family were themselves at the lower end of this social-climbing ladder, granted minor offices and titles by Henry II and the Farneses. Such powerful patronage no doubt kept the mouths of their smooth-skinned fellow officials shut, or at least kept criticism of the hairy courtiers limited to whispers.

People on the bottom of the social heap, too, created new identities or fashioned stories about themselves when it suited their purposes. Those who passed as someone else joined monsters and birth defects as "news" in broadsheets and pamphlets. There were women pretending to be men who served as sailors and soldiers, royal infants switched with commoners by conniving midwives, charlatans pretending to be doctors or surgeons, and servants who seemed to be hard-working and faithful, but killed their employers in cold blood.

Favorite fictional stories also involved people who were not what they seemed. Shakespeare's plays are filled with male actors playing women (and sometimes male actors playing women dressed as boys or men), kings' sons in shepherds' clothing, spiteful daughters who pretend to be loving. Fiction about hidden and double identities sometimes masked political critique. A satirical novel published anonymously in 1605 with the title *Description de l'isle des hermophrodites nouvellement découverte* (Description of the Island of Hermaphrodites, Newly Discovered) uses an imaginary island of double-sexed beings to attack the court of King Henry III of France, who had himself dressed occasionally in women's clothing. Not only were the king and his courtiers not what they seemed, suggests the conservative Catholic author, but nor were any moderate Catholics who favored toleration of religious differences instead of trying to wipe out Protestantism. Just as hermaphrodites seem to be women, but are really men—or really monsters of both sexes at once—moderates were only pretending to be Catholics but were really atheists underneath.

Religion provided all kinds of situations in which people were suspected of pretending to be something they were not. The Spanish Inquisition was intent on determining whether people whose ancestors had been Jews or Muslims had "really" converted, testing to see if they would eat pork or could say the Lord's Prayer. Christian authorities viewed religion not simply as a matter of practice and belief, but of one's inner being, one's "blood." Thus no matter how often they went to Mass or prayed to the saints or confessed to a priest, converts still had Jewish or Muslim "blood," and might be just passing as Christians. "Purity of the blood"—having no Jewish or Muslim ancestors—became an obsession in sixteenth-century Spain, but everywhere in Europe people worried about those who outwardly conformed to one religion but secretly practiced another.

In England, these worries about religious impostors were not primarily about Jews, who had been expelled from the country in 1290, or Muslims, who were largely non-existent except for a few slaves and merchants, but about Catholics. During Queen Elizabeth's reign, people were required to attend Protestant services and could be fined for not going. In Catholic families, the men often went while the women stayed home, sometimes secretly sheltering priests and hearing Mass as well. (Under English common law, married women did not own any property independently, so they could not be fined, for all their money belonged to their husband.) Here was another example, to many, of people passing as one thing but really being another. Similarly, on the continent, the religious reformer John Calvin railed against those who accepted Protestant doctrine but continued to go to Catholic Mass or other services, calling this a "perverse subtlety" and labeling people who did so "Nicodemites" after the biblical figure Nicodemus who in fear visited Jesus only at night.

In the 1560s, while Petrus Gonzales was at the French court, people eagerly read about a spectacular case of imposture: that of Martin Guerre, in which a man took on the identity of another man he had apparently befriended while they served as soldiers together. The original Martin Guerre's neighbors, family, and wife fully accepted the impostor until increasing suspicions fueled by battles over money led to a court case, during which the real Martin Guerre returned. The impostor was executed for fraud and adultery, but those who heard about the case were more fascinated than horrified by his skills at deception. (And still are—the story was made into a French movie in 1982, a British stage musical in 1996, and an American movie, with the names changed and the setting moved to the American Civil War, in 1993.)

There is no way to know whether Enrico Gonzales was a Guanche, thought he was a Guanche, or simply pretended to be a Guanche. He most likely—to put it in the terms used in the sixteenth century and still used today—had some "Guanche blood" flowing through his veins, as did his sisters. "Blood" has long been a common way of talking about differences. In the sixteenth century, people in Europe were described as having "noble blood," "French blood," and even "Protestant blood." With the development of colonies came "Indian blood," and in the seventeenth century, "black blood." (None of these differences are apparent in actual blood, of course, although well into the twentieth century physicians and scientists expended much effort trying to prove that they were.)

Enrico Gonzales certainly—to put it in terms used in the sixteenth century and *not* used today—had "Catholic blood." Born in the 1530s on Tenerife, Petrus Gonzales would have been baptized in a Catholic church, whatever the ethnic mix in his background. He was found by individuals who were at least outwardly Catholic, and was probably taken first to a port in Spain or under Spanish control. There the king, Philip II, was a descendant of "their most Catholic majesties" Ferdinand and Isabella and an ardent defender of the faith himself. Petrus was brought to a court that was officially Catholic, and spent most of his life at various Catholic courts, as did his children.

19. *Portrait of Petrus Gonzales* by an unknown artist, 1580s. In this life-size oil painting, made for Duke William V of Bavaria, Petrus is wearing a ruff and a black scholar's robe edged in red. He is standing in what appears to be a cave, a setting the artist used further to highlight the contradictions between his wild hairy face and his sober clothing.

3

Massacring Beasts,
Monstrous Women, and
Educated Gentlemen

THE WORLD OF THE COURT

In 1547, Petrus Gonzales was taken from Tenerife to the court of Henry II and his wife Catherine de Medici in Paris. Giulio Alvarotto, the representative of the duke of Ferrara at the French court, reported on this new arrival:

> Staying with the king was a boy given to him of about ten years old, born in the Indies, very attractive, but he was completely hairy on his face for all his life, exactly like the paintings of wild men of the woods. The fur is about five fingers long. It is very thin, so you can still see all the features of his face. The hair is of a light blond color and very delicate and fine, like the fur of a sable, and it smells good. He speaks Spanish and is dressed like an ordinary person. But the fur frustrated (*frusto*) him for his life. Those who had him gave him to His Majesty.[1]

Ten years later, Julius Caesar Scaliger, an Italian physician and scholar whose students included the apothecary (and later prophet) Michel de Nostradamus and the author François Rabelais, reported on Petrus' arrival in Paris in a long Latin work on natural philosophy. Scaliger's comments were repeated by the Italian physician Realdo Colombo in an anatomy treatise published in 1559, and in 1582, another physician, the Flemish Johann van den Bosch, again described him, adding a few

details about his life at Paris. Aldrovandi read about Petrus in all of
these authors, or so he says in the *Monstrorum historia*, and cites Van
den Bosch directly:"Henry the French king, according to Boscius, was
taking care of a boy in Paris not less hairy than a dog, and having him
instructed in the humanities."[2] There are no paintings of Petrus at the
French court, but the full-length life-size portrait done later by an
unknown court artist and hung on the walls of Ambras castle captures
Aldrovandi's words exactly. Petrus' dog-like hairy face tops a body
dressed in the elegant, yet somber, clothing of a scholar: a black robe,
trimmed with a long velvet band, strikingly similar to the robes worn
by people with doctoral degrees in academic processions today. The
artist places Petrus in what looks like a cave, a reference to the caves
where his Guanche ancestors were thought to have lived. Stories told
later about Petrus said that a cave was made especially for him in the
grounds of one of the French royal palaces so that he would feel more
at home, although we don't know if the painting shows him in a cave
because of those stories, or if the stories came from people looking at
the painting.

We also do not know exactly who brought Petrus to Paris, or
why he happened to be taken there, as opposed to somewhere
else in Europe. He could hardly have landed at a more tumultuous
place, however, or a place more full of "monsters." Catholics and
Protestants accused each other of being "beasts" and "fiends," unnatural beings whose religion made them monstrous. Religious hatred
led to mob violence, massacres, and warfare, which continued
throughout the decades that Petrus was in Paris. His eldest daughter
Maddalena was born shortly after the bloodiest massacre, which in
Protestant eyes was led by the "monster of monsters," Catherine de
Medici. All around the Gonzales family swirled talk of monsters,
and they were not the only ones who seemed both beastly and
human. Not all "monsters" were the same, of course, but this very
variety made monstrosity all the more dangerous.

Monsters could be male or female—or somewhere in between—
but one particular type of woman was always monstrous, in the eyes
of many: a ruling queen. Such "unnatural" women appeared to be
growing more common in the middle of the sixteenth century, and

their opponents argued that they made their countries monstrous as well, deformed because they lacked a proper head. In the decades when first Petrus and then his daughters were growing up, the links between women, monsters, and animals were especially popular themes in sermons, pamphlets, and books. The lines of connection ran differently in the case of the Gonzales sisters than they did for Europe's female rulers, but monstrosity was always a slippery category, and one kind of monster could be read as the sign for another.

Extremes of religious violence and hatred of powerful women shaped the lives of the Gonzales family directly, just as they shaped the courtly worlds in which they lived. International conflicts and tragic accidents had an impact as well, beginning shortly after Petrus arrived as a small boy in Paris.

War and peace, marriage and death

In the sixteenth century, France and Spain were engaged in a long series of wars that pitted the house of Valois, which ruled France, against the house of Habsburg, which ruled Spain and much of central Europe. Habsburg and Valois forces had fought each other in Italy, and along France's southern and eastern borders, off and on (mostly on) since 1494. Shifting alliances on an international scale, and the use of mercenaries on all sides, brought troops from all over Europe into the conflict. Fighting flared up in the 1550s in Italy and along France's eastern border. Henry II's troops plundered Habsburg lands in the Netherlands, but the Habsburgs and their allies were successful in Italy. In 1559 Henry II was forced to accept the Peace Treaty of Câteau Cambrésis, in which France abandoned its claims to Italy. Part of the treaty's complicated negotiations involved a marriage between Henry's daughter Elizabeth and Carlos, the son of Philip II, the Habsburg king of Spain. That marriage was called off when Philip's second wife (Queen Mary of England) died, and Philip decided that he would marry the teenage Elizabeth of Valois himself, though he was nearly twenty years older than she was. (Not surprisingly, this decision made Carlos hate his father even more than he already did, and probably contributed to Carlos' growing mental instability and violent outbursts

of rage. He ended up in solitary confinement, placed there by his
father, and died—still unmarried—as a young man.)

The peace treaty and the royal marriage were cause for celebration in France, and the court sponsored a jousting tournament
featuring the athletic and energetic king as one of the contestants.
To the horror of the splendidly dressed onlookers, a splinter from
the lance of one of his guards went through Henry's visor into his
eye, and on into his brain. Despite the efforts of Ambroise Paré, the
royal surgeon and anatomist, Henry died ten days later, leaving his
sickly sixteen-year-old son Francis II as king. Francis followed his
father into the royal tombs at Saint-Denis the following year, and
his ten-year-old second brother Charles IX became king.

Henry's death was unexpected, but not unforeseen. According to
the memoirs of her daughter Marguerite, Catherine de Medici,
who believed firmly in portents, had dreamt the night before
about the king lying in a pool of blood, and asked him not to joust.
Her fears resulted not only from the dream, but also from the
predictions of two of her favorite authorities on such matters. Luca
Gaurico, the official astrologer for the Medici family, had warned
Henry not to engage in single combat when he was forty, or risk
losing his life.

Another prediction came from the apothecary and almanac writer
Michel de Nostradamus, whose books of prophecies were making
him a sensation at the French court. Catherine had him draw up
horoscopes for her sons, the most alarming of which foretold that
her oldest son Francis would die before he was eighteen, and hinted at
other disasters to come for the royal family. The year before Henry's
death, Nostradamus dedicated a volume of his prophecies to the
king. The dedication describes the coming reign of the Antichrist and
the final triumph of Christ, and gives a few dates for key events, past
and present, based on astrological calculations.[3] It does not predict
anything specifically about Henry, but among the verses in the volume
was one that, after the fact, seemed to foretell the king's tragic death:

> The young lion will overcome the old, in
> A field of combat in a single fight. He will

Pierce his eyes in a golden cage, two
Wounds in one, he then dies a cruel death.

Who else could the old lion be but Henry, and the golden cage his helmet visor? This interpretation does not seem to have been advanced at the time—it first shows up in a biography of Nostradamus written by his son long after the astrologer was dead—but Nostradamus' vague predictions of royal calamities were enough to cement his reputation as a prophet. That reputation grew even more the following year, when Francis II died at sixteen, just as Nostradamus had predicted. Catherine made Nostradamus a royal physician and paid him well.

Catholic wolves and Calvinist beasts

War with the Habsburgs, unexpected deaths, and mysterious prophecies were not the only problems facing France. Religion was tearing it apart. As in other parts of Europe, many people thought that the Catholic Church needed reform. In 1534, single-page broadsheets—the French called them *placards*—appeared one Sunday morning posted all over Paris and nearby cities, right where people would see them on their way to church. The *placards* denounced the Catholic Mass as a "horrible, gross, and insufferable abuse," and described its effects in fiendish terms: "By this [Mass] the poor people are like ewes or miserable sheep, kept and maintained by these bewitching wolves [Catholic priests], then eaten, gnawed, and devoured."[4] One of these broadsheets was even nailed to King Francis I's bedchamber door (though he was in another royal palace at the time), forcing him to respond.

Respond he did. Six suspects were rounded up and burnt at the stake, and the king, dressed in black, led a spectacular religious procession through the streets of Paris with his three young sons accompanying him. A wave of persecutions followed, and many reformers fled France. Among these was John Calvin, whose ideas would prove even more explosive in France than those of earlier reformers. Calvin fled to Switzerland, and became the leader of a new form of Protestant city and church government in Geneva. Here he developed key ideas in a systematic way, and established an academy to train pastors and chaplains. In Calvin's eyes, God is infinite in power and humans are completely sinful, saved only through Jesus Christ. The possibility of redemption and union with Christ is a gift from God, and God has already determined who would receive it. God's decision occurred at the beginning of time, predestining some to eternal damnation and others to eternal salvation. There was nothing anyone could do to change this "terrible decree"—Calvin's own words.

A person's actions could not change fate, but many Calvinists came to believe that hard work, thrift, and proper moral conduct could serve as signs that a man or woman was among the "elect" chosen for salvation. Any occupation or profession could be a God-given "calling," and should be done with diligence, thanksgiving, and dedication. Calvinism appealed to a wide spectrum of people, and in France it proved especially popular with urban residents and nobles. Calvin was himself French and wrote in French, and sent pastors trained at the Genevan academy to French cities and noble households.

Henry II followed his father's example in handling French Protestants (called Huguenots), whom he saw as a poison that would provoke the wrath of God. He had inherited the throne just a few months before Petrus Gonzales arrived in Paris, and immediately created a special court for dealing with heresy, the "burning chamber" (*chambre ardente*). More than a hundred people a year were arrested and tried, with punishments ranging from death at the stake for those who would not give up their beliefs, to banishment and public whipping for those who would. Despite these measures, Calvinist Protestantism continued to gain support in France: the nobles saw accepting Calvinism as a way to combat the growing power of the monarchy, and lower-class urban workers saw it as offering a sense of community during rough economic times. Middle-class city folk were attracted by its emphasis on work and order. Even some judges and officials became Protestant, making it difficult for the king to enforce laws against it.

As Petrus spent his first years at the French court, the conflict between Protestants and Catholics in France was becoming more violent. King Henry II issued a series of increasingly harsh edicts against Huguenots, ordering the death penalty for anyone who went to Geneva, preached Protestant sermons, or attended a Protestant religious meeting. In Paris, a mob broke into a house where Huguenots were worshiping. Over a hundred people were arrested and thrown in prison, and several were soon burnt at the stake. Among the charges leveled at them by Catholic pamphleteers was that they "mixed together indiscriminately, men and women, to make love . . . and offered their own children to be sacrificed, seeing such horrible crime favorably."[5] With the tragic death of Henry II, young King Francis was dominated by several members of the zealously Catholic Guise family, including his mother-in-law, a powerful duke, and a cardinal. Executions increased, especially after a plot to "liberate" Francis from Guise dominance was uncovered.

Huguenots carried out their own mob actions. Protestant teachings called the power of sacred images into question, and mobs in many cities took down and smashed statues, stained-glass windows, and paintings in iconoclastic riots. They ridiculed and tested religious images, throwing them into latrines, using them as cooking fuel or building material, or giving them as toys or masks for children. In the Catholic stronghold of Dijon, Protestants baptized a dog and tied a statue of St Anthony to its collar, which it dragged through the muddy city streets. Though iconoclasm was often inspired by fiery sermons from Protestant clergy, destroying images was a way for ordinary men and women to show that they were rejecting Catholic teachings.

Catholic mobs responded by defending images, and crowds on both sides killed their opponents, often in gruesome ways. According to a Protestant pamphlet, a Catholic crowd of "execrable executioners" burst into the house of a Protestant widow, "slit the throat of this mother, then shot her five times in the breasts with a pistol, and then burned the hands and feet of Faith, her eldest daughter. . . . And after the massacre was completed and the house was ransacked, [the mob] led pigs into the house and enclosed them there, in order to make them eat all those poor dead corpses."[6] Both sides organized local militias, who marched with their weapons through city streets. There was open warfare, as pamphlets encouraged all "to spill your blood for God, even to the last drop." Destroy "the wild beasts of Geneva," urged a Catholic preacher in Paris, for to do so was God's will.[7] Protestants responded with their own animals: "Rabid tiger! Venomous asp! Sepulchre of abomination!" began one pamphlet attacking the duke of Guise, titled *Lettre addressee au Tiger de la France* (Letter addressed to the Tiger of France).[8]

Not only were their opponents more like animals than humans, proclaimed the pamphlets, but sometimes they did things that were even more monstrous. "Our Calvinists are all devoted to carnal desire," wrote one Catholic author. "They are like madmen running like horses after women as soon as they see them. They bray around them; they abandon themselves to their passion. . . . Some among them are so devoted to Venus and to her service that they seek doctors to make their shameful member grow larger than they have by nature."[9] In the Letter addressed to the Tiger of France, the cardinal of Lorraine—brother to the duke of Guise—is described as a "bugger cardinal and villainous sodomite" who "especially brought from Italy eight thousand contaminated sodomites . . . to abandon our daughters and sons to Sodom and Gomorrah."[10]

The court to which the Gonzales family was attached, then, was full of "wild beasts" with unnatural desires whose religion made them monstrous in the eyes of their opponents. Each side charged the other with inner moral monstrosity, relying in their propaganda on people's familiarity with the discussions of unusual creatures and monstrous races that appeared in broadsides, bestiaries, and books of prodigies. Religious hatred actually increased the audience for books of prodigies, as each side could interpret the monsters and portents in them as signs of God's wrath against the other. Petrus Gonzales and his children were a different sort of wild beast, of course, but the language of monstrosity flowed easily from one realm to another. We do not know what the Gonzales family thought about the war of words or the real war that swirled around them in Paris. We do know that this warfare knew few borders, and eventually affected them. They left France after a particularly bloody episode, perhaps given as a present by the king of France to Alessandro Farnese, the general in charge of the victorious Catholic troops.

The Queen of Massacres

Any religious opponent could be a monstrous beast, but in the eyes of Protestants one figure became more beastly than the rest: Catherine de' Medici. To her religious errors was added the fact that she was a woman, for whom political power was unnatural, ungodly, and, indeed, monstrous. "Monster" was a common description not only of one's religious opponents in the sixteenth century, but of any woman ruler. Although the Gonzales sisters would never become rulers, these monstrous and beastly queens lurked in the background of people's minds when they met the girls, enhancing the idea, taken from Aristotle, that women in their basic nature are monstrous.

Why, in Protestant eyes, was Catherine de Medici the worst monster of all? In the midst of the French religious wars, her son King Francis II died shortly after coming to the throne, and Catherine de Medici declared herself regent for her next son Charles IX, the new king. She adopted policies that generally backed Catholics, but dismissed the ultra-Catholic Guise family from court and sometimes took a more conciliatory policy and arranged for truces.

In 1572, it appeared as if the French monarchy wanted to make the truce more permanent, as the royal government invited the leaders of both sides to Paris to celebrate a lavish royal wedding of the Protestant Prince Henry of Navarre to Marguerite, Catherine's daughter and the sister of King Charles IX. A few days later, on August 24 (St Bartholomew's Day), most of the prominent Protestant wedding guests were assassinated on the order of the royal council. Thousands of other Protestants from all walks of life were slaughtered by mobs, often in horrific ways. After killing her mother and father, mobs "baptized" a young woman in their blood, setting her "stark naked in the blood of her mother and father, with horrible threats that, if ever she became a Huguenot, the same would happen to her."[11] People were impaled on spits and had their limbs hacked off; the Seine, which flowed through the middle of Paris, was reported to have filled with blood. The violence spread to other cities, where thousands more were killed, not just as a result of spontaneous mob action but on the direction of municipal authorities. This planned and orchestrated bloodshed, which became known as the St Bartholomew's Day Massacre, drove some Protestants into exile but others to renewed warfare.

The St Bartholomew's Day Massacre provoked vicious battles in print as well as in city streets. After the killings were over, Charles IX admitted that he had ordered at least some of them, and those carrying out the killing clearly believed they were doing the king's will as well as God's. In response, Protestant writers began to argue that the power of a monarch should be limited, that when a ruler became a tyrant, the people—or at least those people who otherwise had some authority, such as nobles or officials—had the right,

20. Francois Dubois, *St Bartholomew's Day Massacre*, 1572. As did many paintings of the massacre by Protestant artists, this includes gruesome scenes drawn from reports, such as blood overflowing from a canal, children's bodies dragged through the dirt, and women impaled on spits. The artist puts Catherine de' Medici herself in the scene at the top in a black dress, dagger in hand.

or even the duty, to rebel. Catholic authors answered these pamphlets by arguing that all political authority came from God and kings were answerable to God alone. No one had the right to resist, or even question, the actions of a divinely ordained monarch. To do so would lead to anarchy, which was worse than the worst tyranny. In making their arguments, both sides used the most extreme language possible.

In Catherine de' Medici the Protestant side had a perfect villain. Two years after the massacre, Charles IX died. His brother Henry was called back from Poland, where he had been installed as king, to assume the French throne. During the months when France had no crowned king, Catherine was officially named regent, and Protestants thought this would be the perfect time to begin the civil war again. A Protestant author published *Discours merveilleux de la vie, actions, et déportments de Catherine de Médicis* (A Marvelous Discourse on the Life, Actions, and Behaviors of Catherine of Medici), a venom-filled tale of Catherine's life and "misconduct," and the ideal vehicle to encourage opposition to the queen, "a woman, a foreigner, an enemy hated by everyone." It was published anonymously, as was so much of the propaganda that appeared during the religious wars, but was probably written by Henri Estienne, a French scholar and printer then living in Calvin's city of Geneva. Despite the French government's best attempts to suppress it, ten editions, in French, German, Latin, and English, appeared in less than two years. It confirmed what many Protestants in Europe thought anyway, that France was ruled by an animal-like monster, whose actions and character were "against the Dictates of Nature."

Catherine, the *Discours merveilleux* proclaims, is the "perfect picture and example of tyranny . . . who holds us between her paws." Her birth had occasioned dire predictions, for when her family—the villainous, social-climbing Medicis—consulted astrologers, they learned that "she would be the cause, if she lived, of very great calamities and finally of the total ruin of the house and the place into which she married." The infamous family contemplated what it should do, the biography tells us: perhaps hang her in a basket on the city walls in the hope that she would be killed by a cannon-ball shot by the armies currently besieging the city? Or put her in a brothel? Or lock her away in a convent? None of these happened. Instead her uncle, Pope Clement VII, arranged for her to be married to Henry, and this "horrible Queen . . . so villainous and stinking" came to France. Here she became demonic as well as beastly, writes the author, plotting various poisonings, including the poisoning of the entire Protestant army "to exercise and satiate her most Devilish inclination . . . . This furious Medea, not satisfied with the bloodshed in this Tragedy," next turned against her own sons, "to attain her ambitious designs with masculine thoughts" and to "exercise and satiate her most devilish inclination." "Never has a woman governed our kingdom without disaster," the author rails, but Catherine's "furious malice" was the worst of all.[12] The queen who provided support for Petrus Gonzales, and later for his children, was thus, in the inflamed rhetoric of the *Discours merveilleux*, also like them, at once human and beastly.

21. Giorgio Vasari, *Marriage of Catherine de' Medici and Henry II of France*, c. 1550. In this allegorical painting, the Italian artist Vasari shows Catherine and Henry being wed by Pope Clement VII (her Medici relative), while courtiers, classical deities, peaceful animals, and dwarves look on. Vasari also painted scenes of the St Bartholomew's Day Massacre from the Catholic perspective, as a triumph over evil Protestants.

The monstrous rule of women

The author of the *Discours merveilleux* was not the first (or the last) to call a woman with political power unnatural. For those who thought this way (and there were many) the situation across the English Channel was even worse. When Henry VIII's sickly son Edward VI died in 1553 after only six years as king, he left two older sisters, the Catholic Mary and the Protestant Elizabeth. Mary became queen, and immediately set about finding a husband, as none of the earlier marriage negotiations that swirled around her—mostly involving various French princes and kings—had resulted in a marriage. She found one in her cousin, King Philip II of Spain, whose first wife had just died. (Philip and Mary were both descendants of Ferdinand and Isabella; that royal couple were Mary's grandparents and Philip's great-grandparents. He went on to have four wives—Maria of Portugal, Mary of England, Elizabeth of France, and Anne of Austria—all of whom except Elizabeth were his blood relatives.) Only through marriage and having a child could Mary make sure that her half-sister Elizabeth would never inherit the throne. (Murder was another option, and Mary did have Elizabeth arrested and sent to the Tower of London, but she decided against executing her.) Philip and Mary were wed in Winchester Cathedral. Mary proclaimed she was in love with Philip, although Philip did not return her feelings, and after little more than a year fled back to Spain.

In Mary Tudor's mind, Philip had done his kingly duty: she was pregnant. Thanksgiving services were proclaimed all over London, and the prospect of a Catholic heir to the English throne was celebrated in Rome, Vienna, Madrid, and other centers of Catholic power. It was regarded with horror by Protestants in England and on the continent, and especially by Protestants who had fled the British Isles to escape Mary's persecution of those who opposed her moves to return England to Catholicism.

One of those exiles was the Scottish religious reformer John Knox, who had been a firebrand preacher in London and a chaplain in the household of Edward VI. When Mary became queen, Knox fled to Geneva, where Calvin was transforming the city into what Knox approvingly viewed as "the most perfect school of Christ that ever was in the earth since the days of the apostles." Just as Mary was marrying Philip, Knox published *A Faithful Admonition to the Professors of God's Truth in England*, attacking Mary and calling on Protestants in England to resist her rule. Knox and other Protestants breathed a sigh of relief when Mary's pregnancy turned out to be a false one and no Catholic heir to the throne appeared. Four years later Mary claimed to be pregnant again, however, and Knox decided even sterner words of warning were needed.

Mary Tudor was not the only Catholic queen who horrified Knox. King James V of Scotland had died in 1542, just as Scotland was going to war—again—with England. He left a week-old daughter, Mary Stuart, who was immediately proclaimed queen, although actual governing was in the hands of a royal council. Mary Stuart spent most of her childhood in France, under the guidance of her mother Mary of Guise, whose brothers were leaders of the Catholic forces in the wars of religion soon to tear France apart. She was at the French court when Petrus Gonzales arrived, and, like him, was educated under the guidance of Henry II. Because of complicated plotting at the Scottish court, Mary of Guise returned from France to Scotland as regent in 1554. When Mary of Guise returned to Scotland, she left her daughter in France, about to marry Francis, the oldest son of Henry II and Catherine de Medici. The two young people wed, and when Henry died in the tournament, Francis became king and Mary Stuart queen of France. It was a very short queenship. A year and a half after becoming king, Francis died, leaving Mary a young widow.

Mary was no longer queen of France, for Francis' younger brother succeeded him as king, but she was still queen of Scotland, and her mother was regent. Three Catholic Queen Marys—Mary Tudor, Mary of Guise, and Mary Stuart—in one island were too much for Knox to bear, and in 1558 he published what was to become his best-known work, *The First Blast of the Trumpet against the Monstrous Regiment of Women* directed against all of them. It was published anonymously, with the author stating he would reveal his identity once he had written all three of his intended "blasts." Everyone knew who had written it, however, and Knox never finished the other two blasts. This first blast was loud enough. "Wonder it is," it began,

> that amongst so many wits as the isle of Great Britain has produced, so many godly and zealous preachers as England did sometime nourish, and amongst so many learned, and men of grave judgment, as this day by Jezebel are exiled, none is found so stout of courage, so faithful to God, nor loving to their native country, that they dare admonish the inhabitants of that isle, how abominable before God is the empire or rule of a wicked woman (yea, of a traitress and bastard) . . . a woman promoted to sit in the seat of God (that is, to teach, to judge, or to reign above man) is a monster in nature, contumely [scornful] to God, and a thing most repugnant to his will and ordinance . . . he that judges it a monster in nature that a woman shall exercise weapons must judge it to be a monster of monsters that a woman shall be exalted above a whole realm and nation.

The monstrous rule of women was like other monsters, only worse:

> For who would not judge that body to be a monster, where there was no head eminent above the rest, but that the eyes were in the hands, the tongue and the mouth beneath in the belly, and the ears in the feet? Men, I say, should not only pronounce this body to be a monster, but assuredly they might conclude that such a body could not long endure. And no less monstrous is the body of that commonwealth where a woman bears empire; for either it does lack a lawful head (as in very deed it does), or else there is an idol exalted in the place of the true head.

Rule by a woman not only *should* be overthrown, but *must* be, for:

> The duty . . . of the people . . . [is] to remove from honour and authority that monster in nature: so I call a woman clad in the habit of a man, yea, a woman against nature reigning

above man . . . [By not resisting] the nobility both of England and Scotland [are] inferior to brute beasts, for that they do to women, which no male amongst the common sort of beasts can be proved to do their females: that is, they reverence them, and quake at their presence, they obey their commandments, and that against God. Wherefore I judge them not only subjects to women, but slaves of Satan, and servants of iniquity.[13]

To Knox, not only was a ruling queen herself a "monster of monsters," but she made everything and everyone around her equally monstrous, including her headless country and her spineless countrymen.

Though his words were extreme, Knox' ideas were not new or distinctive, but his timing was particularly bad. Mary Tudor, the "Jezebel" of England, said she was pregnant again, but the swelling of her body was probably cancer, which killed her. Several months after Knox' pamphlet was published, a new "monster in nature" was crowned queen of England: Elizabeth. Now that there was once again a Protestant ruler, Knox and other exiles began to wend their way back to England and Scotland. Knox would have to take a more circuitous route than the other Scots. They traveled through England, the most direct way from the continent. Furious at what he had written, Elizabeth refused to allow Knox into England—even to pass through it—unless he apologized. He would not.

One of Knox' targets was dead, and another would be soon. Mary of Guise died shortly after Francis II, leaving Mary Stuart an orphan as well as a widow. She was still queen of Scotland, however, and to Scotland she returned, a country nearly as divided by religion as France was. Knox had returned from Geneva, and become leader of the Protestants. The Scottish Parliament had ended the power of the pope and decided in favor of a Protestant form of worship. Mary was Catholic, but at first she kept many of the Protestant leaders as her advisors, and even arranged a series of meetings with Knox. Mary's marriage to her cousin Henry Stuart, a Scottish Catholic nobleman, however, combined with a growing perception that she favored Catholic France, led powerful Protestant lords to oppose her. A first rebellion was put down, but at the same time Mary grew to hate her husband, though she had a son by him. She was implicated in a plot that killed her husband—in fact, she married the chief plotter—and in 1567 was forced to abdicate in favor of her infant son James. She was imprisoned, but escaped. Knox preached sermon after sermon against her, demanding her death. Her small army dissolved and she fled across the border to England, leaving baby James behind. She never saw him again.

Knox died soon after Mary's downfall, but new voices took up the opposition to Mary. An anonymous treatise, *Detection of the Doings of Mary, Queen of Scots* was published in London in 1571, designed to explain to the English why the Scots had thrown Mary out. Like the *Discours merveilleux*, it relates the story of "a woman greedily coveting untempered authority" whose actions showed the "rash violent motion of a muddy and troubled mind." The author was not sure whether Mary was motivated by "unnaturalness, hatred, barbarous fierceness or outrageous cruelty," but concluded that it was all of these. The pamphlet was also published anonymously, but its author was George Buchanan, a Scottish scholar who had earlier taught at French universities and who had actually been Mary Stuart's tutor in Latin when she first returned to Scotland from France. (Buchanan was also close friends with Julius Caesar Scaliger, one of the authors who reported on Petrus Gonzales' arrival at the French court.) *Detection of the Doings* was published in French the year after it had been published in English, the same year as the St Bartholomew's Day Massacre, and was read eagerly by Protestants in France. Here was the story of another evil Catholic queen, perhaps even worse than Catherine de Medici, because she had killed her own husband! And she had close ties to the Catholics in France, for Mary Stuart's mother was one of the evil Guises, who Protestants were sure stood together with Catherine behind the massacre.

Petrus was raised by one "monstrous" queen, Catherine de Medici, and educated alongside another, Mary Stuart, who was just about his age during their years together at the French court. We can hope that his opinion was shaped by his years at the French court, and that he thought better of queens than did many, but this remains speculation.

About the time of the St Bartholomew's Day Massacre, Petrus Gonzales married a Parisian woman named Catherine (no sources give her last name), and several years later their first daughter, Maddalena, was born. Like her father, Maddalena was hairy. She was a very different sort of monstrous woman than those whom Knox rails against in the *First Blast*, but people's notions about one kind of female monster were shaped by what they read or heard about all of them. Knox, for example, directly compares real headless beings (familiar to him from Pliny) with states that lacked a true head because their ruler was a woman.

Animals as well as monsters appear in the works attacking female rule. In the *First Blast*, by not resisting their monstrous queen, nobles in England and Scotland were "inferior to brute beasts." In the *Discours merveilleux*, Catherine is a tyrant who holds poor France "between her paws." The links between women, monsters, and animals were clear in many of the religious and political pamphlets and books that people read avidly—though often illegally—in the decades before Maddalena was born. She and her sisters were not queens, but in their persons or their portraits they provided one more example of the connections between the monstrous, the animal, and the female that were so fresh in many people's minds.

Palaces and princely favor

This was the French court, then, where Petrus Gonzales lived as a boy and young man, where he married, and where Maddalena and his other children were born. French troops fought Habsburg forces, mobs attacked churches and homes in the streets of Paris, and "monstrous" women held power as queens and regents. Life at the court was not all high drama, however. Day-to-day life was also shaped by a regular round of activities and rituals that went on no matter what great political events occurred. Courts were where rulers dispensed favors, offices, gifts, and rewards. Exquisitely dressed courtiers sought to gain the king's and queen's attention, lesser folk served their social betters' physical and emotional needs, and human oddities and animals provided amusement. In the role he came to assume at court, Petrus combined all of these: courtier, servant, and oddity. His distinctive position provides a vantage point for us to examine life at what, through every kind of change, remained the center of wealth and power in sixteenth-century Europe: the court. Of the many courts in Europe, that of the French monarchs was among the most glittering. Like earlier kings of France, Henry moved around between various royal palaces. In Paris there was the Louvre, which he and his father transformed from a medieval fortress to a Renaissance showplace, or the old royal palace of the Tournelles. Just outside Paris was Saint-Germain-en-Laye, and further away the château at Amboise in the Loire valley, with its extensive gardens. After Henry's death Catherine demolished the Tournelles, as this was where the fateful tournament had been held. She began building a separate queen's palace near the Louvre, called the Tuileries (tile kilns) as there had originally been tile-makers' kilns at the site. The Tuileries, designed in the style of the sumptuous palaces in Italy Catherine had known as a child, had long galleries that contained over 250 portraits. Some of these were from the existing royal collection, but many were commissioned by Catherine herself.

After more than ten years with no children, Catherine and Henry had ten in quick succession, beginning in 1544, of which seven survived. Thus when Petrus was a child at the French court, the royal palaces and gardens were filled with children. Along with Catherine and Henry's, there was Mary Stuart, who came to the court at age five in 1548, already engaged to Prince Francis (he was two). In the following year came the ten-year-old Ludovico Gonzaga, the son of the duke of Mantua, a city-state in northern Italy. Ludovico's grand-mother had left a large estate in France that he was to inherit, and his parents decided a French upbringing would be perfect training, and help cement their connections with the French crown as well.

Sending a child away from home at age five or ten may seem cold, but it was a common practice in sixteenth-century Europe. Among artisan families, boys—and some girls—often began apprenticeships at seven or eight, living as well as working and learning in the house-hold of a master craftsman. For the upper classes, the fastest way to climb in terms of title, status, and actual power was through gaining royal or princely favor at court. Because of this, nobles sought positions at court for their adolescent children, especially if the young men or women were physically attractive, intelligent, and talented in music, conversation, or dance. Mary Stuart and Ludovico Gonzaga were a bit younger than normal, but they brought familiar faces with them. Mary, in fact, brought a whole mini-court of children along from Scotland, including four boys and four girls, all of whom were also named Mary.

Henry and Catherine's children were also often separated from their parents, spending much of their time at Amboise, a coach ride of several days from Paris. In order to keep up with their growth, Catherine frequently ordered portraits of her children, and especially liked pencil portraits because they could be done fast. She specified that they were to be done "from life," and be "as true to life as possible." The pencil portraits hung in her private rooms, or were collected in a small book that could be carried around, while the more formal oil portraits of the family hung in the main galleries. (The Tuileries palace was set on fire by political extremists during the Paris Commune of 1871, and burnt to the ground; many of its paintings survived, but much of Catherine's portrait gallery had already been dispersed to other collections.)

Henry's father Francis I had been satisfied with a thousand servants, but Henry and Catherine employed more: there were chaplains, porters, room attendants, footmen, ushers, and secretaries. At the royal stables, there were grooms, trainers, and stable-boys. In the royal kitchens, the hierarchy of servants ranged from master chefs and pastry-makers down to pot-washers and spit-turners. Each one of the children had his or her own nurses and maids. Along with all these people who received a salary from the royal treasury, there were members of the court guard protecting the royal family, gentlemen and nobles seeking the monarch's favor, goldsmiths, furniture-makers, and furriers offering their wares. This entourage easily swelled the court to eight or even ten thousand people. During times of celebration—and there were many—it was even larger, as musicians, firework-makers, actors, dancers, stage designers, and engineers swelled the ranks.

Among those living at the court were dwarves. Dwarves were part of royal and noble households throughout Europe in the sixteenth century. Catherine de Medici had a whole household of dwarves, including soldiers, pages, and monks. They were dressed in elaborate clothing, creating a reflection in miniature of the sumptuous full-size courtiers around them. Those courtiers found the contrast between the dwarves' fancy clothing and their tiny stature hilarious. Even more amusing was the staging of celebrations that paralleled those at court: plays acted by dwarves, jousts with dwarves on horseback, and once even a wedding between two of the queen's favorite dwarves. To some observers, dwarves also had a more serious purpose. When they stood next to a monarch, their small size reminded "those who desire to approach near Princes" that they "ought not to be ambitious of any greatnesses, but [ought] to acknowledge all their courtly lustre is but a reflection of the beam of the royal sun their master."[14] Dwarves thus could serve rulers as a symbol of the hierarchy they hoped their courtiers would remember.

The royal household was also home to animals. Along with horses, there were dogs of all types, from trained hunting dogs to tiny lap dogs. There were songbirds in cages and peacocks walking the grounds. The palaces in Paris and at Amboise held a menagerie of exotic animals, including lions, bears, and monkeys.

Petrus came to a court that was full of both servants and oddities, and his role there was somewhere in between. When he was in his late teens, Henry II gave him a position as an assistant bearer of the king's bread, one of several young men assigned to carry the bread from the bakery to where the king was dining. For this he received a salary, as did most servants, but this position also put him near the king, so his status was higher than that of many others at court.

Petrus was a servant, but he was also a courtier, and to understand his position we need to look at the court as a whole, not simply those in it who received wages from the king. The primary job of everyone at court was to keep the ruler content and happy, which meant that Petrus, and later his children, shared their dependent situation with everyone else. All encounters with the king were regulated by an increasingly elaborate code of social ritual that in

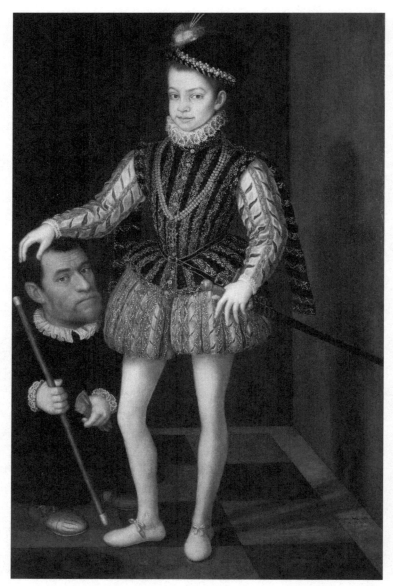

22. Giambattista Aleotti, *Charles Emanuel, Duke of Savoy, with a Dwarf, c.* 1600. The artist highlights the contrast between the two not only through their stature, but also through the nobleman's far more elegant clothing. Aleotti paints the dwarf with a beard, an indication that he is an adult, but a further blurring of his status, as he would not have the privileges that normally went with being an adult man.

the eighteenth century came to be called "etiquette." Even the very high nobility could not approach the king without arranging this in advance and following a prescribed set of gestures. Nobles vied with each other to carry out tasks associated with the physical needs of the monarch—bringing in breakfast, handing napkins, emptying the royal chamber pot. As Petrus carried the king's bread, he may have walked beside, or at least close behind, some of France's most powerful individuals. Though we may view such service activities as demeaning or even disgusting, they offered great opportunities for personal access to the ruler.

Two or three days a week were marked with religious observances of some sort, often several hours long, with music and processions. In addition to Sundays, there were feast days of the Christian calendar and saints' days for local and national saints. Courtiers missed such events at their peril, for the king himself was often at their center, covered by a canopy held up by courtiers that was modeled on the canopies that sheltered sacred objects. Indeed, the king *was* a sacred object, anointed by holy oil and consecrated in a coronation ceremony that took many things from religious liturgy. The gravity of religious ceremonies shaped other sorts of court rituals as well, all of which could fill long hours for the gentlemen- and ladies-in-waiting who waited on (and waited for) the ruler.

Success at court for either an adult or adolescent called for deference, understanding of ceremony and protocol, discretion, charm, and skill. Astute courtiers also used these qualities in their relations with anyone higher up the social scale, not simply the monarch. Leading office-holders, major army commanders, other members of the royal family, prominent church officials, and high nobles all had powers of patronage. They distributed offices and positions— which brought an income—and their support could open doors. Some of those doors might lead to the monarch, but even if they did not, being known as in the favor of Cardinal So-and-so, or Duke So-and-so, or General So-and-so, could increase a person's status. Power was especially diffuse in areas of Europe that were not nation-states and so lacked a central royal court, such as Italy. Here the patronage of regional rulers and high church officials was paramount, as Petrus Gonzales and his sons came to find in their connections to the Farnese family.

One's position in the hierarchy at court was initially set by inherited social rank and lineage, symbolized by the four images on a family crest that represented the families of one's grandparents. (These are called "heraldic quarterings.") But by making the right connections, knowing the right thing to do, and having more than a little luck, fortunate courtiers could add to the honor that came from family background. Courtly hierarchies were thus not rigid or set in stone, and this allowed individuals without family connections—of which Petrus was one—to insert themselves, or be inserted, somewhere on the social ladder, at least on its lower rungs. Battles over honor or precedence, fought in dining rooms, bedrooms, and hallways, and occasionally on dueling fields, provided regular drama.

By the time Petrus came to the French court, courtiers throughout Europe had an excellent guide for how to proceed, Baldassare Castiglione's *The Book of the Courtier (Il libro del cortegiano,* 1528*).* Castiglione had been a courtier in the ducal courts of Urbino, Mantua, and Milan in northern Italy in the early sixteenth century, and had written an advice manual setting out proper behavior for courtiers and court ladies, or those aspiring to such positions. This sold very well in its original Italian, and was translated into Spanish, French, English, German, and Polish. Life at the French court was guided by its suggestions, as was that at the Italian courts where the Gonzales family lived later. The personal qualities Castiglione praises—reserve, discretion, good manners, solidity, and learning worn lightly for men, and purity, modesty, beauty, agreeableness, and graciousness for women—actually became ideals for people much further down the social scale than his original audience. Middle-class urban people sought to learn and imitate courtly manners as a demonstration of their improving economic status, providing a wide market for conduct books such as *The Courtier.*

Special events and entertainments gave courtiers additional opportunities to display and enhance their honor. The most spectacular of these were tournaments and jousts, often sponsored by one of the chivalric orders created or re-created by rulers in the sixteenth century. Chivalric orders—associations of nobles who swore their devotion to honor, faith, and the ruler—were established in the fourteenth and fifteenth centuries by various rulers in Europe: King Henry II of England founded the Order of the Garter, Duke Philip III of Burgundy the Order of the Golden Fleece, King Louis XIII of France the Order of St Michael. Their fanciful names derive from romantic notions of knightly glory, but in reality they served more mundane purposes. Membership was strictly limited to only a few of the highest nobles, so chivalric orders were one more way for those nobles to prove they were better than everyone else. Initiation was marked by an elaborate ceremony in which the new member swore his loyalty to the king on the Bible and received insignia with Christian symbols. The chivalric orders were also a way for kings to affirm the sacredness of their power and the holiness of the bonds between them and the nobles. These idealized bonds did not shape the actions of Huguenot nobles during the French wars of religion very much, but French kings still regarded the chivalric orders as important. Shortly after the St Bartholomew's Day Massacre, Henry III established the new Order of the Holy Spirit, an even more limited and

23. Jacques Callot, *Combat a la barriere: The Tournament*, engraving, 1627. Royal ceremonies culminated in staged tournaments at which various sorts of real and stylized combat were performed. These became increasingly elaborate, designed more for spectators than as actual tests of skill.

higher-status group than the Order of St Michael, with membership confined to Catholics.

Tournaments on tour

Courtly magnificence was not restricted to palaces, but was also taken on the road during tours designed to parade the king and his family in front of his subjects. The royal tours of Henry II and Catherine de Medici displayed their power and wealth, and also demonstrated their interest in the exotic to the crowds who thronged to watch. That widely known interest may be one of the reasons that Petrus Gonzales was brought to Paris rather than to one of Europe's many other courts.

As the royal entourage traveled, each city along the way offered a ritualized "entry;" these grew increasingly elaborate as cities competed with one another. These entries were truly imagined worlds come to life. When Henry II made his formal entry into Paris in 1549, the decorations and events used classical themes, with the first arch through which the king rode crowned by a French Hercules. For a 1550 royal entry, the city of Rouen built an entire Brazilian village complete with parrots, trees, monkeys, hammocks, and fifty men and women brought from Brazil. The people were displayed completely naked, other than having polished stones stuck through body piercings. The Brazilians were joined by French sailors who—as accounts of the entry tell it—had all been to the Americas and could mimic the language and actions of real Brazilians well. As the king looked on, the actual and pretend Brazilians staged a battle with clubs and arrows, burning some of the houses to the ground. The king was pleased by this spectacle, and those who had been to Brazil swore that it was close to the truth.[15]

In 1564, Catherine de Medici decided that she and the young king Charles IX should tour the southern part of France so that they could demonstrate royal power, and also visit Charles' sister Elizabeth, now married to King Philip II of Spain. The tour lasted two full years, with the king and court making a formal entry into more than one hundred walled cities. On this tour, ten companies of foot soldiers made sure the king was safe along the way, while hundreds of servants and thousands of horses transported everything the royal household could possibly need along the muddy roads of France, including furniture, dishes, and silverware. Charles' younger brother Henry and sister Marguerite came along as well, although their youngest brother Hercule François stayed behind, as he was only nine.

Catherine and Charles were so attached to their animals that they took them along when they traveled. A drawing by the court painter Antoine Caron shows the royal tour leaving the castle at Anet, with the procession headed by a bear and its cub, several lions, monkeys on horseback, birds carried on poles, and a variety of dogs. The account books for the tour list payments to a certain Captain George, "manager of the king's beasts."

The entry into each city—for which an advance team had made extensive preparations—began with a long set of speeches, known officially as "harangues." Showing off their civic pride and hoping to win the king's favor through their flowery, flowing prose, city officials compared the king to Hercules, Alexander the Great, Charlemagne, and the god Apollo. Charles was like St Louis, they proclaimed, for like that earlier king of France he was also guided by his wise mother. Catherine herself was like the Greek princess Ariadne—just as Ariadne had helped the hero Theseus defeat the monstrous Minotaur, so Catherine helped Charles defeat the civil unrest of the wars of religion. Or she was like the goddess Athena, or Juno, who had suckled Hercules. On and on they droned, often for hours, and the teenaged Charles could only hope that something unexpected would happen. Usually it did not, so then there was a procession, more speeches, and a formal gift-giving ceremony. Charles might be asked to lay his hands on people ill with scrofula or "the king's evil," a type of externally visible tuberculosis that people believed could be cured by a touch from royalty. He and his mother also attended baptisms, where they stood as godparents to noble children.

Each city tried to outdo the others in splendor, providing tournaments, naval battles, banquets, bullfights, plays, dances, and jousts for the young king. The city of Fontainebleau constructed a huge "enchanted castle," where "maidens"—young male courtiers dressed in women's clothes—were guarded by "giants"—more courtiers in costume—until they were rescued by valiant knights.

Bordeaux offered "three hundred well-armed men who represented twelve vanquished foreign countries and paraded in front of
the king, with each nation dressed in its own style." The report of
the entry notes that these were "Greeks, Turks, Arabs, Egyptians,
Ceylonese, Americans, Indians, Canary Islanders, savages, Brazilians,
Moors, and Utopians."[16] The captain of each group professed his
loyalty to the king "in his own language," which was then translated.
Unfortunately, the contemporary report of this royal entry is not
illustrated, so that we don't know exactly what "in its own style"
meant. Nor do we know who these people really were. Bordeaux
was a port city, and an important center of the slave trade as well
as that in wine and sugar. People from all parts of the globe could
be found on the ships and docks in its harbor, so it is possible that
at least some of the well-armed men who marched in front of
the king were actually who they were claimed to be. Perhaps the
Canary Islanders really were Canary Islanders, for traders in
Bordeaux had direct contact with the Canaries. Perhaps this group
was even wearing *tamarcos*, although more likely they were dressed
in whatever the city officials of Bordeaux imagined Canary
Islanders wore.

The "Utopians" in the procession gave city officials even more
opportunity to use their imagination, for unlike Greeks, Turks, Arabs,
Egyptians, and the rest of the parade marchers, "Utopians" came
from a completely fictional place. Thomas More's *Utopia*, published
several decades earlier, depicted an island where life was orderly and
reasonable, so different from Europe. Utopia was a product of More's
fertile imagination, but many people thought he was describing
an actual place. Thus in their collection of exotics to parade before
the king, Bordeaux officials include a group of "Utopians." If they
had read the book, they would have known that Utopians dress in
very plain skin, wool, and linen garments of natural colors, and that,
"everyone on the island wears the same sort of clothes, except that
they vary slightly according to sex and marital status." More contrasts
the Utopians' simple garments with the multi-layered ones of the
wealthy in his own day: "Whereas in other countries you won't find
anyone satisfied with less than five or six suits, and as many silk

shirts, while dressy types want over ten of each, your Utopian is content with a single piece of clothing every two years. For why should he want more? They wouldn't make him any warmer or any better looking."[17] Simple brown outfits would not have fit with the splendor of the procession, of course, so it is doubtful that the dress of the Utopians in the parade matched More's description very closely.

More's discussion of the language of the Utopians was very brief. He simply noted that it has "quite a rich vocabulary," is "pleasant to listen to and extremely expressive" and "contains some traces of Greek."[18] This certainly gave the men marching as Utopians in the Bordeaux procession free rein to use whatever language they wanted, and their "translator" the opportunity to let his rhetoric soar wherever his fancy took him. What he might have said, or who these people actually were, is anyone's guess.

The city of Bayonne, right by the Spanish border on a river near the Atlantic, was not to be outdone by Bordeaux. For the initial

24. Jacques Callot, *Combat a la barriere: Entry of his Highness Duke Charles IV, representing the sun*, 1627. Horses in a royal entry pull a large wagon, with Duke Charles IV of Lorraine standing on the top symbolizing the sun. The high nobility of an area would often participate in royal entries, paying for their own elaborate costumes and decorations.

procession, hundreds of courtiers and servants were dressed in red velvet and silk, decorated with silver. Even those who led horses wore the same splendid outfits, designed to impress every onlooker, and especially any Spaniards. A French account describes the dress of the Spanish nobles who watched as "sober and frugal" (by which he meant dark, boring, and cheap), though whether the more plainly dressed Spanish were suitably impressed by the extravagant expenditure and French finery is not known.[19] The festivities at Bayonne included a week's worth of enormous events, each more fabulous than the previous. First there was a Tournament of Diverse Nations, in which knights representing France, Spain, Rome, Greece, Albania, and the Moorish kingdoms, all dressed in sumptuous outfits decorated with gold, silver, and semiprecious stones, jousted with one another in an outdoor arena. Some of the groups included winged creatures in masks and warriors dressed in hairy robes, described by one observer as "Tartars" and another as "savage Scots." Not surprisingly, in the joust that followed, France won, a clear sign of Charles' triumph over nations present and past, near and far, mythological and real.

The Tournament of Diverse Nations was followed two days later by another assault on an enchanted castle. This time the king was a participant as well as a spectator, which must have pleased the teenaged Charles immensely. At one end of a huge ballroom a fairy, dwarf, and giant guarded a castle complete with rocks and trees, and through magic or strength defeated all who attempted to enter. Only the king, dressed in armor, was able to defeat them and take the castle, where a beautiful lady led him to the summit. Then the entourage moved outdoors again, onto decorated boats this time. They sailed up the river, but their way was blocked by a huge (artificial) whale, defeated after a fight by some of Bayonne's (real) whale hunters. More feasting, more dances, more songs. Two more day-long tournaments with chariots and jousts (which the king won, of course), and then a final series of plays that lasted until four in the morning, lit by colored lights, torches, and fireworks. All of this occurred in a nine-day period, after which the king and his entourage might have wanted to collapse, but the royal tour continued. One imagines that his entry into the next town, which offered simply "girls of the area who danced in the Basque style with tambourines," was something of a relief.[20]

Descriptions of the festivities often mention dwarves. They guarded the enchanted castles, rode the dragons, and accompanied the goddesses. At Bayonne, dwarves accompanied each knight, and Charles IX's personal dwarf, Thonin, announced who would be fighting in the jousts. All of the knights, Thonin proclaimed, wished to prove themselves valorous before the king of France, who fought in the joust himself. Antoine Caron's drawing of one of the jousts at Bayonne shows Thonin, dressed in a long tunic and a tight-fitting cap with little ears, watching intently as his master attempts to run his lance through a ring held in the mouth of a carved wooden dragon. The drawing depicts Charles as a well-muscled full-grown man, though as he was actually only fourteen he was probably not much taller than Thonin. (These drawings later served as the basis for a series of vast tapestries, but by the time the tapestries were made Charles was dead, and neither he nor Thonin is shown in them.) Like the "Brazilian" forests and "Utopian" speeches on the tour itself, the portrayal of the tour in art was full of illusion.

Learned beasts

Whether in Paris or on tour, the royal court provided a number of models for the way Henry II could have handled the hairy little boy from the Canary Islands. He could have treated him like one of the royal animals, giving him food and shelter and a caretaker. He could have treated him like one of the court dwarves, dressing him in fancy, but odd, clothing and expecting him to mimic what he saw. He could have treated him like one of the exotic savages he had seen at the royal entry into Rouen, dressing him in feathers and stone jewelry. He could have treated him like a menial servant, giving him duties in the royal forests or gardens. Instead he followed a different model: he treated him much like the other children at court, training him in the skills expected of a courtier, and even went beyond this. Shortly after Petrus came to the court, Henry II

decreed that he should be "educated in the humanities." Petrus
was to be trained, as were the non-hairy children and adolescents
around him, in reading and writing through studying the classics, a
new model of learning recently brought to France from Italy. Henry
directly oversaw the schooling in Latin of his children, bringing
noted scholars to court for the task, and one or several of these must
have tutored Petrus.

This new program of education, termed humanism, advocated the
study of ancient Greek and Roman literature as the best type of
learning. Humanists viewed an education in the classics as the best
preparation for a political career as either a ruler or advisor, for it
taught one how to argue persuasively, base decisions on historical
examples, write effectively, and speak eloquently. Conversely, humanists taught that a public political career or the creation of a public
reputation through writing should be the aim of all educated individuals, for the best life was not a contemplative one, but a life of action.
In this they disagreed with many medieval scholars, who had viewed
the best use of an education to be the glorification of God through
prayer, manuscript copying, writing, or teaching. Education, humanists taught, was not simply for individual or religious purposes,
but directly benefited the public good by providing knowledgeable
public servants. Not surprisingly, many rulers of the sixteenth century,
Henry II among them, supported programs based on humanist principles. Learning Latin became part of the training for many at court,
not simply those destined for a scholarly life.

But why on earth would Henry decide to have Petrus educated
in this new style of learning? Henry was known to be fond of
children, and perhaps he arranged for Petrus' education because he
cared for the little boy. Although Petrus owed his position at court
to the fact that he was an oddity, the king decided to "normalize"
him as far as was possible, eventually giving Petrus his position as
an assistant bearer of the king's bread, for which training in courtly
protocol was necessary. For this Petrus did not need to speak
Latin, however, and a higher position would have been impossible.
Appointing commoners created enough trouble with the nobility,
who regarded this as an "unnatural" overturning of proper social

hierarchies. One can only imagine what their reaction to an official "not less hairy than a dog" might have been. Whatever Henry's motivation, to most of those at court Petrus was no doubt a source of amusement, for a Latin-quoting beast was even more absurd than dwarves dressed in fancy clothing or bears walking on their hind legs.

Listening to Petrus speak Latin might have been funny, but it was also amazing. Here was a creature whose appearance put his rational capacity in doubt, but he was speaking that most difficult and elegant of languages! Who could have imagined this? Actually some who heard him might have, for they must have been reminded of other creatures of uncertain rational capacity whose abilities in Latin were also sources of marvel: young women. Although humanist academies were not open to women, a few women in Italian and French cities were educated in the classics by their fathers, tutors, or programs of self-study. The daughters of Henry II, for example, learned Latin alongside their brothers, and were reputed to be more skillful at it than the boys. Young learned ladies occasionally gave public speeches at official occasions in Latin and even in Greek, with crowds of onlookers. The young Mary Stuart was one of these, presenting a Latin oration to the assembled French court when she was about thirteen. Many of those who listened admired the young women, praising them as "illustrious virtuosas."

Others were not so sure. Were women even capable of advanced learning, or was reason a masculine quality? Did women really have the rational capacity for their own thoughts, or were they simply repeating what male teachers had written and taught them? Could a woman be both eloquent and chaste, or was a woman's speaking in public (or publishing her words) a clear sign of her lack of virtue?

Petrus' tutors at the French court were well aware of this debate. Just after he arrived from Tenerife, Louise Labé, who had received a solid humanist education through the efforts of her father, published a collection of her writings and sonnets written by men in her honor. This book, published in Lyons in central France, received praise in some circles, but was also severely criticized. From Geneva, Calvin accused her of gaining popularity by providing sexual services to local nobles and clergy. Similar charges were frequently leveled at eloquent women. Labé defended herself, writing to a supporter:

> The time having come, Mademoiselle, when the stern laws of men no longer bar women from devoting themselves to the sciences and disciplines, it seems to me that those who are able ought to employ this honorable liberty, which our sex formerly desired so much, in studying these things and show men the wrong they have done in depriving us of the benefit and honor which might have come to us. . . . The honor which knowledge will bring us cannot be taken from us . . . in addition to the recognition our sex will gain by this, we will have furnished the public with a reason for men to devote more labor to virtuous studies lest they might be ashamed to see us surpass them when they have always pretended to be superior in nearly everything.[21]

Might this have been how Petrus regarded his own education? We have none of his words directly, but the Flemish artist Joris Hoefnagel puts these words in his mouth in the verse that accompanies his portraits of the family:

> I am Petrus Gonsalus, cared for by the king of France
> I was born in the Canary Islands,
> Tenerife brought me forth
> The miracle of nature covered my whole body with hair.
> France, my other mother, nourished me as a child up to my adulthood.
> She taught me to put aside my wild ways
> And taught me the liberal arts and to speak Latin.

At least as Hoefnagel envisions him, Petrus is as proud of his learning as Labé is of hers.

Did the Latin classics that Petrus was taught include Pliny's *Natural History*, with its discussion of hairy peoples from around the world? Had his tutors read the story of Hanno's voyages, which told of

Hanno's discovering—and then killing and skinning—hairy people on an African island? Did they relate this story to Petrus, or did he read it himself? Any of these was possible. Hanno was available in Greek, Latin, and French when Petrus lived at the French court, and Pliny in any number of editions. We know that none of his children was described as being able to read Latin, so Petrus apparently did not transmit his learning to them. None of his daughters gained the "benefit and honor" of classical knowledge that Labé envisions as possible for women, but then neither did any of his sons. (Enrico did learn to read and write Italian, and Orazio probably did as well; whether any of the girls did is impossible to say.) This was no surprise, as language training is easily forgotten if one has no chance to use it. Petrus is listed among the servants at the court of Henry's son Francis II in 1560, but again as an assistant bearer of the king's bread, an office that required little speaking, to say nothing of a Latin education. After that he disappears from the records, because the royal accounts no longer list the holders of such minor offices by name. We do know something about his activities during these years, however, for when the written and visual trail of his life picks up again, he has acquired a wife and children.

25. Jacob Hoefnagel or Dirck van Ravesteyn, *Gonzales Family*, *c.* 1600. In this painting, based on earlier separate portraits, the artist poses the Gonzales family in a way that suggests both care and dignity. Later the painting was included in a collection of natural history paintings by various artists, done for Emperor Rudolf II.

4

The Sanctity of Marriage, the Marvel of Birth

THE WORLD OF THE FAMILY

The large portrait of Petrus in a scholar's robe did not hang alone on the walls of Ambras castle, for the same artist painted matching life-size portraits of his wife and two hairy children. These paintings hung as part of Archduke Ferdinand II of Tyrol's collection of portraits at Ambras, but they were not originally made for Ferdinand. Instead they were made for his nephew, Duke William V of Bavaria, whose court was in Munich, and who later gave them to his uncle. Other members of William's extended family were also interested in paintings of the Gonzales family. In 1583, Archduke Charles of the Steiermark—like Ferdinand, a member of the Habsburg family—thanked William in a letter for sending him small copies of paintings of the "wild man with his wife and children." He asked for paintings that showed the children full-length, and his wife Maria, who was William's sister, seconded his request. A month or so later William wrote to Maria:

> Concerning my wild guy: I will have him painted full length and send it to you shortly. I wrote to France asking about his background and what he does. He himself would not know very much, because he came when he was very young and was given as a present to the king. But he is not wild, as one would think. The man is actually a refined and courteous fellow, but just

shaggy. The little girl is also actually nicely brought up. If she didn't have hair in her face, she would be a pretty girl. The little boy can't speak, but he is silly and amusing. The mother and father of the man were not wild, but like other people, and, if I have it right, they were Spanish. I will send you a copy of the man's picture, which I have in full length; he is not very tall.[1]

William's letter, written in a breezy style to a family member, suggests that he already had the full-size paintings, and artistic evidence backs this up. Shortly before this exchange of letters, Joris Hoefnagel, a court artist to both William and Ferdinand, used the huge portraits as the basis for his own smaller depictions of the family, which he included in his book of miniatures.

Several decades later, Joris Hoefnagel's son Jacob, like his father a court artist for the Habsburg family, combined features of his father's portraits and those in Ambras castle, and painted the whole family together. This small oil painting was placed at the beginning of a collection of natural history paintings produced for the Holy Roman Emperor Rudolf II, who, like his cousin William V and his uncle Ferdinand of Tyrol, was an avid collector of art and objects. (Some art historians conclude that the person who made the small painting was actually a different artist at the Habsburg court, Dirck van Ravesteyn. The work is not signed, and the styles of van Ravesteyn and Jacob Hoefnagel are very similar, so it is impossible to know for sure who made this painting.)

Jacob Hoefnagel (or whoever painted this) shows the family arranged in formal, yet relaxed poses. Petrus stands, wearing the same robes that he wears in the individual portrait made for William V, but with a classical pillar behind him instead of the wall of a cave. His wife wears a starched white head-covering, which indicates her status as a respectable married woman, and a simple, yet nicely cut, dress. The children are also in respectable, but not too elegant, clothing, quite different from the elaborate court dress they wear in most of the other portraits. Here they have no brocade and no jewelry, although the little girl has a charming ruffled collar like that of her mother. The little boy holds an owl, an unusual—but not

26. & 27. Portraits of Catherine and Enrico Gonzales, *c.* 1580. These large portraits by an unknown artist hung alongside those of Petrus in his scholarly robe and Maddalena in her yellow dress on the walls of Ambras castle. All four were given by William V, who apparently commissioned them, to his uncle Ferdinand II, who had a huge collection of portraits of famous nobles and kings, and of human oddities.

unknown—family pet. The owl's face looks much like that of the little boy. As they are today, owls were symbols of wisdom, and Jacob Hoefnagel may have chosen this particular pet as a reference to this, or to the children's animal-like nature, or—most likely—to bring these together. Like the owl, the hairy Gonzaleses were creatures of wisdom despite their beast-like appearance.

Hoefnagel places the children in contact with one another and with their mother—her arms nearly encircle the youngest child, while his older sister holds his hand. Such suggestions of family intimacy were increasingly common in family portraits by 1600. Along with her portraits of the Gonzales sisters, Lavinia Fontana painted the portraits of many other children, sometimes alone, sometimes with siblings, sometimes with their fathers, and sometimes in a family group with multiple generations. As does Hoefnagel's painting, hers show family members with their arms around children, and children touching their parents or hanging onto their clothing. Dogs gaze at their owners and cats ignore them.

28. Lavinia Fontana, *Portrait of a Family, c.* 1585. Fontana, the daughter of a painter, received commissions to paint single portraits and family groups in her native Bologna and other Italian cities. Here the men's lace collars and the women's red coral beads indicate their wealth, while the dog—a symbol of loyalty—and the protective gestures suggest family bonds.

Family portraits such as these are common on walls and shelves today, but they contrast with what has been a long-standing idea about childhood in past times: that it was grim. In the 1960s, historians began to study family relationships in past times. They read child-raising manuals that advocated strict discipline and warned against coddling or showing too much affection, and concluded that children were largely ignored and were raised harshly. They looked at portraits of children that showed them dressed as little adults, and deduced that childhood was not recognized as a distinct stage in life. Family inter-actions were cold, historians asserted, with mothers indifferent to their infants, siblings jealous of the power of the oldest brother, parents callous toward their children's wishes, and spouses formal and uncaring in their relations with one another. Most families were units of work, and no one expected them to be warm and loving.

In the last several decades, however, a closer look at the way children were actually treated has revealed that this view of childhood is wrong, or at least incomplete. Many parents showed great affection for their children, making toys for them, playing with them, and singing them lullabies. Half of the children born in the sixteenth century died before they were five, but this did not make parents complacent. Instead they tried to protect their children with religious amulets, pilgrimages to special shrines, and home-made medicines. Even practices that to us may seem cruel, such as tight swaddling in which a child's legs and arms were bound to its body, were motivated by a concern for the child's safety and health at a time when most households had open fires, domestic animals wandered freely, and mothers and older siblings engaged in productive work that prevented them from continually watching a toddler. Parents were deeply saddened, sometimes to the point of madness or suicide, by the deaths of their children. Portraits such as Hoefnagel's and Fontana's do show children dressed as little adults, but they also show those children encircled in protective arms. Such portraits are idealizations, of course, and do not necessarily represent reality, just as the smiling faces in contemporary family portraits may hide intense anger and bitterness. They do suggest, however, that familial and parental love and affection were valued highly in earlier centuries, whether or not they were always practiced.

The painting of the Gonzales family group is even more of an idealization than most family portraits, as it is based completely on earlier illustrations. Most likely neither Jacob Hoefnagel nor Dirck van Ravesteyn met any member of the family, for they were all in Italy at the time these two men were court artists in Vienna and Prague. The painting showed the children as they had been in the 1580s, not as they were in the 1600s when it was actually made. The arrangement of the family in the painting paralleled the arrangement of family members in many paintings of noble families, including those of the artist's Habsburg patrons. In presenting the cosy group, Hoefnagel may also have been attempting to portray in paint what his father had said in the verse that accompanies his own paintings of the family members. Speaking in the voice of Petrus, the elder Hoefnagel writes:

A wife of outstanding beauty fell to my lot by a gift of God
As did the most dear children of our marriage chamber.
It is proper to admire the gifts of nature given to you: the
children.

Like any family portrait, then, this painting cannot show us what
the Gonzales family was really like. What it *can* show us, though, is
that there was a Gonzales family, that Petrus married and had children, a fact that written records support. The various portraits and
the letter from William V suggest that his oldest daughter was about
seven or eight in 1583, and his oldest son about two. The report
William had received from France about the family described the
girl as a "little girl" and the boy as "silly and amusing," but not yet
able to talk, typical toddler behavior. So she would have been born
in the mid-1570s, with the wedding some time before that. From
later sources, we know that Petrus' wife was named Catherine, his
oldest daughter Maddalena, and his oldest hairy son Enrico, named
after the French king who was his father's protector. ("Enrico" in
Italian or Spanish is the same name as "Henry" in English and
"Henri" in French.) Those sources reveal no further details about
the marriage or the births of the children, but these could not
have broken completely with patterns in the society around them.
Examining those larger patterns can provide us with clues about the
Gonzales family history on which the records are silent.

Marriage for money, marriage for love

Acquiring a spouse was a complex process for anyone in sixteenth-
century Europe. Marriage created a household, the basic social unit
and the site of most economic production. Through marriage, sexual
desire was channeled in appropriate ways and wealth was passed down
to the next generation. Particularly among the upper classes, complicated marriage strategies cemented family alliances and expanded
family holdings.

At the very highest level, royal marriages were important tools of
state policy. Because almost all of Europe was ruled by hereditary

dynasties—the papal states and a few cities being the exceptions—claiming and holding resources also involved shrewd marital strategies, for it was far cheaper to gain land by inheritance than by war. The benefits of an advantageous marriage, particularly if the wife had no brothers and thus inherited territory, stretched across generations, a process that can be seen most dramatically with the Habsburgs. The Holy Roman Emperor Frederick III, a Habsburg who was the ruler of most of Austria, acquired only a small amount of territory—and a great deal of money—with his marriage to Princess Eleonore of Portugal in 1452. He arranged for his son Maximilian to marry Europe's most prominent heiress, Mary of Burgundy, who inherited the Netherlands, Luxembourg, and the County of Burgundy in what is now eastern France. Maximilian learned the lesson of marital politics well, marrying his son and daughter to the children of Ferdinand and Isabella, the rulers of Spain, much of southern Italy, and eventually of the Spanish New World empire. His grandson Charles V would eventually rule about half of Europe. Habsburg successes gave rise to the saying: "Let others wage wars; you, happy Austria, marry" (*Bella gerant alii, tu Felix Austria nube*). The frequency with which the Habsburgs went to war made this aphorism somewhat ironic, but other ruling houses still followed their example in brokering marriages. The marriage between Henry II of France and Catherine de Medici was arranged by his father and her cousin, who happened to be Pope Clement VII. (Catherine's father had died before she was born, and her mother when she was less than a month old.) Henry II in turn arranged the marriages of many of his children when they were still very young, and freely rearranged them when circumstances changed.

Popes and city leaders were part of such marital strategies. As the story of the Farnese and Medici families shows, papal nieces, nephews, and sometimes children—whether born in or out of wedlock—were coveted marriage partners, as were the rich daughters of urban elites. Wealthy urban families, especially in Italy, also transformed themselves into hereditary dynasties through coups and alliances during this period, and cemented their position by marriages with more established ruling houses. Catherine de Medici's marriage to Henry II was a spectacular example of this, as was that of a later Medici daughter, Marie, who married King Henry IV of France in 1600.

The decision about whom to marry was thus far too important to leave up to young people themselves. Family, friends, and neighbors played a role in finding an appropriate spouse and bringing the marriage to realization. Children and parents sometimes fought bitterly over the choice of a spouse, but in most marriages, the aims of the people involved and their parents, kin, and community were largely the same. For ordinary families, the best husband was the one who could provide security, honor, and status, and the best wife one who was capable of running a household and assisting her husband in his work. Therefore even people who were the most free to choose their own spouses, such as widows and widowers or people whose parents had died, were motivated more by what we would regard as pragmatic concerns than romantic love. This is not to say that their choice was unemotional, but that the need for economic security, the desire for social prestige, and the hope for children were as important emotions as sexual passion. The love and attraction a person felt for a possible spouse could be based on any combination of these, with intense romantic desire often viewed as more likely to be disruptive than supportive of a marriage.

Once a prospective spouse had been chosen, financial negotiations began. The fathers of the bride and groom, or the groom himself if he was older, or some other male relatives if the fathers were not available, began bargaining. They considered what the wife would bring to the marriage as her dowry. For most women, this would include clothing, cooking implements, dishes, bed-linens, and perhaps the marital bed itself. Wealthier women might bring sheep, cows, jewelry, cash, and the all-important land. Even wealthier women brought estates and manor houses, and those at the top of the social heap brought provinces or counties or vast amounts of cash. The dowry usually remained the property of the wife in legal theory, though her husband had control over it during his lifetime. In return for the dowry, husbands often gave their wives a smaller gift of money, termed the "morning gift" in some parts of Europe because it was formally given the morning after the marriage had been consummated. Granting a "morning gift" was a very old practice in Europe. It symbolized the sexual transaction at the heart of marriage, in which a husband rewarded his wife for her sexual loyalty, but she had no expectations of sexual fidelity in return.

Dowries brought by the bride also had a long history, stretching back to Roman days. Among wealthy families in some parts of Europe they had become astronomical by the sixteenth century, so that families could afford to dower only one daughter. In fact, they sometimes used the money brought in by the marriages of her brothers to do so, so dowries were important ways that money circulated among the wealthy. The other daughters simply remained with their parents, or were sent to convents, which required an entrance fee much smaller than a dowry. These young women wanted to live in the convent just as they had outside, surrounded by servants, friends, and fine furnishings. Not surprisingly, standards of piety and religious devotion in many convents declined, but the wealthy families who supported the convents did not object, for to them, the convent was serving its primary purpose: as a respectable storage facility for unmarriageable daughters.

Once the financial aspects of the marriage were set, they were recorded by a notary in a written marriage contract. Marriage contracts were not limited to the wealthy, and by the sixteenth century in some parts of Europe quite ordinary people, including servants and craftsmen, made them as well. Signing the contract was sometimes part of a formal betrothal ceremony, in which the men of each family—and occasionally the bride—declared before witnesses their agreement to the contract. The bride and groom might exchange small gifts, and perhaps clasp hands, but they did not seal the betrothal with a kiss. A meal or party often followed the betrothal ceremony at which there was plenty of beer or wine, along with dancing and raucous behavior. If such festivities led to kissing or even sex, most people did not take this very seriously, as the betrothed were about to marry anyway and what was the harm if a child was born a little early. The law regarded all children born after their parents were married as fully legitimate, no matter how soon before the birth the marriage had occurred.

The actual wedding was another ceremony followed by a party, much as weddings are today. Catholic doctrine held that a valid marriage involved the consent of the couple freely given, so vows exchanged by the spouses themselves, often sealed with a ring and a kiss, were the center of the wedding. This might be in a church, but it might also be in a private household. Family, friends, and neighbors looked on, and sometimes led the couple to and from the ceremony or their new home in a procession that might be stately and dignified, but more often was noisy and rowdy. The party that followed could be even more unruly, with as much food and wine as the family could afford. It ended only when the group led the bride and groom off to bed, tucking them in with jokes about his sexual prowess and her fertility. Or it continued long after the bride and groom had left, sometimes for days if the families were extremely wealthy. Officials fretted over how much money was spent on weddings, and tried to restrict this by passing all sorts of laws limiting the number of guests, type of wine, amount of food, and cost of wedding clothes, but these laws were never very successful.

Secret weddings and parental consent

Most weddings were public events, but Catholic doctrine developed in the Middle Ages held that consent between the spouses was the only requirement for a marriage to be valid. Witnesses, parental consent, and a priest were good things, but not essential. As long as the two people agreed—"let's get married . . ." "sure"—and especially if some sort of gift had been given, and the words had been followed by sex, the couple was legally married. It did not matter if this had occurred in a tavern, barn, or haystack, nor how much the couple had been drinking beforehand. Secret betrothals and weddings were part of plays in the sixteenth century—*Romeo and Juliet* is the best known—but also part of real life. The real ones led more often to court cases than to dramatic suicide pacts, however, with the standard scenario a pregnant woman claiming there had been a marriage, and a man denying it.

City, state, and church officials worried about secret marriages because they created uncertainties in this essential part of life, and could also allow young people to escape the authority of their fathers. (Which is exactly what Romeo and Juliet did.) Most secret marriages involved people of low social standing, but occasionally love (or sex) led the rich and famous into secret engagements or marriages as well. A spectacular case happened at the French court when Petrus was there: Henry II arranged a marriage between his illegitimate daughter Diane de France and François de Montmorency, the son of Henry II's friend Anne de Montmorency, who was the constable, or highest general, in France. (Diane had earlier been married to Orazio Farnese, the great-uncle of Ranuccio and Odoardo Farnese, but the marriage had lasted less than a year because Orazio was killed in battle.) François suddenly announced that he had already married secretly, which made his father and the king furious. Their desire and ability to bend church rules were stronger than François', the earlier marriage was annulled, and François sullenly wed Diane.

Henry II decided that no other father should have to go through what Anne de Montmorency had, and enacted a law in 1557 that required parental consent for marriage, which became the first of a long series of such laws. Severe penalties, including capital punishment, were prescribed for minors who married against their parents' wishes. (Minors were defined as men under thirty and women under twenty-five.) Marriages without parental consent were defined as *rapt* (abduction), even if they had involved no violence (such cases were termed *rapt de seduction*). Young people who defied their parents were not actually executed, but were sometimes imprisoned by what were termed *lettres de cachet*, documents that families obtained from royal officials authorizing the imprisonment without trial of a family member who was seen as a source of dishonor. *Lettres de cachet* were also used against young people who refused to go into convents or monasteries when their families wished them to, or against individuals whose behavior was regarded as in some way scandalous, such as wives whose husbands suspected them of adultery or men from prominent families who engaged in homosexual activities. This practice was often abused, and individuals were imprisoned for years

if their families refused to agree to their release. These laws and practices were proposed and supported by French officials because they
increased their personal authority within their own families, and
simultaneously increased the authority of the French state *vis-à-vis*
the Catholic Church, which had required at least the nominal
consent of both parties for a valid marriage.

Protestant reformers agreed with Henry about the importance of
parental consent, and in addition, Protestant marriage laws required
witnesses and a minister for a wedding to be valid. Catholic reformers
reaffirmed the idea that freely given consent made the marriage, but
at the final session of the Council of Trent in 1563 they also decided
that because of "the grievous sins which arise from the said clandes-
tine marriages" this consent had to be exchanged before a priest and
witnesses for the wedding to be valid. Planned marriages were to be
announced three times publicly in church—"reading the banns"—to
make sure that no one had an objection, and in particular to make
sure that neither of the parties had earlier wedded someone else in
a secret ceremony. This decree slowly changed Catholic marriage
practice, but it would take centuries before the public ceremony
as envisioned by the reformers at Trent became standard Catholic
practice everywhere and for all classes of people.

None of the men who discuss Petrus Gonzales and his family
talk about his wedding, but it would have fit the pattern approved by
the Council of Trent, for this was already standard for prominent
people. There would have been a priest and witnesses. There were
probably onlookers, although not many, as none of the usual sources
of goings-on at court reports the wedding. In this it contrasted with a
wedding between two of Catherine de' Medici's dwarves, which
drew a huge crowd. The wedding between Petrus and Catherine was
most likely similar to the dwarves' wedding in some regards, however.
Catherine de' Medici herself arranged the marriage between her
dwarves, and the marriages of many of the other young men and
women of her court. She probably arranged Petrus Gonzales' marriage
as well, or at least promised financial support for the couple.

Looking at the paintings of Catherine Gonzales, we want to know
what made her agree to the match, for without her agreement, the

marriage could not have gone forward. She would have known that her husband's status as an oddity meant that he would probably be supported at some noble court for the rest of his life. She would have decent clothes and enough to eat, as would her children. She was a Catholic, and so was he, so religious disagreements would not split the family as they did others in Europe at this time. Like many women, she had to weigh these material advantages against negative factors—other women had to decide whether to marry men known to be violent drunkards or gambling wastrels—and she had to decide whether to marry a man who was unusually hairy. She was significantly younger than Petrus, so perhaps her parents convinced her that this was a good match, or threatened her if she did not agree. She was no doubt of too low social standing for her family to have arranged for a *lettre de cachet* if she did not follow their wishes, but she had certainly heard stories about what happened to young people who refused to marry their parents' choice of spouse.

Money, combined with pressure from her family and perhaps from the queen, was probably behind Catherine's acceptance of a marriage with Petrus. Because the sources are silent, however, we are free to imagine that other factors played a role as well. Perhaps she was better able than most people of her day to ignore standard ideas about monsters, beasts, and wild men, and to see the person within the animal-like exterior? The ability of love to overcome all boundaries is a modern romantic notion, but it was not unknown in the sixteenth century. Love leads to suicide in one of Shakespeare's plays, but in many more it leads to marriage. The weddings happen only at the very end, however, for the plots in these plays are driven by women and men falling in love with people they could never marry—shepherdesses fall for princes, men fall for men, women for women. Eventually the lovers reveal they are not what they seem to be, but instead someone who is an appropriate spouse, and the wedding festivities begin.

In *As You Like It*, the final scene is a quadruple wedding through which all plot complications are resolved. To this celebration of marriage Shakespeare adds a teasing epilog, however, in which Rosalind, the main female character who had been dressed as a boy throughout most of the play, comes out in her female clothing. She reminds the audience that she is really not a woman, but a boy actor playing a woman. "If I were a Woman," she/he says, "I would kiss as many of you as had beards that pleased me, complexions that liked me, and breaths that I defied not." Like Rosalind, Petrus Gonzales had an exterior that did not fit with his interior. His wife may have been willing to overlook the discrepancy— as were many of Shakespeare's characters when confronted with a similar scenario—or she may have been fascinated by it—as were Shakespeare's audiences.

Stories of love and marriage involving people who were not what they seemed were told in plays, poems, and songs, and one in particular might have had a special meaning for Catherine. From Greek mythology came the tale we now call "Beauty and the Beast," in which a lovely young woman is married to a horrible beast, who turns out to be a prince in disguise. In the original Greek version, the young woman agrees to the marriage out of love for her father, who otherwise will die. By the sixteenth century, in stories told and published in Germany, Italy, and France, she is motivated by her love for the man within the animal-like exterior. The artists who painted the Gonzales family were all familiar with the story, and those who saw the paintings of the lovely Catherine and the hairy Petrus—or saw the couple themselves—could not help but be reminded of it. Petrus would never turn into a handsome prince, of course, but he was connected to princes and educated in a princely fashion, qualities in a husband that any woman would have valued.

Marriage and the Gonzales children

Along with Petrus and Catherine, the Hoefnagel paintings show two other members of the Gonzales family, their children Maddalena and Enrico, both of whom also later married, Enrico actually four times. Speculations about what Catherine was thinking can thus extend to the spouses of her children, both those who married these two older children and the wife of the younger son Orazio, who also married. Money leaves far more traces in the records than love, and there are a few hints about the circumstances in which they wed. Duke Ranuccio Farnese bought a house in 1593 in Parma for a woman described as "Maddalena the hairy," which no doubt served as her dowry. The next time Maddalena is mentioned in the sources is at her daughter's confirmation ceremony, and here Maddalena's husband is named as well: Giovan Maria Avinato. Like the Gonzales family, Avinato was attached to the Farnese court in Parma and in Rome, where he was the keeper of the family's hunting dogs. Did Ranuccio or Odoardo Farnese choose a man with this particular occupation as a husband for the hairy Maddalena because they thought it appropriate, or because they thought it amusing? Perhaps both. Did Maddalena's husband agree to the match solely because of the money, or was he also attracted to the young woman, about whom William V had earlier commented "if she didn't have hair in her face, she would be a pretty girl"? Might Maddalena have shaved her face, so that she looked more attractive and less strange? Like his mother-in-law, and like most spouses in the sixteenth century, Avinato left no record of his motives. The couple had at least one daughter, but then or now, children are no proof of love, or even of fondness.

Money was clearly the centerpiece of Enrico's first marriage, for the bride brought no dowry at all, which was almost unthinkable. Most Italian cities had charities that provided dowries for very poor girls, with the funds supplied by well-to-do citizens who saw this as a way to help young women achieve the honorable status of marriage. The Catholic Church and many city governments ran special houses for young unmarried women where they were supposed to learn a trade and be given the opportunity to earn a dowry. These institutions were attractive charities for those interested in religious and moral reform, and were sometimes also supported by taxes on registered prostitutes. By the time Enrico married he had moved to the small village of Capodimonte, however, and was no longer living in a city. There were few charities to provide dowries in villages as small as the one where Enrico married, but a bride's extended family could usually scrape something together, at least a little clothing or a few blankets. Since Enrico's wife brought absolutely nothing, the dowry was supplied to Enrico by Duke Ranuccio Farnese, so her family must have been extremely poor. The marriage lasted until her death more than twenty-five years later, and during this time Enrico's younger brother Orazio also married in the village, most likely also to a girl from a poor family.

Enrico's subsequent marriages were very different. His second and third wives were the daughters of officials, not poverty-stricken villagers, and brought dowries to the marriage. Enrico's second and third marriages followed standard Italian patterns in other ways as well as the dowry arrangements. In each case the bride was decades younger than the groom, a common situation in the remarriage of a widower and not that unusual in first marriages, either. A significant difference in ages between husband and wife was typical in southern Europe at this point, in contrast to northern Europe, where women waited until later to marry and then married someone close to them in age. The marriages took place within months of the death of the previous wife; a bit hasty, but again fairly typical. Both Catholic and Protestant preachers sharply criticized their parishioners for remarrying when the body of their spouse was barely cold, and laws required women to wait at least nine months—to be sure they weren't pregnant—before running to the altar again. Somewhere around a fifth of all marriages were remarriages for at least one of the partners, and widowers everywhere were more likely to remarry than widows, and to remarry faster.

Enrico's fourth—and last—marriage took place when he was about sixty, again to a much younger woman, Emilia. Marriages in which the spouses were very different in age were also condemned by preachers, and satirized by artists. Woodcuts and paintings showed wrinkled old men or women embracing attractive younger spouses, whose hands are in the older person's money pouch and eyes turned away. Martin Luther commented on this to his dinner companions: "If an old man takes a young wife, this is a very ugly spectacle, for there is no pride or lust in such a man, for the opportunities for this are past. There is nothing attractive or strong about him any more. For this reason an old man with a young wife is contrary to nature. It is best if like and like are paired together."[2] Ordinary people voiced their disapproval of such marriages in many parts of Europe through rituals in which they shouted insults, beat drums, clanged metal implements together, and sang bawdy songs in front of the house where the couple was in bed together after the wedding. This "rough music," as it was called in English, sometimes led to more serious violence as masked and drunken revelers hurled stones through windows or burnt carts or sheds with their torches.

Enrico's fourth wife Emilia bore him several children, so apparently there must have been some lust left in him, and his letters to the Farneses indicate there was certainly pride. Enrico and Emilia worked together in various business transactions in their little village, mostly loaning small amounts of money, so at least in their desire to improve their circumstances they were "like and like." Given Luther's attitude toward marvels and monsters, he would no doubt have discounted this, and seen their marriage as even more "contrary to nature" than one between an old man and a young woman. The fact that Enrico found four wives in the village suggests that at least some people there did not share this opinion, or that Enrico's connection with the Farneses was enough to overcome their reservations. Some villagers may have contemplated "rough music," but they owed Enrico money, and by the time of his fourth marriage the Gonzales family had lived in their midst for decades, and were familiar to one and all.

Bringing forth a child

To return to Petrus and Catherine. Within a few years of the wedding, Catherine Gonzales was pregnant, just as were most wives. Catholics and Protestants alike—and the Jews and Muslims who lived in Europe as well—saw the procreation of children as one of the most important functions of marriage, and viewed childless couples with pity.

Determining whether she was pregnant would not have been an easy matter for Catherine. Her menstrual period stopped, but she would know from speaking with her female relatives and friends that this was not a clear sign, because it might have been due to other medical conditions. Nausea, breast enlargement, and thickening around the middle also pointed to pregnancy, but only at quickening—that is, when a mother could feel the child move within her body, which usually happens during the fourth or fifth month— would she, or any other expectant mother, have been regarded as veri- fiably pregnant. Quickening was also viewed as the point at which a child gained a soul (the word "quick" is an old word for alive, as in the phrase "the quick and the dead"), so that charges of abortion could not be brought against a woman who had not yet quickened. Pregnancy was not a condition affirmed externally and visually the way it is today with home pregnancy tests and ultrasound screenings, but inter- nally and in a tactile way, with only the mother able to confirm that quickening had happened.

Like any pregnant woman, Catherine Gonzales would have received lots of advice. Some of this came from printed manuals designed especially for midwives, of which the most important was the *Rosegarden for Pregnant Women and Midwives*, first published in German in 1513 by Eucharius Rösslin, the city physician in Frankfurt. The *Rosegarden* was instantly popular, and was translated into Dutch, Czech, French, Danish, Latin, and English. Other manuals appeared, circulating the same pieces of advice and stories of warning, which midwives shared with their clients. Much of what they advise is still recommended today: pregnant women should eat moderately of nourishing foods, including a good amount of protein, and avoid foods that make them nauseous or that are highly spiced; they should moderate their drinking and avoid strong liquors; they should get regular exercise but avoid strenuous lifting; pregnant women should wear low-heeled shoes and loosen their lacing or corsets. Not following such advice could lead to miscarriage or stillbirth, or to children that were deformed.

Ambroise Paré, the French royal physician who cared for King Henry II after his accident at the jousting tournament, published a long book on reproduction in 1573, about the time that Catherine and Petrus were married. The first part provides guidance for handling delivery and illnesses in pregnant women, and the second part, later separately titled *Des Monstres et prodiges* (On Monsters and Marvels) discusses the causes of abnormal births. Most of the causes of human monsters, which Paré defines as "things that appear outside the course of Nature, such as a child who is born with one arm, or another who will have two heads," are physical: the mother fell, or her womb was struck, or she had a disease, or there was too little or too much "seed" so that limbs were missing or there were extra ones. "Children are sometimes born bent, hunchbacked and misshapen," Paré comments, "on account of [the mother] having almost always held her legs crossed during pregnancy—as seamstresses and women who work tapestries on their knees often do so quite readily—or bound or strapped her belly too tight."[3] In warning against physical dangers during pregnancy, Paré was following a long tradition. In his lectures on the Book of Genesis, for example, Luther commented that "A woman has a body created for pregnancy, for the nourishment of the fetus, and she is exposed to very many dangers. Therefore she must be treated with wisdom and moderation."[4]

A mother's imagination

To the physical causes of monstrous births, Paré adds another: "The ancients, who sought out the secrets of Nature (i.e. Aristotle, Hippocrates, Empedocles) have taught of other causes for monstrous children and have referred them to the ardent and obstinate imagination or impression that the mother might receive at the moment she conceived."[5] On this he was repeating an idea held not only by the ancient philosophers he cites, but by highly educated scholars and unlearned villagers alike in the sixteenth century. They were certain that what a woman saw or experienced during pregnancy could affect the child. Being frightened by a hare caused harelip; eating strawberries caused red birthmarks; seeing an animal slaughtered or a person executed might cause a miscarriage.

The Bible provided support for the notion that what a mother saw could influence her offspring. Genesis 30 tells the story of Jacob's agreement with his father-in-law to take only the spotted goats from the flock, leaving the unspotted for his brothers-in-law to inherit. He increased his stock by putting a partially peeled branch in front of the goats as they were drinking; the goats saw the mottled branch, and gave birth to more spotted and striped kids. In what is one of the first records of selective breeding, Jacob further improved his flocks by putting the "stronger of the flock" in front of the spotted rods, but left the weaker alone, so that his flocks grew increasingly superior to those of his brothers-in-law. (Not surprisingly, they were furious with Jacob.)

In his lectures on Genesis to his students at the University of Wittenberg during the 1530s and 1540s, Martin Luther uses this chapter to tell a story affirming that what it relates still happens:

> I remember that when I was a boy at Eisenach, a beautiful and virtuous matron gave birth to a dormouse. This happened because one of the neighbors had hung a little bell on a dormouse in order that the rest might be put to flight when the bell made a sound. This dormouse met the pregnant woman, who, ignorant of the matter, was so terrified by the sudden meeting and sight of the dormouse that the fetus in her womb degenerated into the shape of the little beast.[6]

When a child was born weak or malformed, the mother and those surrounding her searched back through her pregnancy, trying to determine what she had seen or experienced that had caused this.

Midwives agreed with learned men about the influence of the mother's experiences on the fetus, although they drew their examples from life as well as from reading. Catharina Schrader was a professional midwife in the Netherlands who kept notebooks of all of her cases between the years 1693 and 1745, more than 3,000 in all. When she was in her eighties, she decided to collect all of her most complicated cases into a single book, dedicating it to the women she had delivered. This casebook includes several instances of abnormal births:

> 1710 on 5 February with Jan Gorrtzacke's daughter Hinke, whose husband, Wattse, was a corn merchant, who was visiting her mother. And delivered her quickly of a son. Lived but half an hour. But, The Lord works mysteriously, I [was] terrified. Found that between the stomach and the belly [there] was an

opening as big as a gold coin, all round it grew a horny border. Out of this hung the intestines with the bowels. Had grown outside the body. One saw there the heart, liver, lungs clear and sharp, without decay. One could touch wholly under the breast. It was worthy to be seen by an artist, but she did not want it shown. I inquired [of] the woman if she had also had a fright or mishap. She declared that she was unaware of anything, but that [when] it had been the killing time they had slaughtered a pig. They had hung it on the meat hook, and the butcher had cut out the intestines and the bowels.

1733 on 10 November with Maryken, wife of the servant to the orphanage. A son. But had a face like an ape. At the back of the neck an opening as big as a hand. Its genitals were also not as they should be. She [the mother] had seen apes dancing. It did not live long. O lord, save us from such monsters.[7]

Quick thinking on the part of the mother might lessen the impact of accidental dangers. She could immediately pray that what she had seen would have no effect on her child, or take direct action:

If a mouse, rat, weazel, cat, or the like, leaps suddenly upon a woman that has conceived, or if an apple, pear, plum, cherry, etc. fall upon any part of her body, the mark of the thing, (be what it will) is instantly imprinted, and will manifestly appear on the same part or member of the child; unless the woman (in that very moment) wipe that part or member, and move her hand to some more remote, private, or convenient place of the body; which one, the mark is actually averted, or at least stamped upon the other part touched.[8]

Not only could a mother's experiences lead to abnormal births, but her thoughts, desires, and imagination could as well. Luther ends his story of the dormouse with the comment, "Such examples are all too common when pregnant women are often excited by sudden emotions and fears at the risk of their life." Simply wanting to eat hare could cause harelip, just as wanting to eat strawberries or drink red wine could cause red birthmarks.

In a long Latin poem, *The Callipaed, or The Art of Creating Beautiful Children*, the French doctor Claude Quillet explained how this worked, comparing a mother's imagination to a baker forming bread:

> The spirits descending from the brain mingle in the womb with the prolific [child-making] essence and penetrate it through and through; there they imprint with invincible force the same images by which they have themselves been struck. . . . In a baker's trough, the flour, mixed with warm water and set in motion by the yeast, swells up into one single mass; if the baker sets a hand to it, he can make all different kinds of cakes of many different shapes: so in women, ideas make the same sort of impressions on the fetus.[9]

As the title of the poem indicates, the maternal imagination was also thought to work in a positive way, so mothers were encouraged to look at pleasant and beautiful things in order to improve their chances of having attractive children.

Paré was a bit more skeptical than most about the power of the maternal imagination, limiting the time that this could harm a child to the point of conception and early pregnancy. He still includes stories from ancient authorities about children whose form was shaped by the power of their mother's mind operating throughout the pregnancy, however. From the eighth-century Christian scholar John Damascene comes the story of a girl "as furry as a bear, whom the mother had bred thus deformed and hideous, for having looked too intensely at the image of Saint John [the Baptist] dressed in skins, along with his [own] body hair and beard, which picture was attached to the foot of her bed while she was conceiving." The Greek physician Hippocrates, Paré reports, "saved a princess accused of adultery, because she had given birth to a child as black as a Moor, her husband and she both having white skin; which woman was absolved upon Hippocrates' persuasion that it was [caused by] the portrait of a Moor, similar to the child, which was customarily attached to her bed."[10]

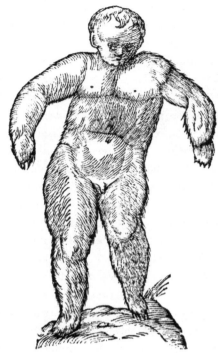

29. A boy "as hairy as a bear," from Ulisse Aldrovandi, *Monstrorum historia*, 1642. Aldrovandi repeats a number of stories of the power of the maternal imagination, including the standard one about a child who was born covered in fur because its mother stared too long at a picture of John the Baptist.

Paré's accounts were widely repeated. In his *Essays*, published in 1580, the French writer and statesman Michel de Montaigne also spoke about the power of a mother's imagination, using the same examples:

> We know by experience that women transmit marks of their fancies to the bodies of the children they carry in the womb; witness the one who gave birth to the Moor; and there was presented to Charles, king of Bohemia and Emperor, a girl from near Pisa, all hairy and bristly, who her mother said had thus been conceived because of a picture of St. John the Baptist hanging by her bed.[11]

The hairy girl and black baby were shown in pictures as well as words in Paré's book. Paré actually took both the stories and the illustrations from recently published books of monsters and prodigies, especially Conrad Lycosthenes' *Prodigiorum ac ostentorum chronicon* (Chronicle of Prodigies and Portents) (1557) and Pierre Boaistuau's *Histoires prodigeuses* (Marvelous Stories) (1560). These books, as well as Paré's *Monsters and Prodigies*, went through many editions and translations, with the hairy girl and black baby appearing in every one. They were shown on broadsides and in pamphlets as well. Ulisse Aldrovandi included the pictures in *Monstrorum historia*, near one of the places where he makes reference to the Gonzales family. The images were picked up by the anonymous compiler of a guide to pregnancy and childbirth called *Aristotle's Masterpiece*, first published in English in 1684, where they appeared directly across from the title page. This book went through several versions and many editions over the next hundred years, and remained the best-selling book on reproduction in English into the nineteenth century, on both sides of the Atlantic. Various publishers altered the image considerably over the years, but a hairy young woman and black baby were the first thing any reader saw in most editions of *Aristotle's Masterpiece*.[12]

Most people who saw the Gonzales sisters would have known the story of the hairy girl, and would have seen her picture somewhere. Thus along with Mary Magdalene, hairy saints, and wild women, this hairy young woman shaped the way that people saw the sisters. The maternal imagination was one of many reasons that Ulisse Aldrovandi proposed for how the Gonzales family came to be hairy. In their case, of course, the woman with the terrible experiences or fertile imagination was Petrus' unknown mother back in the Canary Islands.

Catherine Gonzales did not have to see a picture of John the Baptist or contemplate sex with animals to give birth to a hairy child; she simply had to have sex with her husband. This did not mean, however, that ideas about the maternal imagination had no relevance for her. Hairy children would confirm that her children were her husband's, and also confirm that she had not let her

30. Black child and hairy young woman, from Ulisse Aldrovandi, *Monstrorum historia*, 1642. This pair was depicted in nearly every collection of stories about prodigies, as well as many guides to childbirth, published from the sixteenth to the nineteenth centuries.

imagination roam too widely during pregnancy. She had not tacked a picture of a smooth-skinned prince on her wall in the hopes of producing smooth-skinned children, or prayed too fervently to God for the same outcome. Catherine's giving birth to hairy children was proof that she was a good wife, while for any other woman it suggested the opposite. If a child looked like something its mother saw or imagined, it did not look like its father, of course. Thus the power of the maternal imagination could erase the father's role in producing a child, a fact that was not lost on some commentators. In Marvelous Stories, Pierre Boaistuau attributes monstrous children to mothers who, instead of desiring their husbands, desire sex with someone else, or perhaps even contemplate sex with animals: "God allows [women] to produce such abominations because they hurl themselves forward indifferently, like savage beasts that only follow their appetites, with no consideration of age, place, time, and other laws established by Nature."[13] Catherine's giving birth to beast-like children would, by contrast, demonstrate that she herself was not the sort of beastly woman that Boaistuau envisions.

Most of the children of Petrus and Catherine were hairy, but at least one was not. Joris Hoefnagel provides one clue about this, commenting in the inscription that accompanies his portrait of the family that "some [children] take after their mother in form and color. Some follow their father, adorned with hair." Yet none of the portraits (including Hoefnagel's own) show any non-hairy children, nor does any doctor or scientist who commented on the family mention them. Records from the small village in Italy where the family ended up appear to confirm Hoefnagel's comment, however, for a daughter of a Gonzales brother named Paulo came to live with the rest of the family there. Paulo shows up in no other source about the family, which suggests he was not hairy. Did his birth raise suspicions about Catherine's behavior, or at least her desires? Probably not. People recognized that in many families, not just the Gonzaleses, some children take after their mother and some after their father, so that Paulo's lack of hair simply confirmed the normal pattern.

Midwives and the experience of childbirth

Friends, neighbors, and relatives helped women in villages and smaller towns through childbirth, perhaps under the direction of a woman known to be more knowledgeable than most about the process of delivery. Childbirth was strictly a female affair in the sixteenth century. The husband was not present unless his wife was dying, and male physicians and surgeons took little interest in delivery. Male doctors were only called in if the child or mother or both were dead or dying, so their presence was dreaded.

For any woman, an approaching birth brought questions and decisions, beginning with the issue of which friends and neighbors she would invite to assist her. This was something taken very seriously in real life, not simply in fairy stories. Witchcraft accusations sometimes arose from the curses and anger of a neighbor who had not been invited.

If a woman lived in a city, as did Catherine Gonzales, she could call not only on friends and relatives to help her, but also on a professional midwife. Women were appointed as official city midwives in German, French, Flemish, and Dutch cities beginning in the late fourteenth century. By the end of the fifteenth century, most towns of any size had several midwives on the city payroll, who would receive either an annual salary or else a payment for each woman they cared for who was not able to pay herself. Most clients paid the midwife directly, with women from a city's wealthiest families often paying ten or twenty times what the city gave midwives when they cared for poor mothers.

Midwives trained through apprenticeship, assisting an experienced midwife for several years, and were then examined by city doctors and in some places by a group of what were termed "honorable women," women from prominent city families appointed to oversee the midwives. First came questions about training and experience. With whom had she studied, and for how long? Had she had children herself? How many births had she seen or taken part in? Had she read Rösslin's *The Rosegarden for Midwives and Pregnant Women* in one of its many variations, or had it read to her if she could not read?

Then came questions about the content of her training: What food, drink, and baths will help a woman have an easy birth? How does she know if a woman is pregnant and does not simply have some other kind of swelling? How does she tell if the pains are really labor pains, and if the time for delivery has come? What is the normal position for birth, and how is this to be brought about if the baby is emerging in an unusual way? What should be done with the umbilical cord and afterbirth, especially to make sure all of the latter has emerged? How are the new mother and infant best to be taken care of, and what advice should she give the new mother? Only after successfully completing her exam was a woman allowed to swear an oath and become an official midwife. Even then city officials sometimes had reservations, noting in one case that "even though she has the desire and love for this office, she is in some points rather weak." They set limitations on what this particular midwife could do: "Because she is a beginner and experience comes only through daily practice, especially in this occupation, she must learn a number of things by daily application, and in difficult or precarious situations that she is not ready for, she is to call in another older and more experienced midwife."[14]

Cities passed ordinances regulating midwives, as they did for many other officials. The first of these was in Regensburg in 1452, then Munich in 1488, and Strasbourg in 1500. Many cities followed in the sixteenth century, including Frankfurt in 1509, Nuremberg in 1522, and Paris in 1560. Just as the midwives' guides copied from one another, so did the ordinances, though they got longer and more complicated as time went on and new issues emerged.

The Munich ordinance had many clauses that were copied identically in later ordinances in Germany and France. The midwife was to swear to come to anyone who asked her, rich or poor, day or night, and to handle all to the best of her abilities. She was not to leave the city without the permission of the council, so that she could always be found at home when needed, and was to leave a message as to where she could be found if she was out attending to a woman. "She should also encourage and comfort the pregnant woman and not be sharp or coarse with her, not even with a poor woman from whom she could expect no special reward." If a woman were dying, on no account was she to leave her side; she was to encourage her to confess her sins and believe in God and the Savior. If the child was born alive and healthy, she was to care for it and the mother. If it was born dead or nearly dead, she was to perform an emergency baptism, or she "would have to answer to God for her laziness and irresponsibility."[15] God rewards as well as judges in the Frankfurt 1509 ordinance: "For the very poor the midwife should work for free and wait for her payment from Almighty God, who does not let works of mercy go unrewarded."[16] The 1560 Paris ordinances, which were in force when Catherine Gonzales gave birth to her first children, prescribe similar behavior, and forbid midwives to discuss "the modesty, corruption or pregnancy of girls and women . . . on the occasion of the illnesses which often accompany their pregnancy." Before they were licensed, midwives in Paris were to "provide evidence of the place where they live, their way of life, sober conversation, and under which mistresses or mothers, they have learnt the vocation of midwife." In addition, every year the midwife "will be shown Woman's Anatomy by one of the two sworn surgeons of the King, in order to learn what belongs to the practice of the said midwives."[17]

During the sixteenth century, city officials became increasingly worried about births out of wedlock, and required midwives to report all such children—whether they were alive or dead, who and where the mother was, who the father was, if possible. "When they come upon a young girl or maid or someone who is pregnant outside of marriage," the Strasbourg ordinances prescribe, "they should speak to them of their own accord and warn them with threats of punishment not to harm the fetus in any way or take any bad advice, as such foolish people are very likely to do."[18] Midwives were to report "the name of the one who is exclaimed during the pains of birth [that is, the father]" and actually to go further than that: "When she [a midwife] is called to an unknown person or a person pregnant out of wedlock who has been overcome by the pains of childbirth, she must then ask her, before she gives her a helping hand, who the father of the child is so that justice is not neglected and children come in to the city's orphanage or otherwise seek public support who should be taken care of elsewhere."[19] In Paris midwives were instructed to closely examine any abandoned child "to see whether they recognize it" and to report any "debauched women" whose child they had delivered. Such rules did not apply at the very top of the social scale, of course. When Diane de France was born, no one asked Henry II's mistress "during the pains of birth" who the father of her child was, for everyone knew that it was the king, and he did not deny this.

Diane de France's birth, like that of any royal child, would have been attended by the best midwife that could be found. Nobles advised rulers and their wives about who would make a proper royal midwife, for good advice on this most important decision was one more way to gain the monarch's favor at court. When Marie de Medici, the wife of the French king Henry IV, became pregnant in 1601, for example, discussion at the court about the appointment of a royal midwife involved her physician and a number of the king's noble advisors. Marie had her own discussions with friends and associates, and ended up successfully maneuvering for Louise Bourgeois, a licensed midwife in Paris who had served one of Marie's childhood friends and several other noble clients. Bourgeois joined the royal household for a month before each of six royal births from 1601 to 1609, and stayed a month after each child was born. For her two months' service, she was paid 900 *livres*, at a time when the average pay of a normal licensed midwife in Paris was about 50 *livres* per *year*. Her connections with the royal household led to work with more noble and well-to-do professional families, and created a wide audience for books that Bourgeois published over the next several decades, including manuals of practical advice, discussions of the problems associated with reproduction and pregnancy, and a collection of medical recipes.

Whether the mother was a queen or a more ordinary woman, once labor had begun, the women assisting in the birth transformed the room, or in small houses the bed or part of a room, into a "lying-in chamber," according to local traditions of what was proper. Air was viewed as harmful to the mother, so doors and windows were shut and candles lit. Special objects thought to help speed delivery were brought in, such as amulets, relics of saints, or certain herbs. Special prayers were offered. Women bustled about, preparing broth or mulled wine to nourish the mother through the delivery, and arranging swaddling clothes for the infant. Dr Christoph Scheurl, a Nuremberg lawyer, describes just such a scene in his household account book at the birth of his son George: "The birth occurred at the back of the house, in our normal eating room along Rosenpadt street. I was banished before the bed was prepared. Frau Margaretha Endres Tucherin, Ursula Fritz Tetzlin, the widow Magdalena Mugenhoferin, and Anna the midwife assisted her."[20] Louise Bourgeois advised midwives to make sure the mother was not surrounded by too much commotion, however: "the midwife must never make nor allow others to make any noise in the room of a woman giving birth . . . whatever may happen, never seem to be at a loss, for there is nothing so unpleasant to witness as those households all at sixes and sevens. Never be surprised if something does not go right, because fear troubles the senses."[21]

Midwives varied in their techniques of delivery. Some midwives and mothers preferred to use a birthing stool, a special padded stool with handles that tipped the mother back slightly. Paré shows one of these birthing stools in his treatise on reproduction, and most midwives' manuals do as well. Other mothers lay in bed, kneeled, stood, or sat in another woman's lap. Louise Bourgeois recommended whatever made the mother most at ease: "I have often noticed that one of the most essential things for a woman in labour is to find the best position, for the comfort of the mother and child."[22] "Nature," she commented, "works miracles when one least expects it," so midwives should not try to hurry the birth.[23] Most midwives agreed with her, and tended to intervene only if something was going wrong, which was usually a case of abnormal presentation. If the child was emerging feet or knees first (breech), it could generally be delivered, but if it emerged arm or face first it often needed to be turned. Until the invention of the forceps, the best way to do this was to reach inside the uterus and grasp the feet, then turn the child to bring about a feet-first birth (this technique is termed podalic version). Midwives' manuals beginning in the sixteenth century recommend this, and records of births handled by professional midwives indicate they handled this technique successfully.

31. Illustration from a midwives' manual, 1587. In this engraving, the mother leans back on a birthing stool, while the midwife sits in front of her and other women assist and encourage her. The foreground accurately presents birthing techniques of the sixteenth century, while the astrologers looking at the stars in the background are a more fanciful addition.

Most women experienced multiple childbirths successfully, but all knew someone who had died in childbed and many had watched this happen. Historians using English statistics have estimated that the maternal mortality rate at this time was about 1 percent for each birth, which would make a lifetime risk of 5 to 7 percent. Women knew these risks, which is why they attempted to obtain the services of the midwife they regarded as the most skilled. Living in Paris, Catherine Gonzales would have had an experienced midwife to assist her in each of the deliveries of her older children, as she would have living at the Farnese court in Parma where her younger children were born.

Children and grandchildren

Judging by the later illustrations and written records, the Gonzales children were born somewhere between two and five years apart, common birth intervals. Mothers recognized that the dangers of childbirth might be intensified when children were born too close together, and attempted to space births using a variety of means. Many nursed their children until they were more than two years old, which acted as a contraceptive, for suckling encourages the release of the hormone prolactin, which promotes the production of milk and inhibits the function of the ovaries. They sought to abstain from sexual relations during the time of their monthly cycle regarded as most fertile, though this "rhythm method," based on an incorrect view of the menstrual cycle, was even less effective than that practiced in the twentieth century. Couples also regularly attempted to restrict fertility through coitus interruptus, magical charms, and herbal potions, all of which were officially condemned by religious authorities.

Catherine and Petrus Gonzales had at least seven children, and may have had more. Their last son, Ercole, born after they moved to Italy, apparently died young, and it would have been unusual if he were alone in this fate. Many children died very young, a pattern that stretched across the social spectrum. Of the ten children born to Queen Catherine de Medici, three died before they reached their first birthday, including her last children, a set of twins whose birth nearly killed their mother as well. Enrico Gonzales' four wives bore him at least five children, all of whom died young, and Orazio Gonzales' wife three children, two of whom died right after they were born.

Catherine Gonzales was still alive when her older grandchildren were born, and no doubt assisted her daughters-in-law through their labor and delivery. Catherine's own last child, the short-lived Ercole, had been born only a decade before her oldest grandson, so her pregnancies and deliveries were not all far in the past. By the time the Gonzales sons were fathering children, the family had moved to the small village of Capodimonte, where giving birth was very different than it was in cities like Paris or Parma. Village midwives had no opportunity to receive the professional training that their urban counterparts did and could rarely read, so that they could not learn from midwives' manuals. They learned by watching and assisting older midwives, but more highly educated urban midwives such as Louise Bourgeois were often scornful of the level of their knowledge. In many small villages there was no midwife at all, so older female family members or friends who had themselves given birth to children were a woman's only support. Catherine watched three of her grandchildren die as infants, although, as the fate of Catherine de Medici's children demonstrates, even the best midwife and highest level of medical care could not prevent this. Catherine Gonzales did not watch any of her daughters or daughters-in-law die in childbirth, however, which made her luckier than many women.

The hairy Gonzales children passed their condition on to at least some of their children. Enrico's oldest son was hairy, and at least one child of Maddalena's was as well, for Aldrovandi reports that "recently at Parma in the most serene court of the Farneses" the girl with the hairy face "was married and bedded and gave birth to other children likewise hairy on their faces."[24] The non-hairy brother Paulo's daughter is nowhere described as hairy, however, nor are her daughters when they were later born in the village. Whether Orazio's three children were hairy is not clear. They died very young, as did their uncle Ercole, too soon to make their hairy condition, or anything else about them, worthy of record. Maddalena's hairy children have similarly left no trace. In contrast to their mother, their portraits were never painted, never copied, and never hung on castle walls.

32. & 33. Joris Hoefnagel, miniatures of the Gonzales family from *Elementa depicta*, 1580s. In Hoefnagel's tiny paintings, Petrus wears a brilliant blue robe and the children bright pink gowns, while Catherine is dressed in a more sober black dress. Hoefnagel includes suggestions of natural settings within each oval, and frames the ovals with verses, most from the Bible.

5

God's Miraculous Creation

THE WORLD OF RELIGION

At just about the time that Maddalena Gonzales was born, the Flemish artist Joris Hoefnagel began to paint brightly colored watercolors of plants and animals on small sheets of vellum. Each tiny oval painting showed one or several animals, with a saying or Bible verse inscribed above or below. Hoefnagel copied some of the creatures and mottoes from earlier illustrations, such as the engravings in Conrad Gesner's huge book of animals, or albums of animals, birds, and fish that other Flemish artists had painted. He took his paintings with him when he left Antwerp in 1576 after his house was burnt down and the town was nearly destroyed by Spanish troops fighting Protestants in what became known as the "Spanish fury." Hoefnagel went to the court of the Wittelsbach duke Albrecht V in Munich, where he continued to add new paintings to his collection, gathering those of fish under the heading "water," those of birds under "air," and those of animals under "earth," and eventually binding these into books. Such collections of illustrations with sayings, called emblem books, were popular as reading material and even more as gifts, much like coffee-table books today. They ranged from exquisite hand-made masterpieces such as Hoefnagel's to cheap printed booklets in paper covers.

Water, air, and earth were three of the four basic elements in the classical understanding of what made up the world, and there was a fourth—fire. For this, Hoefnagel gathered his paintings of insects, drawn mostly from life, rather than copied, as no large collection of insect illustrations existed. How fish, birds, and animals fit with water, air, and earth is clear, but why classify insects as "fire"? Because, for Hoefnagel, the key quality of insects was their ability to transform into something else: larvae into beetles or caterpillars into butterflies. He often chose to show the insects sitting on flowers or plants that were also in the process of mutation, such as flowers bursting into bloom or withering into a seed pod.

Hoefnagel also added miniatures of several other subjects to the insects in "fire," and when he bound the paintings into a book, these are the first pages. On the very first vellum sheet is a picture of Petrus and Catherine Gonzales, he wearing a blue robe with black sleeves and she a black dress with a tight-fitting bodice and lace collar. On the second vellum sheet are two of the Gonzales children, Maddalena and Enrico, in brilliant pink gowns. Like her mother, Maddalena is in a gown with a tight bodice and lace collar, although the fabric is fancier than that of her mother, and she is wearing a necklace with a large teardrop pearl and a hair decoration that entwines flowers, pearls, and her own hair. Like his father, Enrico is wearing a long gown, with clasps running down the front—a miniature version of the standard scholar's robe, but shocking in color, an even brighter pink than his sister's. All of the family have sober expressions, quite different from the smiles in the family portrait done later by Joris Hoefnagel's son Jacob, and stand near large rocks. The third sheet has an empty oval, but the inscriptions note that it was to contain a dwarf and a giant. The fourth sheet is completely blank, and on the fifth begin seventy-eight pages of insects. The title page of this volume reflects these two types of contents: "Fire: Rational Animals and Insects" (*Ignis: animalia rationalia et insecta*).

God's wondrous and mysterious hand

Why did Hoefnagel choose to include the Gonzales family with insects, and mean to include other human wonders, such as a giant and a dwarf? Why does he call them "rational animals"? He does not tell us directly, but leaves clues in the words and verses that accompany the paintings. Above the painting of Petrus and Catherine is the following, in beautiful Latin penmanship: "Greater than all the miracles made by man is MAN. Among all visible things he is the greatest world; among those invisible, GOD [is the greatest]. When we see that [man] is a world, we believe there is God." Beneath the painting is a verse from the Book of Job, "MAN, born of a WOMAN, living for a short time, is filled with many miseries" (Job 14: 1). Job is the Old Testament figure whose faith is tested through a series of dreadful events—he loses his wealth, his children die, and he is afflicted with a terrible and disfiguring illness. Like Job, Hoefnagel suggests with this verse, Petrus has also been afflicted, and like Job—and any human— his life is short. The verse above the painting of Petrus and his wife also connects with Job: don't get too proud of the things you have or make, it implies. Even if they seem miraculous, God can make things that are even more miraculous, and what he made in this world (including man) proves it.

Hoefnagel describes man as a miracle, and he also describes him as a "world." What does he mean by this? Here he is bringing in the idea, developed first in classical Greek philosophy, of the macrocosm/microcosm, and the connections between these two realms. The macrocosm ("large world") is the whole universe, but its parts are understood to have similarities with the human body and mind. The microcosm ("little world") is the individual person, whose physical, mental, and spiritual parts correspond with parts of the universe. The same four elements—earth, air, fire, and water—made up both human beings and the cosmos. Just as humans have a soul and the quality of reason, so does the universe. Just as blood spurts out of a person's veins if they are opened, so water spurts out of the veins of the earth, or minerals harden into veins of silver or gold. The macrocosm of the planets and the stars affects the microcosm of human temperament, so that people born when certain planets or constellations were visible show certain personality characteristics. Those born under the sign of the planet Jupiter are generally happy and "jovial," for example, a word that comes directly from Jove, another name for Jupiter. For political theorists, the political structure was also a macrocosm with affinities to the human being, so that the king is the head, the nobles the hands, and the peasants the feet.

In the sixteenth century, notions of the connections and similarities between the macrocosm and microcosm pervaded art, philosophy, and scientific writings. Learned men developed complex systems about exactly how the two were related. Some of these involved beliefs in the properties of certain objects, numbers, or relationships later discounted as occult, but widely accepted at the time by scientists, physicians, and many members of the clergy. Hoefnagel took his specific presentation of the microcosm/macrocosm from another emblem book recently printed in Antwerp, *Mikrokosmos parvus mundus*. The very first emblem in that book lets the reader know exactly what the "little world" was, showing a familiar image: an idealized nude male figure superimposed on the globe, with the words "man" and "microcosm." Underneath this was the same verse from Job that Hoefnagel used, highlighting man's short and miserable life. Yes, man is a microcosm of the universe, and the greatest of all visible things, the verse reminds us, but God is far greater. Hoefnagel's presentation of Petrus and Catherine as microcosms, rather than the more common idealized male figures, further emphasizes the power of God. If even this hairy man is among the "greatest things" of the visible world, surely God's majesty must be astounding.

Apart from the few pages at the beginning, Hoefnagel's emblem book is primarily about insects, but the lines written above Petrus and Catherine can apply to insects as well. Other than humans, what better example of the visible miracles created by God could there be than insects, whose weird shapes and body parts still inspire Hollywood filmmakers when they create space aliens? To us in the twenty-first century, Petrus Gonzales may also look like a space alien, and a very specific one—Chewbacca the Wookiee, Han Solo's faithful sidekick in *Star Wars*. Hoefnagel is not presenting him as a creature from a distant planet, however, but, with the insects, as a sign of God's creative powers in *this* world.

Across from Petrus and Catherine in Hoefnagel's emblem book, on the back of the previous page, is the poem the artist writes in Petrus' voice:

I am Petrus Gonzales, cared for by the king of France
I was born in the Canary Islands,
Tenerife brought me forth
The miracle of nature covered my whole body with hair.
France, my other mother, nourished me as a child up to my
adulthood.
She taught me to put aside my wild ways
And taught me the liberal arts and to speak Latin.
A wife of outstanding beauty fell to my lot by a gift of God,
As did the most dear children of our marriage chamber.
It is proper to admire the gifts of nature given to you: the
children,
Some of whom take after their mother in form and color,
Some follow their father, adorned with hair.

Here Petrus is again a miracle—of nature, which is under the power
of God—and his wife and children are gifts. Like all the gifts of
God's creation, they are to be marveled at and admired.

The phrases that accompany the picture of the Gonzales children
on the next page reinforce this point. Above and below them, in
Latin, are inscriptions from the Book of Psalms: "Praise the Lord,
children! Praise the name of the Lord!" (Psalms 112: 1)[1] On the
page facing the picture of the children, Hoefnagel added other verses
from Psalms. At the top he wrote: "Out of the mouth of infants and
of sucklings thou hast perfected praise, because of thy enemies"
(Psalms 8: 3) and at the bottom: "Lord, what is MAN, that thou art
made known to him? or the son of man, that thou makest account
of him? MAN is like to vanity: his days pass away like a shadow."
(Psalms 143:4–5)

Hoefnagel gives a book and chapter notation with these verses,
directing any reader to the relevant psalm. Reading those psalms
provides further clues to why Hoefnagel might have begun his books
with the Gonzales family. After the verse he includes, Psalm 8 goes on:

5 What is man, that thou art mindful of him? or the son of
man, that thou visitest him?

6 Thou hast made him a little less than the angels, thou hast crowned him with glory and honour:

7 And hast set him over the works of thy hands.

8 Thou hast subjected all things under his feet, all sheep and oxen: moreover, the beasts also of the fields.

9 The birds of the air, and the fishes of the sea, that pass through the paths of the sea.

10 O Lord, our Lord, how admirable is thy name in the whole earth!

Verse 5 from Psalm 8 is almost the same as verse 4 from Psalm 143 that Hoefnagel includes on this page, and verse 10 from Psalm 8 is an echo of the sentiment on the preceding page above the picture of Petrus and his wife. Verses 6–9, however, expand on the place God has given man in the world, emphasizing his place as the pinnacle of creation ("little less than the angels"), with authority over the rest of God's creatures, those beasts, birds, and fishes whose paintings make up the rest of Hoefnagel's book. But the painting across from this verse is not that of a man "crowned with glory and honor," but two little hairy children. So do these children, and their parents, also have "dominion over the fishes of the sea, and the fowls of the air, and the beasts, and the whole earth, and every creeping creature that moveth upon the earth" (Genesis 1: 26), in Hoefnagel's opinion?

The verses above and below their picture (Praise the Lord, children! Praise the name of the Lord!) imply that they do, but later verses in Psalm 143 suggest that Hoefnagel's opinion may have been more ambivalent. The whole psalm is one in which David (or whoever wrote it) first praises God, and then asks God to come down with lightning, smoke, and arrows to deliver him from his enemies. Twice the psalmist puts his pleas the same way: "rescue me from the hands of strange children." These verses are not written in the book, but Hoefnagel directs any reader to the entire chapter, and both he and his audience were very familiar with the Bible. So here is this psalm, and here are the Gonzales children, as strange (the word in Latin is *alieni*) as anything that the psalmist might have imagined. Are the Gonzales children the "strange children" we want God to rescue us from? Or are they part of the creation that ordinary humans have dominion over? But how does this more negative view fit with the verses that accompany the painting of the parents on the previous page, in which Hoefnagel describes children as a gift of God? Or with the verse earlier on this page in which "infants and sucklings" provide perfect praise?

Hoefnagel was not alone in his ambivalence about the human condition, particularly when considering those who for one reason or another deviated from the norm. Twenty years after Hoefnagel painted the Gonzales family, Shakespeare wrote *Hamlet, Prince of Denmark*. In the play, Shakespeare gives Hamlet lines that parallel those Hoefnagel added to his painting: "What a piece of work is a man! How noble in reason! How infinite in faculty! In form, in moving, how express and admirable! In action how like an angel! In apprehension how like a god!" These lines are spoken in a scene where people are trying to figure out whether Hamlet is insane or just pretending to be, however, so that it is not clear how Shakespeare meant them. Is Hamlet's speech a sign that he *is* insane, as only a person who had lost his reason would compare humans to the gods? Or does he just say this because he knows people will judge him insane for saying it? Is Shakespeare mocking the human condition or celebrating it?

Trying to determine what Hoefnagel meant is as difficult as trying to decide what Shakespeare meant in Hamlet's speech, but there is no doubt about the context. Hoefnagel framed the Gonzales family—both actually and metaphorically—within his religious understanding. Like the animals that follow them in Hoefnagel's emblem books, they are demonstrations of the magnificent range of God's creation.

Religious devotion and destruction

The verses that Hoefnagel uses point to God's creative powers, but they also point to destruction. "Out of the mouth of infants and of sucklings thou hast perfected praise, because of thy enemies," wrote Hoefnagel next to the children, and other psalms that he quotes plead with God for rescue and deliverance. Such entreaties are common in prayers and psalms, but they may also reflect Hoefnagel's own experience, for he was directly caught up in the religious violence of the era, and had seen at first hand the death and destruction that it brought. Hoefnagel's home city was Antwerp, the second-largest city north of the Alps and a thriving center of business in spices, textiles, and silver. Spanish troops sent by King Philip II to fight Protestant rebels in the Netherlands saw that wealth. In 1576, when their wages were delayed many months and they heard that ships carrying much of the money had been captured by the English, they sacked the town in a frenzy of destruction. In three days this "Spanish fury," as it came to be called, killed 6,000 people, burnt down hundreds of houses, and destroyed vast amounts of property. The city threw out the Spanish soldiers, and became the center of the Protestant revolt in the Netherlands. The Catholic Hoefnagel decided to leave for more peaceful surroundings, taking the completed paintings of fish, birds, and animals for his emblem book with him. When he added the Gonzales family several years later, and chose verses to accompany the tiny paintings, the disastrous effects of religious disagreements were still fresh in his mind, so it is no wonder that he included verses noting the fleetingness and misery of human life, or asking God for rescue.

In 1582, when he penned the words, the enemies that these "infants and sucklings" pointed to might have been Spanish troops that had sacked the city. Or they might have been the Protestant forces currently holding Antwerp, making it impossible for Hoefnagel to return. But like any prodigy, the Gonzales children hinted at things to come as well as past misfortunes. In this the words were particularly prophetic, for several years after Hoefnagel wrote them Antwerp fell to Catholic troops after a year-long siege. Half the population fled the city, and the lead in Dutch commerce was taken by Amsterdam. The head of the victorious Catholic forces was Alessandro Farnese, to whose court the Gonzales children and their parents were later sent. Hoefnagel could never have imagined when he wrote them how appropriate the verses he chose to accompany the "strange children" would be.

Hoefnagel did not have to look back to Antwerp for religious conflicts, however, but could see them closer to hand in Munich. By the middle of the sixteenth century, many of the middle-class citizens of Munich and some of the nobility from the state of Bavaria that surrounded it had converted to Protestantism. They hoped to convince the Wittelsbach dukes of Bavaria to convert as well, but Duke Albrecht V, who ruled from 1550 to 1579, instead became a major figure in reinvigorated Catholicism. His forces attacked the castles of the most prominent Protestant nobles, whom he charged with treason and conspiracy. He was successful in crushing Protestantism in Bavaria, forcing Protestants to reconvert to Catholicism or leave Bavaria. Many left, joining the stream of religious refugees of all types seeking new places to live in this era when the ruler of each state of Germany could determine whether his territory would be Protestant or Catholic.

Albrecht's son William V was even more intensely devoted to Catholicism than his father, and so devout that he became known as "William the Pious." He often heard several masses a day—at which courtiers were expected to be in attendance—and sponsored frequent processions, pilgrimages, and huge religious plays. He set up a special council to regularly investigate the theological ideas and depth of spiritual conviction of the duchy's clergy and officials. Jesuits were brought in to staff high schools in many towns of Bavaria, and as faculty at the University of Ingolstadt, where the religious ideas of the next generation of Catholic political and church leaders were molded.

William and his wife Renate of Lorraine were specially devoted to the Virgin Mary, who was named the patron saint of Bavaria. Enormous columns in Mary's honor were set up in the central market square of every major town, and religious brotherhoods devoted to Mary were established. Bavarians of all social classes, including the duke, made pilgrimages to the shrine of Mary at Altötting, a small chapel with a statue of the Virgin in southern Bavaria. Here in the late fifteenth century a grieving mother had brought her drowned son, and, according to tradition, the statue had miraculously revived him. Altötting became the most important pilgrimage site in Germany, the heart of a strong Bavarian Catholicism that has lasted until today. (Altötting now receives over a million visitors a year, some of them pilgrims on special tours of all the major shrines to Mary in Europe.)

William's support of Catholicism included military measures. In 1583, the archbishop of Cologne, one of the most important church leaders in Germany, became a Protestant and declared that Cologne would from that point on be a secular state. William sent Bavarian troops to depose the archbishop, armies on both sides plundered a number of towns, and eventually William's brother Ernst was appointed as archbishop. Wittelsbachs held this position for the next two hundred years, which meant the Wittelsbach archbishop was one of the seven men who elected the Holy Roman Emperor, and could help make sure that the emperorship remained in Catholic hands.

In the same year as the Cologne war, William began planning a new church for the Jesuits in Munich, the St Michael's Church. He ordered a number of houses in the center of the city demolished to make room for it, envisioning this as the heart of Catholic piety north of the Alps. William made a pilgrimage to Rome, where he saw the Church of the Gesù, the mother church of the Jesuits, and decided St Michael's should be modeled on it. He may also have visited Gesù's primary funder, Cardinal Alessandro Farnese, the great-uncle of Cardinal Odoardo Farnese, who later owned Enrico Gonzales and his portrait. William returned to Munich determined to build a church just as enormous and spectacular as those he had seen in Rome, and he did. The vault was larger than that of any other church except St Peter's in Rome. When a tower collapsed during construction, William decided God wanted a still bigger building, and the church was redesigned on an even more massive scale. William's religious and architectural endeavors nearly bankrupted Bavaria, and he finally abdicated, leaving his son to handle the financial mess.

To his subjects, William V was best known for the piety that was on constant display, but to artists, scholars, and dealers in rare objects, he was also known as a collector. In this, as well, he built on his father's interests. Both Albrecht and William employed agents to search all over Europe for extraordinary items, and hired artists and craftsmen to create them. Among these was the unknown artist who painted the huge pictures of the Gonzales family that William later gave to his uncle Ferdinand II to hang in Ambras castle, and, of course, Joris Hoefnagel, who based the portraits of the Gonzales family in his emblem book on these large paintings. Both of them made sure that William's religious devotion was not ignored, showing Maddalena Gonzales wearing a huge cross among the decorations on her dress. In Albrecht's and William's collections, religious objects such as crucifixes, communion chalices, and relics stood side by side with plant and animal specimens, clocks, globes, and carved ivory. Did their collections ever include the Gonzales family itself? Probably not, for there is no evidence that any member of the family was actually at the Wittelsbach court in Munich. In 1583, William wrote to someone in France asking for more details about the "wild guy" in his pictures and his family, details he would not have needed to seek from such a far-away place if the Gonzales family had been with him.

The pictures of the family were in Munich, however, owned by this most pious Catholic duke, and surrounded, in the case of Hoefnagel's tiny emblem book, by Bible verses. But Hoefnagel and his patron were not alone in viewing the world primarily through the lens of religious beliefs. Although religion was tearing Europe apart, Christian beliefs shaped the ways that most people understood the Gonzales family, particularly their views of them as monsters or as creatures somewhere between human and animal. Their reactions to the Gonzales sisters were also framed by religious understandings of the role God had set out specifically for women.

Monsters and prodigies in God's creation

Beginning with St Augustine in the fourth century, most Christian writers saw both marvelous species and monstrous individuals as signs from God. Augustine makes no distinction between the two, but by the late twelfth century theologians and scholars asserted that what God was saying through them differed. The marvelous species, whether it was the one-legged tribe who used their feet for umbrellas described by Pliny, or the people who lived for hundreds of years described by Pierre d'Ailly, was a wonderful (in both senses of the word) symbol of God's broad creative powers operating in the natural world. In his *Topography of Ireland*, Gerald of Wales discusses barnacle geese that grew on trees rather than being hatched from eggs, judging them to be a marvelous work of God in nature. Edward Topsell views unicorns in the same way in the *History of Foure-Footed Beastes*, and scolds those who don't believe unicorns exist:

> We are now come to the history of a beast, whereof diverse people in every age of the world have made great question . . . [but such] people scarcely believe any herb but such as they see in their own gardens, or any beast but such as in their own flocks, or any knowledge but such as is bred in their own brains . . . . It appears to me that there is some secret enemy in the inward degenerate nature of man, which continually blinds the eyes of God's people, from beholding and believing the greatness of God's works.[2]

Unicorns, and the many other exotic species of creatures he includes in the bestiary, were to Topsell a demonstration of the great variety of God's creation, for God could (and did) create more things than anyone could imagine from his or her own experience alone. This point of view is similar to Hoefnagel's, for Hoefnagel's emblem book, a bestiary of sorts, opens with praise of God's entire creation, the greatest of visible miracles. Most of the creatures in it were members of a species to be marveled at and admired.

The Gonzaleses were not a species, however, but a small group of individuals. Thus Hoefnagel's understanding of their place in the world—and that of others who saw them—was also shaped by religious notions about monstrous individuals. In contrast to marvelous species, monstrous individuals were usually viewed with fear and horror, not wonder. God and the saints could produce beneficent miracles, of course, but generally such creatures represented God's judgment for evils that had taken place, or foretold catastrophes to come, or both. Such warnings from the realm beyond appeared throughout the Middle Ages, but they were growing ever more common, in many people's opinion, in the sixteenth century.

Monstrous births were sometimes interpreted as signs of God's wrath against individual sinners, often the parents or the mother. An illustrated broadside describing a "monstrous childe" born in Essex in England in 1562 blamed its parents for their "want of honesty and excess of sin" because the child was born out of wedlock. Another detailing a monstrous birth in Kent in 1568 blamed the mother, "who being unmarried played the naughty pack, and was gotten with child."[3] These births were never simply punishment for the parents, however, but were also signs of God's anger at the entire community and calls to repentance. The child born in Kent was a "terror as well to all such workers of filthiness and iniquity," while that born in Essex was a word of warning to everyone in "this monstrous world."

God sometimes sent monsters as a message to a particular group. In 1512, Luca Landucci, an apothecary in Florence, reported that

> We heard that a monster had been born in Ravenna, of which a drawing was sent here; it had a horn on its head, straight up like a sword, and instead of arms it had two wings like a bat's, and at the height of the breasts it had a Y-shaped mark on one side and a cross on the other, and lower down at the waist, two serpents, and it was hermaphrodite, and on the right knee it had an eye, and its left foot was like an eagle's. I saw it painted, and anyone who wished could see this painting in Florence.

Not three weeks later, according to Landucci, troops "took Ravenna and sacked it, being guilty of many cruelties. . . . It was evident what evil the monster had meant for them! It seems as if some great misfortune always befalls the city where such things are born."[4]

As he tells it, Landucci first learned about this monster by seeing a picture of it, the way that many people learned of monstrous births and prodigious events. The story he heard about it had become somewhat garbled in transmission, however, as the monster was first described as born in Florence, not Ravenna. It was the subject of printed broadsides that circulated as far away as Germany and France. There commentators viewed it as a sign not for Ravenna alone, but for all of Italy. The French chronicler Johannes Multivallis connected each of its abnormalities to a certain sin, all punished by the French invasion of Italy:

> The horn indicates pride; the wings, mental frivolity and inconstancy; the lack of arms, a lack of good works; the raptor's foot, rapaciousness, usury and every sort of avarice; the eye on the knee, a mental orientation solely toward earthly things; the double sex, sodomy. And on account of these vices, Italy is shattered by the sufferings of war, which the king of France has not accomplished by his own power, but only as a scourge of God.[5]

Like the monsters sent as warnings to individuals, those sent to specific groups also carried a message to all of society, and in the mid-sixteenth century several authors turned to interpreting the phenomena as a whole. They gathered stories from broadsheets, pamphlets, and chronicles into whole books of prodigies. Conrad Lycosthenes' huge *Prodigiorum ac ostentorum chronicon* (Chronicle of Prodigies and Portents), published in Basel in 1557, included nearly 1,500 cases and 2,000 woodcuts. These ranged from the beginning of time—the first monster was the talking snake that led Eve astray—to his own day. In the introduction, Lycosthenes does not deny that natural explanations were possible for some of the occurrences, but "nature is God's minister in matters both favorable and unfavorable, and through her agency he aids the pious and punishes the impious . . . it is impossible to deny that a monster is an imposing sign of divine wrath and malediction."[6] Lycosthenes was a Protestant, but most of his monsters point toward moral failings that were shared by Protestants and Catholics, rather than toward specifically Catholic sins. Like the Ravenna/Florence monster, Lycosthenes' prodigies had deformities that linked with particular sins: swollen bellies stood for gluttony or greed, enlarged heads for pride, malformed sexual organs for lust, fingerless hands for sloth.

The French Catholic Pierre Boaistuau, author of another collection of prodigy stories, agreed that monsters had a general meaning.

34. Monster of Ravenna, from Ambroise Paré's *On Monsters and Marvels*, 1573. Verbal and visual depictions of this "monster" appeared throughout Europe, with its deformities often tied to specific sins or events.

"They do for the most part reveal to us the secret judgment and scourge of the ire of God," Boaistuau wrote in the preface to his collection, "which makes us to feel his marvelous justice so sharply, that we are constrained to enter into ourselves, to knock with the hammer of our conscience, to examine our offences, and have in horror our misdeeds."[7]

There were some differences between Protestant and Catholic understandings of the role of monsters. To Protestants, monsters warned of the rapidly approaching end of the world: the Last Judgment is upon us and God is sending these shocking prodigies to warn us to repent. An English broadside ballad of 1562, *A discription of a monstrous Chylde, borne at Chychester in Sussex*, began:

> The Scripture says, before the end
> Of all things shall appear,
> God will wondrous strange things send,
> As some is seen this year.[8]

We may not know exactly what they mean, but we can be sure that through them God is telling us to live pious lives.

Catholic interpretations of the same creatures or events often read them as warnings about the heresy of Protestant teachings rather than as signs of the end of the world. *Ecclesia militans* (The Church Militant), a 1569 broadsheet composed by the Dominican friar Johannes Nasus, shows the Catholic Church being attacked by a host of monsters, each labeled with a numbered caption. All of the creatures, which included two-headed, headless, and huge-headed infants, as well as the monk-calf and other deformed animals, come from reports about monstrous births in Protestant areas. To Nasus, they represented the deformity and disunity of Protestant teachings, all brought about by Luther, "who led a cow's life."[9]

Most authors read prodigies negatively, as warnings from God about human failings, but a few saw them in a more positive light, or at least ambivalently, as Hoefnagel did the Gonzales family. After describing a small boy with a parasitic twin attached to his stomach and a man who had "no sign of genital parts," Michel de Montaigne commented in one of his essays: "What we call monsters are not so to God, who sees in the immensity of his work the infinity of forms that he has comprised in it; and it is for us to believe that this figure that astonishes us is related and linked to some other figure of the same kind unknown to man. From God's infinite wisdom there proceeds nothing but that is good and ordinary and regular; but we do not see its arrangement and relationship."[10] In this, however, as on other topics—such as his notion that people of the New World might be as civilized as those of Europe—Montaigne's remained the minority opinion. It was shared by Hoefnagel, for whom Petrus and his children were also demonstrations of the infinity and immensity of God, but by few others.

Rational animals

The verses surrounding the Gonzales family in Hoefnagel's emblem book point to their status as one of God's (many) wondrous miracles, and the title of the book indicates another of their features: *Animalia rationalia*, rational animals. In these two words Hoefnagel captures what was seen as the key distinction in the sixteenth century between animals and humans, the quality of reason. In their animal-like appearance, however, Petrus and his children challenged that distinction. Looking like this, were they truly rational humans, or were they animals? Hoefnagel has no doubts, which may be why he was the only commentator on the family who did not compare them with animals. Petrus is hairy and wild in the poem Hoefnagel writes in Petrus' voice that accompanies the pictures, but he is not like a dog, and his daughter is not like a monkey, animals other writers associated with the Gonzales family. Others were not as sure where the Gonzales family belonged, particularly because the line between humans and beasts seemed to them increasingly blurry.

Medieval and Renaissance thinkers looked to Aristotle on the difference between humans and animals, as they did on so many other topics. Although Greek mythology contained many tales of human–animal hybrids and shape-shifting gods, for the Greek philosopher these were simply stories, and the distinction was clear. Aristotle held that there are three kinds of "souls" among living beings: vegetative, sensible, and rational. Plants had only the vegetative, animals the vegetative and sensible, and only humans all three. The English philosopher Daniel Widdowes repeated Aristotle's ideas succinctly in his 1631 description of the world: "All Creatures are reasonable, or unreasonable. They which lack reason, are Beasts, who live on Land or in Water."[11] Christian understandings modified Aristotle, but continued to focus on reason as the key difference. Reason was given to humans by God, and not destroyed by the sin of the Fall, when Adam and Eve disobeyed God's command. As John Woolton, the bishop of Exeter, wrote in 1576:

> God has left unto [man] . . . *a power to discern between things honest and unhonest*, and to understand the grounds of liberal arts, of good laws, and of honest actions. This knowledge of reason, as the Philosophers call it, was not altogether extinct in man's ruin. For it was God's good pleasure, that there should yet be some difference between reasonable man and brute beasts.[12]

This quality of reason gave man dominion over animals. God had not only "endowed him with reason," wrote the English clergyman Thomas Rogers in 1576, "but has brought all other things as well senseless as having life: as fowls, fishes and four-footed beasts, under his power either to kill or keep them."[13] Reason allowed humans to know that there was a past and a future, which animals did not, and to have self-knowledge, another quality animals lacked.

Alongside this confident trumpeting of difference there were also some doubts, however. How did we *know* that humans had reason? This could be asserted on the basis of ancient authorities or the Bible, but visible proof was also important. Since no one could peer inside people's heads, finding proof meant looking at actions. But that led to a host of problems. At what point in their development did people gain their rational souls? Most authors doubted that it was at the moment of conception, a point termed "generation" in the sixteenth century. Instead a fetus acquired a rational soul when it began to move in the womb. As the anatomist Thomas Vicary wrote in 1548, "then it [the embryo] receives the soul with life and breath, and then it begins to move itself alone."[14] Humans thus had their rational soul while still in the womb. But if rational capacity was to be judged through visible actions, what about infants and children? They certainly did not act in ways that anyone would judge rational, so were they human?

Answering that question in the affirmative required complicated logical gymnastics. Yes, infants were human, and their rational capacity—the source of their humanity—was a quality given to them by God, but it was limited by their physical weakness. It was also limited, according to most authors, by their imagination and feelings; what we call emotions and the sixteenth century called passions. Those passions were strong in young children, and might grow even stronger if children were not taught to control them through their reason. Children, as the English author Thomas Wright wrote, "lack the use of reason, and are guided by an internal imagination, following nothing else but that pleases their senses, even after the same manner as brute beasts do."[15] Wright's comment highlights the problem with this widely shared line of thought. If reason is a natural and God-given quality that separates humans from animals, why do humans have to be trained to use it? Are humans born, or are they made? Hoefnagel's poem suggests he thinks it is the latter, for only when "France, my other mother . . . taught me to put aside my wild ways and taught me the liberal arts and to speak Latin" does Petrus Gonzales become fully human. But then what about children who never learned to put aside their wild ways? Were they animals or humans? Many preachers and writers of the time were not sure. As the English clergyman John Moore wrote in 1617, "What is an infant but a brute beast in the shape of a man? And what is a young youth but (as it were) a wild untamed ass-colt unbridled?"[16] If any infant or youth could blur the distinction between animal and human, the Gonzales children did so even more dramatically.

The beast within

Not only did the behavior of children reveal problems in the human/animal distinction, but so did that of adults. Even those who had been trained to use their reason and so had become fully human might lapse and let the passions again decide their actions. Doing this was generally described in animal terms: people "descended to the realm of the beasts" or "let their inner beast emerge." Alcohol offered an easy way for this to happen, for, as the English soldier and poet George Gascoigne put it bluntly, "All drunkards are beasts."[17] Many others agreed, and Thomas Young expanded on this idea to specify which kinds of animal men became when they drank:

> The first is Lion drunk, which breaks glass windows, calls his hostess whore, strikes, fights, or quarrels, with either brother, friend or father. The second is Ape-drunke, who dances, capers, and leaps about the house, sings and rejoices, and is wholly ravished into jests, mirth, and melody. The third is sheep drunk, who is very kind and liberal, and says, by God captain I love you . . . . The fourth is Sow drunk, who vomits, spews, and wallows in the mire, like a Swine . . . . The seventh is Goat drunk, who is in his drink so lecherous, that he makes no difference of either time, or place, age or youth.[18]

Drink offered the easiest path to the realm of the beasts, and, as Young's list of animals indicates, it often led to other sorts of beastly behavior. Drunkenness could result in violence and cruelty, which was brutish even without drink, because it turned a human into something other than a rational being. As the Spanish humanist Juan Luis Vives noted early in the sixteenth century, "it is inhuman and cruel when we relinquish human judgment and feeling to adopt that of the beasts."[19] Claude Prieur, the French author of a treatise on werewolves, agreed, commenting that although werewolves were violent, the French wars of religion revealed that "there is no savage beast wilder than man if he is left to himself."[20]

Sexual passion was a powerful transformer of men into beasts, with or without alcohol. This idea had strong roots in Christian teachings. St Augustine, the most important thinker in the western Christian Church, commented that during intercourse "there is an almost total extinction of mental alertness; the intellectual sentries are overwhelmed."[21] Men's erections, to Augustine, were "bestial movements," both because they were uncontrollable by human reason or will and because they were an experience shared by animals. Augustine viewed sexual desire as a result of the Fall, of Adam and Eve's sinfulness. Adam and Eve disobeyed God to eat of the Tree of Knowledge, and one aspect of the knowledge they gained was sexual, or as the Book of Genesis puts it: "They knew that they were naked." This original sin, in Augustine's view, was passed down to every human afterwards through the semen emitted in sexual acts motivated by desire, and was thus inescapable. Only God's grace could allow one to overcome it, or to overcome any other human sin or weakness.

Augustine's idea about original sin became Christian doctrine in the western Church, and sex continued to be seen as an activity in which humans' animalistic natures emerged. As the thirteenth-century philosopher Thomas Aquinas put it bluntly: "in sexual intercourse man becomes like a brute animal."[22] Actually, when driven by lust, man was *worse* than a brute animal. Lust was a natural state for animals, so that when they engaged in sex they were simply carrying out natural behavior. Reason is the natural state for humans, so that lust-driven sex made them unnatural, and therefore even more beastly than a beast. Virginity and celibacy were thus the preferred states of human existence in medieval Christian theology, spiritually superior to marriage.

The Protestant reformers rejected the value of celibacy, in large part because they saw the power of lust as so strong that a truly chaste life was impossible for all but a handful of individuals. In countless sermons, lectures, and letters, Martin Luther emphasizes that sexual passion is "a malady common to the entire human race." He speculates that in the Garden of Eden before the Fall there was (or would have been) sex without lust: "If we had not fallen, it would have happened that everyone had to produce young. The blessing had been pronounced [Adam's saying to Eve in Gen. 2: 23 that she is 'bone of his bone, flesh of his flesh'] so that this should take place without pain and without evil lust." Sexual relations would have taken place without sin, and here Luther makes an analogy with animals: "We observe in all animals that they are not in a condition to sin. So it also was with human beings. But now that is past."[23]

The Fall changed human sexuality so that it was both less and more like that of animals. It was less like that of animals because it was sinful, but more like that of animals in its outward appearance.

In commenting on Genesis 1: 28 ("Be fruitful and multiply") Luther says that through lust "the body becomes downright brutish and cannot beget in the knowledge of God," and that human "procreation [is] only slightly more moderate than that of the brutes."[24] (Luther also equates lust with disease, terming it an "unavoidable leprosy of the flesh" and commenting that it is "so hideous and frightful a pleasure that physicians compare it with epilepsy.")

To many authors, women who lust were particularly animalistic. As Dorothy Leigh, author of *The Mother's Blessing*, an advice manual for women that went through many printings in the seventeenth century, put it: "The Woman that is infected by the sin of uncleanness, is worse than a beast, because it desireth but for nature, and she, to satisfy her corrupt lusts . . . let women be persuaded by this discourse, to embrace chastity, without which, we are mere beasts, and no women."[25]

Lust made all human sexuality brutish, but some sexual relations were worse than others. Incest, same-sex relations, and sex with animals were all regarded as "crimes against nature" as well as sins, and those who practiced them were viewed as both monsters and animals. King Henry III of France, the third son of Henry II and Catherine de Medici, was particularly subject to such charges. He married and had children, and visited courtesans when he traveled to Venice, but also wore women's clothing to balls and parties and surrounded himself with male favorites, his so-called *mignons*. According to a contemporary description, an anonymous broadside attacking the king included portraits showing him with the head of a "furious lion" because of his "audacity and arrogance," and with the "breasts of a woman underneath [which] show that this effeminate prince sinned against nature by his excesses as a hermaphrodite. They also wished to show that this monster enlarged his breasts with the blood of the people so he could nourish his blood-suckers."[26]

"Unnatural" sex could sometimes have dramatic consequences. According to one pamphlet, a monstrous infant born in Hereford in England in 1600 was the result not only of sex out of wedlock, but of "incestuous copulation between the brother's son and the sister's daughter" and so was a "notable and most terrible example against incest and whoredom."[27] A French pamphlet told of an infant born in

Paris in the same year, the product of sex between a chambermaid and a monkey. The mother admitted this while being tortured; she and the child and the monkey were all burnt together, and readers of the pamphlet warned to "pray constantly to God" so that Satan would not lead them into such "sinister evil doing."[28] Those who saw the Gonzales children all knew of such stories, and may have wondered if they, too, were God's punishment for unnatural sex. Seeing or learning about their father just made such questions more complicated—was he so animal-like that sex between him and Catherine was, indeed, unnatural? And what about *his* mother?

Sex and marriage

Lust did not usually lead to monsters, but it was always dangerous. For Protestants, the best Christian life was not one that fruitlessly attempted ascetic celibacy, but one in which sexual activity was channeled into marriage. (This is what Dorothy Leigh, a good Protestant, means by "chastity," in her advice to women.) God had established marriage as the first human institution when he created Eve out of Adam's rib and brought her to him. This happened *before* the Fall, so before human sin had led to lust. Thus the purposes of marriage were not only controlling the sex drive and having children, but companionship. Lust might make humans like animals, but those who criticized marriage were, to Luther, also like animals. In a wedding sermon preached in 1531, he comments:

> We should honor and praise this estate [marriage] and not do as the filthy sows who think and talk about nothing else other than shameful whoredom and adultery. They are abominable filthy beasts, who soil their own nests and love to root round in the filth with their dirty snouts and roll around in their own excrement . . . . We should also not do as the clever ones do, who rebuke this dear estate and criticize it because there is much dissatisfaction, strife, trouble, and toil in it, and who say "God keep me from this estate—he who takes a wife gets a devil." People like this are rabid dogs who shame this dear

estate with their vicious muzzles and tear at it with their poisonous teeth, just as sows do with their snouts.[29]

The Catholic response to the challenge of the Protestant reformers, usually termed the Catholic Reformation, included a response to the Protestant elevation of marriage. As with many other issues, Catholic thinkers reaffirmed traditional doctrine. They agreed that the most worthy type of Christian life was one both celibate and chaste. Catholic leaders also realized, however, that most people in Europe would marry, and so preached sermons and published works that presented a more positive view of marriage than had classical or medieval Christian thinkers. Sermons praising Jesus' mother Mary increasingly noted that she was a wife and mother as well as a virgin, and Mary's husband Joseph became the patron saint of marriage. Hoefnagel, himself a Catholic, captures this emphasis in his poem. Petrus praises his beautiful wife and his dear children as gifts from God, a sentiment on which Protestants and most Catholics agreed, at least in theory.

Women's inferiority

A wife might be a gift of God, but this did not make her equal to her husband. Children, drunkards, and people having sex were not the only humans whose diminished rational capacity brought them closer to animals. To most people in the sixteenth century, all women, not just girls, had less reason than did men. On this issue people looked, once again, to Aristotle and the Bible. In the *Generation of Animals*, Aristotle had noted that women were monstrous because they were less than perfect, and nature always aimed at perfection. In the *Politics*, Aristotle discussed a different reason for women's inferiority. In this work, he considered the origins of government, which he saw as rooted in households and families. Within a family, he remarks, "A husband and father . . . rules over wife and children . . . although there may be exceptions to the order of nature, the male is by nature fitter for command than the female, just as the elder and full-grown is superior to the younger and more immature . . . . When one rules and the other is ruled we endeavor to create a difference of outward forms and names and titles of respect . . . . The relation of the male to the female is of this kind, but there the inequality is permanent." Women do have rational capacity, according to Aristotle, "but the temperance of a man and of a woman, or the courage and justice of a man and of a woman, are not, as Socrates maintained, the same; the courage of a man is shown in commanding, of a woman in obeying . . . . All classes must be deemed to have their special attributes; as the poet says of women, Silence is a woman's glory."[30]

But what about the women who married into the Gonzales family? The marriage of Petrus and Catherine, and later of their sons Enrico and Orazio to their wives, set one rational-human vs. irrational-animal hierarchy against another. In physical appearance the men appeared closer animals, but in their gender the women were. Which hierarchy should take precedence? On this question there would have been little doubt, because the women's inferior position was the result not simply of their gender's lack of reason, but also of their position as wives. A married woman was legally subject to her husband in all things; she could not sue, make contracts, or go to court for any reason without his approval, and in many areas of Europe could not be sued or charged with any civil crime on her own. In much of Europe, all goods or property that a wife brought into a marriage and all wages she earned during the marriage were considered the property of her husband, a situation that did not change legally until the nineteenth century.

The legal dependence of wives on their husbands means that married women are the most difficult group to trace in the sources, for they simply disappear. Not even her hairy condition kept Maddalena Gonzales, the one Gonzales sister who married, in the historical record for very long. In 1593, the duke of Parma bought "Maddalena the hairy" a house. Maddalena—the little girl in the pink dress in Hoefnagel's emblem book—was about eighteen at the time, the perfect age to get married for women in Italian cities. With that, she vanishes from the records, other than a brief mention later as the mother of a girl who was being confirmed in her

Catholic faith. By contrast, Maddalena's husband, the keeper of the duke's hunting dogs, appears regularly in letters and account books, as do her brothers. In Maddalena's case there was no contradiction between the human/animal and male/female hierarchies, of course, and no one would have doubted that her husband was the superior of the pair.

Married women's legal inferiority had divine support, in the eyes of most people, for the Bible provided reinforcement for male rule of women. On this point Martin Luther was especially eloquent. Commenting on Genesis 1: 27 ("So God created man in his own image, in the image of God created he him; male and female created he them"), he notes:

> Eve, too, was made by God as a partaker of the divine image and of the divine similitude, likewise of the rule over everything . . . . In the household the wife is a partner in the management and has a common interest in the children and the property, and yet there is a great difference between the sexes. The male is like the sun in heaven, the female like the moon, the animals like the stars, over which the sun and moon have dominion. In the first place let us note from this passage that it was written that this sex may not be excluded from any glory of the human creature, although it is inferior to the male sex.

Where does this inferiority come from? From Eve's sin in the Fall, Luther says plainly:

> If the woman had not been deceived by the serpent and had not sinned, she would have been the equal of Adam in all respects. For the punishment, that she is now subjected to man, was imposed on her after sin and because of sin, just as the other hardships were: travail, pain, and countless other vexations. Therefore Eve was not like the woman of today; her state was far better and more excellent, and she was in no respect inferior to Adam, whether you count the qualities of the body or those of the mind.

Adam and Eve are thus equal before the Fall. Why then, did Satan choose to tempt Eve rather than Adam? When he turns to this issue later in the lectures on Genesis, Luther has changed his mind about the original equality in the Garden of Eden:

> Satan's cleverness is perceived also in this, that he attacks the weak part of the human nature, Eve the woman, not Adam the man. Although both were created equally righteous, nevertheless Adam had some advantages over Eve. Just as in all the rest of nature the strength of the male surpasses that of the other sex, so also in the perfect nature the male somewhat excelled the female. Because Satan sees that Adam is the more excellent, he does not dare assail him; for he fears that his attempt may turn out to be useless. And I, too, believe that if he had tempted Adam first, the victory would have been Adam's. He would have crushed the serpent with his foot and would have said: "Shut up! The Lord's command was different." Satan, therefore, directs his attack on Eve as the weaker part and puts her valor to the test, for he sees that she is so dependent on her husband that she thinks she cannot sin.[31]

Although he loudly (and proudly) rejected Aristotle's ideas on many issues, here Luther agrees with Aristotle that the inequality between men and women was present from creation. In statements made offhand to the people gathered around his dinner table and recorded by his students and followers, he expresses this more succinctly: "God created male and female—the female for reproduction, the male for nourishing and defending." "It appears from this that woman was created for housekeeping but man for keeping order, governing worldly affairs, fighting, and dealing with justice." "There is no dress that suits a woman or maiden so badly as wanting to be clever."[32]

Luther was no more contradictory or inconsistent in his opinions about women than any other religious thinker in the sixteenth century. Although they challenged tradition on many things, Protestant reformers did not break sharply with medieval Catholic theologians in their ideas about women. For Protestant reformers, including Ulrich Zwingli, John Calvin, and many English Protestants as well as Luther, women were created by God and could be saved through faith; spiritually women and men were equal. In every other respect, however, women were to be subordinate to men, a position with which Catholic reformers agreed.

Sermons, marriage manuals, and household guides from all over Protestant and Catholic Europe repeated the same message: Women's subjection was inherent in their very being and was present from creation. Eve was primarily responsible for the Fall and the introduction of sin, which made women's original natural inferiority and subjection to male authority even more pronounced. God created Eve out of Adam's rib, which was proof that God wanted women to stand by the side of men as their assistants and not be trampled on or trod underfoot (for then Eve would have been created out of Adam's foot), but women should never claim authority over men, for Eve had not been created out of Adam's head.

Women were to be obedient to their husbands, even if this was difficult. As the Tudor homily on marriage, which the crown required to be read out loud regularly in all English churches, put it: "Truth it is, that they [women] must specially feel the griefs and pains of matrimony, in that they relinquish the liberty of their own rule."[33] Men were also given very specific advice about how to enforce their authority, which often included physical coercion; in both continental and English marriage manuals, the authors use the metaphor of breaking in a horse for teaching a wife obedience. In Luther's lectures on Genesis, women share in men's dominion over animals as the moon shares the sun's dominion over the stars, but in more commonly repeated metaphors, women are subject to men's dominion just as animals are.

Are women human?

Anyone who was uncertain about where various members of the Gonzales family fit into God's plan had yet another issue to consider in the late sixteenth century, particularly when considering the girls.

Even if they were not monstrous marvels or irrational animals, were they, as women, human? Women's status as part of their husbands led a few legal theorists to debate whether, technically, women were human beings at all. If women were not separate persons, did laws of homicide apply to their murder, particularly as the word "homicide" was derived from the Latin word "*homo*" that could mean "man" as well as "person"? Works arguing that women were *not* human also circulated as satirical in-jokes among highly learned humanists, and in 1595 one of them was published anonymously in central Germany. The author of this elegantly written and provocatively titled *Disputatio nova contra mulieres, qua probatur eas homines non esse* (New disputation against women, which proves that they are not human) sets out fifty-one theses demonstrating that women are not human. These included statements from classical authorities, such as Plato's comment that woman was more an irrational animal than a rational one. There were arguments from language: the word "*homo*" came originally from "*humus*"—dirt— and because Eve was made from Adam's rib, not dirt, she was not human. There were proofs from biology: only man provided the "active" principle in reproduction, while woman was simply the tool, and just as a hammer did not become part of a smith when he created something, so woman did not become part of mankind when men used her to perpetuate the human race. There were many demonstrations from the Bible: only men are mentioned in its genealogical tables of the Old Testament, and Saint Paul had said "by one *man* did sin enter the world." In the Book of Numbers, God had empowered the prophet Balaam's (female) ass to see God's angel messenger before her master did, and even to speak the truth to her master, although he beat her three times (Numbers 22: 21–30). This did not make the ass human, so that the fact that women spoke or had faith did not prove that they were human. The treatise does not say exactly what women *are*, although it does connect them with dogs and with demons.

Within a month, the *Disputatio* provoked a furor of controversy. It was answered by the long *Defensio sexus muliebris* (Defense of the female sex), written by Simon Geddicus, a Lutheran theologian and professor of Hebrew. The publisher was hauled into court, and ordered to reveal the identity of the author of the *Disputatio*, which he did: Valens Acidalius, a German scholar of the classics who had also received degrees in philosophy and medicine from universities in northern Italy. Geddicus' fellow Lutheran pastors joined the chorus attacking Acidalius, and publishers realized they had a sure hit. The two pamphlets were issued, together and separately, many times, translated into French, German, and Italian, and continued to be published in new editions until the late eighteenth century. Stories spread as widely as the pamphlets themselves did. A university student in Cologne was beaten to death by angry mothers after he defended Acidalius' ideas, went one story. Acidalius himself, who died several months after the pamphlet was published, had supposedly committed suicide or been driven insane.[34]

Acidalius had given the pamphlet to his publisher, but may not have written all of it, for the various arguments it presented were not new. Humanist scholars, such as those in Acidalius' circles of friends in Germany and Italy, were active participants in the "debate about women" (often known by the French version of the phrase: *querelle des femmes*), an argument about women's character and nature that had been going on for centuries. As part of the debate, misogynist critiques from both clerical and secular authors denounced females as devious, domineering, and demanding. In answer, authors compiled long lists of famous and praiseworthy women, exemplary for their loyalty, bravery, and morality. In Italy, a number of learned women wrote spirited defenses that directly refuted the works of misogynist writers. The Venetian poet Modesta Pozzo, writing under the pen-name Moderata Fonte ("moderate fountain"), produced *The Worth of Women: Wherein is Clearly Revealed their Nobility and their Superiority to Men* (first published 1600), whose main point is captured in the title. Women's activities as wives and mothers have been undervalued, Fonte argued, and if women received the same education as men, their innate moral superiority would clearly emerge. Her fellow Venetian Lucrezia Marinella agreed, penning in the same year *The Nobility and Excellence of Women and the Defects and Vices of Men.*

Some authors, such as Baldassare Castiglione in *The Courtier*, included both sides of the argument in their writings, so that it is difficult to gauge their true opinions. Acidalius himself was a member of a humanist group that included females, although his most intense friendships and connections were with other highly educated men. Some of these men may have contributed various theses to the *Disputatio*, using this as a way to show off their rhetorical skills and classical or biblical knowledge.

Was the disputation proving that women are not human simply a joke, then? A literary game among intellectuals that tedious theologians such as Geddicus took too seriously? From Acidalius' perspective, perhaps, but the pamphlet's long publication history suggests otherwise. The arguments that it made were not new, but they never seemed to become old. The arguments that it raised about women's humanity, and related arguments about their vices and virtues, continued on and on, in popular songs, jokes, jests, and stories as well as learned works. Prints that hung in taverns or people's homes, as well as pictures on plates and drinking cups, juxtaposed female virtues and vices. Artists frequently portrayed misogynist stories involving classical figures, such as Socrates' wife Xanthippe nagging him or Aristotle being so seduced by the beauty of the younger Phyllis that he allowed her to ride him around a garden, so that these became part of popular culture as well as that of Europe's learned elite.

Whether in words or images, attacks on women appeared more often than defenses. In part this is because satire and insults are always more fun than praise, but they also represented deep-seated feelings. One of the most elaborate comparisons of women with animals in the sixteenth century was Hans Sachs' poem, *The Nine Skins of a Bad Wife*, which retold a popular story and was itself read and recited widely. In the poem, the wife has nine layers of skin, eight of which have the properties of certain animals, such as a bear, cat, fish, pig, and dog. These must be beaten off before her human skin can be reached, which her husband does with various implements. The animal skins of the Gonzales sisters could not be beaten off, of course, but those who saw them may well have been reminded of the story that Sachs told, for it was a familiar tale in Italy as well as Germany.

Die Neunerley heudt
einer bösen Frawen / sambt
jren Neun Eygenschafften.

Mehr das Bitter Süeß Ehlich
Leben.

Hans Sachs.

35. Title page of Hans Sachs' satirical poem, *The Nine Skins of a Bad Wife*, 1554. The woodcut shows a furious husband beating his wife with a chair, trying to remove the nine animal skins that cover her human skin, while two other men stand calmly to one side. The German playwright and poet often wrote literary works based on popular stories and moral tales, which were performed and sold widely.

The learned scholars and more ordinary folk at the Italian courts where the Gonzales sisters lived knew the debate about women well. Before he published the work that made him infamous, Acidalius earned his medical degree at Padua and Bologna, arriving in Italy around 1590, about the same time that the Gonzales family did. Like many scholars, he lived at the villas of wealthy benefactors, where humanist discussion circles applied their learning and wit to the contemplation of topics such as whether women were human. Those circles may have included Ulisse Aldrovandi, who was teaching philosophy and science at the University of Bologna when Acidalius was a student there. Acidalius had returned to Germany by the time Aldrovandi saw Antonietta Gonzales at the home of yet another nobleman with scholarly interests, but their circles of friendship—a topic that Acidalius often considered in his poetry—overlapped. Those circles included others who were educated as physicians, or in the newer fields of natural history and natural philosophy, as well as men learned in theology and literature. Such men of the new sciences examined the Gonzales sisters with eyes that were somewhat different from those of artists such as Hoefnagel, but no less interested in the variety of God's creation.

Puella pilofa annorum octo alterius foror.

36. Woodcut of one of the Gonzales sisters from Ulisse Aldrovandi's *Monstrorum historia*, page 18. The caption reads "a hairy eight year old girl, the other sister." This may have been Antonietta, as she looks much like the girl in Lavinia Fontana's oil portrait.

6

Medical Marvels and Cabinets of Curiosities

THE WORLD OF SCIENTISTS AND COLLECTORS

After the birth of several children, the growing Gonzales family left France and wended its way southward. En route to Italy, Catherine and at least two children stopped in Basel in Switzerland. Basel was an important center of printing, where the "Periplus of Hanno" saw its first modern publication. It was also a university town, with a medical school renowned in much of Europe. Here Felix Platter was the city physician, and a professor at the university medical school. Among the many medical examinations contained in *Observations*, his three-volume book of cases, was the following:

Some hairy and exceedingly hirsute men

It is commonly believed that there are men among the savages with hairy skin on their whole body surface, except for the tip of the nose, the front part of the knees, buttocks, palms, and soles of the feet, as they are usually described. But we can understand that this is false, based on the following. Cosmographers, who described the whole world, never mention these men, although they never forget the fiercest of peoples, like Amazons, Cannibals, Americans, and others, who walk naked yet are not hairy and shave their naturally growing hair. This, instead, is true: There are humans of both sexes, especially males, whose legs, arms, chest and face are shaggy, with long hair, and I know and have seen several of those individuals.

In Paris there was one of those men, exceptionally hairy in his whole body, very dear to King Henry II and attending his court, with his whole body covered in long hair, and his face all covered as well, except for a small part under the eyes, with eyebrows and hair on the forehead so long that he had to pull it up to be able to see.

After marrying a hairless woman, similar to other women, he had by her some children, hairy as well, who were sent to the Duke of Parma in Flanders. I saw them, with their mother, a nine-year-old boy and a seven-year-old girl, in Basel in 1583, while they were in the process of being sent to Italy, and I made sure to have them portrayed. They were hairy in the face, especially the boy, a little less the girl, whose dorsal region along the vertebra of her spine was exceedingly hairy.

After all, since we have hair in each pore of the body, as we explained in the *Anatomy*, it's no wonder that in some people, as in many animals, their hair is longer and continuously grows, like fingernails. It is strange, instead, that in some parts where it grows, it maintains the same length, like in the eyebrows, while in other parts it is so much shorter that it is barely visible. In fact, though, not even the palms [of these people] are hairless, as can be seen in the youth; instead, because the hair is short and continuously shaved, the hand just appears balder.[1]

Platter is the first medical doctor to examine members of the Gonzales family, or at least the first whose report was published and became widely known. He was a careful observer, of his medical cases and of the world around him. His *Observations* includes thousands of cases of all types of medical problem and abnormality, some that Platter had only heard or read about, but many that he had himself seen and attended. His study of the Gonzales children is one of these, but the date he attaches to it, 1583, creates some problems. In 1583, Maddalena Gonzales would have been about seven, just the age Platter notes, and the age at which she is shown in all the paintings made in Germany and Austria. But who was this older boy? The paintings all show a much younger boy, who was certainly Enrico, and Platter was not the sort of observer who would mistake a two-year-old for a nine-year-old, particularly a child that he had studied closely enough to know that his palms were hairy. Was this boy an older Gonzales son, who had died by the time the family got to Italy? Perhaps, but another possible explanation is that Platter got the date wrong. This report was published in 1612, long after he examined the children, and based on notes taken down much earlier. So perhaps Platter actually saw the children when they were on their way to Italy in the early 1590s. At that point Enrico would have been about nine, so fitting the age that Platter notes for the boy. Maddalena would have been much older than seven, but the second Gonzales daughter, Francesca, would have been about the right age, so perhaps this was whom Platter examined. We cannot know exactly, but we do know from his report that she was at least partially undressed as he studied her, for he comments that her back was very hairy all along her spine.

Like all records of the Gonzales family, Platter's examination of the Gonzales children is frustratingly brief, and it leaves open many of the questions we have about them: What were they like as children—quiet and obedient, troublesome and mischievous? Did they speak only French, or had their father also taught them the Spanish of his childhood or perhaps a little Latin? What were their relations with their mother, and with each other? Platter notes that he had them portrayed, which meant he hired an artist, but the illustration has not survived. Platter's case history actually reveals more about Platter than it does about the children. His report, like the writings of his more famous contemporary Ambroise Paré, reveals the ways that physicians and natural scientists understood abnormalities in the natural world.

Several years after Platter looked at the children, the Bolognese scientist Ulisse Aldrovandi also examined some members of the family. His report was not published during his lifetime, but was included in the *Monstrorum historia*, the huge book of human and animal abnormalities published later under his name by one of his

followers. There the verbal descriptions of the family are accompanied by woodcut illustrations, showing, according to the captions,
"an eight-year-old hairy girl, the daughter of a fifty-year old wild
man . . . [his] twelve-year-old daughter and twenty-year old son."[2]
Although Aldrovandi nowhere gives their names, the ages more or
less match those of Petrus, Enrico, Francesca, and Antonietta in the
mid-1590s. These are their portraits, or at least what the artist hired
by Aldrovandi imagined they looked like. Aldrovandi does include
the name of the woman who possessed Antonietta, and where he
had seen the little girl: "this wild kind of person was first seen
at Bologna when the most illustrious Marchesa of Soragna was
received by the most illustrious man Mario Casali, for she brought
with her an eight-year-old hairy girl." Aldrovandi's description of
Antonietta follows, and then the text and illustrations turn to hairy
people found in newly discovered parts of the world.

Platter and Aldrovandi were physicians and scientists, and they
were also collectors. Platter primarily collected natural objects and
plants. He had a garden full of exotic species, including Switzerland's
first silkworms and its first canaries. Whether he knew that the
hairy father of the children he examined came from the same island
as his birds is not clear from his report, but he probably did. This
was such a well-known part of the Gonzales story, and he could
have heard it directly from Catherine Gonzales as well, conversing
in the French he learned on the streets of Montpellier. Aldrovandi
collected everything. His collection eventually came to include
more than 18,000 items, and later formed the basis of the natural
history museum in Bologna.

These two men were not alone in their pursuits, for in the decades
around 1600 collecting became a mania. Princely collectors gathered
gems, coral, ivory carvings, shells, paintings, scientific and musical
instruments, antique coins, and countless other expensive and exotic
objects in what were termed "chambers of art and wonders."
Physicians, apothecaries, and scholars put together herbariums of dried
plants, and collections of plants, crystals, and minerals useful as medicine. Merchants collected luxury items from China, weapons from
the Americas, animal skins from all over, and anything else strange or

interesting that they could afford. By the early seventeenth century there were hundreds of encyclopedic collections in palaces and city houses around Europe, and their owners traded objects regularly. These "cabinets of curiosities," as they are usually known, ranged in size from an actual cabinet to many rooms. The cabinet itself was often something to be marveled at—made of tropical woods, inlaid with ivory, ebony, and amber, with doors and drawers everywhere, all offering the possibility of something astounding within. The profusion of stuff crammed in or bursting out was part of the show. Visitors discussed what they had seen or wrote about it in letters and essays. Some collections issued printed catalogs, so that even those who could not afford to visit could know the wonders they contained.

Among the most important princely collectors were the Wittelsbach rulers of Bavaria, the Farnese dukes and cardinals, and many of the Habsburgs. And among the curiosities in their collections, as we have seen, were portraits of the Gonzales family, placed among stuffed crocodiles, suits of armor, paintings of gods and kings, ivory inkwells, and skeletons of humans and animals. The largest portraits, those in Ambras castle, were given as gifts from one collector—William V of Bavaria—to another—Archduke Ferdinand of Tyrol. The Gonzaleses themselves were also presented as gifts for collections. Enrico went to Cardinal Odoardo Farnese as a gift from his brother, a living specimen of a Herculean wild man to complement the cardinal's collection of classical sculpture and exotic species. Antonietta went to the marchesa of Soragna, known for her patronage of writers and artists. They were not the only living people in such collections. William V's sister apparently possessed a young bearded woman, and the Italian nobleman Ferdinando Cospi was said to have a dwarf who acted as a guide to his collection for visitors.

The scientists and collectors who studied and marveled at the Gonzales family or their pictures were all educated, many of them extremely well, and were almost all men. They all wrote, some of them in quantities that nearly matched the size of their collections. Through their words and their collections, we can trace the ways in which learned men sought to create systems of meaning in which everything had a place, what they termed natural philosophy and

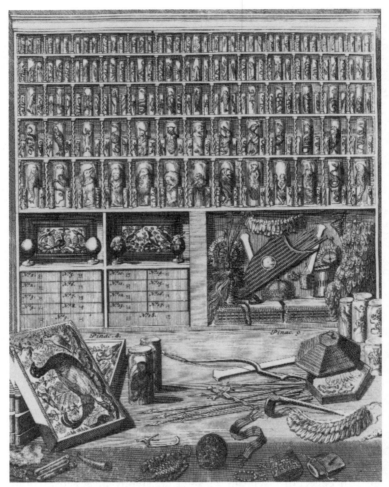

37. Cabinet of curiosities, from a series of illustrations of a Dutch collection of the "marvels of nature," 1719. Here there are animal specimens in jars, with exotic objects and paintings of nature below. Collectors arranged their holdings in various ways, sometimes based on colors, or on theories of the correspondence between macrocosm and microcosm, or on ideas about other affinities between objects in form or function.

we term science. Those systems were challenged by objects that seemed to stand on the border between one category and another, or mixed categories, such as coral that appeared to be animal, vegetable, and mineral all at once, or patterns in rock that looked as if an artist had made them but were actually the result of natural processes. The Gonzales family—animal and human, courtier and monster, wild folk and Christian—was a fascinating example of this hybridity, and so perfect subjects for scientific inquiry or princely collecting.

Tolerance and dissection: the Swiss doctor

The two men who examined the Gonzales children were alike in many ways. Both were trained as physicians and taught at universities; both had well-known collections that attracted visitors from all over Europe. Their ways of seeing the Gonzales children were similar, which is not surprising given their training. They were not exactly the same, however. Felix Platter viewed the children's condition as a medical issue, comparing them with other cases he had seen of people who had unwanted hair and suggesting remedies. Ulisse Aldrovandi set them in several different contexts, and compared them to people he had read about in the works of classical authors and recent travelers. Thus to his actual observations he added the whole intellectual history of unusual hairiness, applying and demonstrating his scholarly expertise. These two approaches—narrow and strictly empirical, broad and scholarly—were shaped by the earlier experiences of the two men.

The family backgrounds of Platter and Aldrovandi were very different. Felix Platter's father Thomas came from a very poor shepherd family in the Swiss hills. He was extremely bright, however; he taught himself Latin, Greek, and Hebrew, and eventually rose to be director of the Latin school in Basel. Thomas Platter made sure that his son had every advantage that he did not have, and sent him to the best medical school in Europe, Montpellier in southern France. Felix kept a journal during his student days in Montpellier and his first years back in Basel, where he worked as a doctor and taught medicine at the university. From his journal, we can learn much about the man Felix was becoming, as well as details of the medical training he received and life in Montpellier. Those early experiences shaped the way he later looked at the Gonzales children, providing him with examples of tolerance and intolerance toward those who were different.

Montpellier drew men from all over Europe to study medicine. Living there could be expensive, and many families arranged exchanges if they could, in which their son stayed in a household in Montpellier while someone from that household lived with them. Thomas Platter was fortunate to find such an arrangement for Felix, with an apothecary's family named "Catalan." This was not normally a family name in the sixteenth century, but a place— Catalonia, part of the kingdom of Aragon in Spain. The first member of the "Catalan" family in Montpellier had come from Catalonia early in the sixteenth century, adopting his place of origin as his name. This is one piece of evidence that the family was Jewish, for many families of Jewish ancestry adopted—or were given— place names as family names. Platter provides more evidence in his journal, discussing the religious ideas and background of his hosts quite openly, as these were writings intended for Platter's eyes alone:

> After supper, when we were warming ourselves by the hearth, Monsieur Catalan gave me an old Latin Bible, from which the New Testament was missing. I read it to him, and commented upon it. When I read the prophet Baruch, who preaches against images and idols, Catalan was delighted. He was a Maran, and loved idols no more than the Jews; but he did not dare to declare so openly. He interrupted me often with the words 'Ergo nostri sacerdotes,' that is to say, Why do our priests have them?[3]

Platter calls his host a "Maran," a slang term for Jewish convert that was regarded by many of Jewish background as insulting because it also meant "swine" or "pig." (The word came from the Jewish and Muslim prohibition against eating pork.) The term, and the Catalan family's presence in Montpellier, reflects the long history of Christian persecution of Jews in Europe. Around 1300, Jews had been expelled from England and France, and many had settled in Muslim and Christian areas of the Iberian Peninsula. Initially rulers of both faiths welcomed them, but during the late fourteenth century attacks and riots against Jewish communities in Christian areas became more common, and many Jews converted (or were forced to convert), becoming *conversos* or "New Christians." *Conversos* were often well educated, serving as lawyers and physicians, local and royal officials, and even bishops and abbots. Their success enhanced popular resentment on the part of "Old Christians," and with the accession of Isabella as queen of Castile in 1474, this sentiment gained a royal ear. Isabella was very devout, and she regarded *conversos* as a cancer within the Christian community. She and her husband Ferdinand, the ruler of Aragon, gained papal permission to establish an Inquisition to distinguish those who were hiding their "real" identity as Jews and passing as Christians.

Investigations, trials, and executions of *conversos* began immediately, with officials of the Inquisition charged to search out the least sign of an incomplete conversion, such as not eating pork, or wearing clean clothes and not cooking on Saturday (the Jewish Sabbath). Some individuals and communities engaged in more clearly Jewish practices such as circumcision and Sabbath services, and maintained a kind of dual identity, blending Jewish and Christian beliefs and practices. Evidence of these practices has led some scholars to argue that most *conversos* were "crypto-Jews," while others view them as entirely Christian until the Inquisition invented their devotion to Judaism. When brought before the Inquisition, most *conversos* argued that they were fully Christian and had been for generations, and that their food practices were simply a matter of habit, not religious rules. We have no way of knowing whether such an argument was the truth or a realistic response given the situation, which is why historians disagree. It was probably both in many cases, as conversion from one religion to another is a process, not a sudden event, but hybridity of any type was viewed as threatening.

The armies of Ferdinand and Isabella conquered Granada, the last Muslim state in the Iberian Peninsula, in 1492, and immediately the monarchs ordered all Jews to leave this area and the rest of Spain without taking any of their property with them. About 200,000 Jews and Jewish converts left, some to southern France, including the Catalan family of Montpellier. Like *conversos* in Spain, the Catalan family blended Jewish and Christian practices: they owned a Bible that contained only Jewish scriptures, and, as Platter reports, "abstain from the same foods as do the Jews," never eating pork or cooking meat in butter.[4] When "Catalan's wife was brought to bed of a child . . . she gave birth in the dining room, behind a curtain, and brought forth a son. He was called Laurent, and was secretly circumcised and baptized according to their custom."[5] They were careful to follow the dietary practices of the Christian community around them, however. Platter notes that during Lent in Montpellier "meat and eggs are forbidden under pain of death," so that Madame Catalan became "very annoyed" with him when eggshells were discovered in his room during this period of fasting.

Why did Platter have eggshells in his room? Because he was a Protestant, not a Catholic, and no longer followed Catholic practices of fasting during Lent. He could not be too open about his religion, however, writing that "I learned how to cook eggs in butter on a piece of paper held over live charcoal. I did not dare to use any utensil for this purpose." His caution was wise, for only several months later "five [Protestant] martyrs were burned, who had studied at Lausanne, and who on their return had been arrested, thrown into prison, and condemned to the fire."[6] This was 1553, just a few years after Petrus Gonzales was brought to Paris, and a time when Henry II was ordering death to those who attended Protestant services. Platter himself saw several executions of Protestants, and describes them in detail. On the face of one accused man "the sweat stood out in great drops, as big as peas," while another "sat down on a log at the pyre and himself took off his clothes as far as his shirt, and arranged them beside him tidily, as though he would be putting them on again."[7]

Platter felt more open discussing religion with his host than he would have had he been boarding with a good Catholic family. To Monsieur Catalan's criticism of religious images, Platter notes, "I replied that the priests were wrong, and that our religion rejected such images and idols, and I cited a host of passages in which God had forbidden them."[8] On the street both Platter and Catalan kept their religious ideas to themselves. *Conversos* who were "really" Jewish were a primary target of the Inquisition in Spain, but for the teenaged Platter they were a welcoming community, and models in other realms as well as medicine. His tolerance for differences among people appears to have been strengthened by his stay in Montpellier, and he never lost it. In the hundreds of cases of medical problems and abnormalities Platter describes in his *Observations*, he comments often about possible causes, but rarely lays blame.

Platter did not let his religious allegiance get in the way of his medical studies, but sometimes those studies themselves put him in danger, or so he tells us. "My principal study was anatomy," he writes, and he watched every dissection he could. "At another session the subject was a handsome courtesan who had died in childbirth. Her womb was still swollen, since the delivery had only recently occurred."[9] Montpellier was not that large a city, and Platter sometimes knew the individual:

> Beatrice, Catalan's former servant girl, who had drawn off my boots when I first arrived in Montpellier, was executed on the 3rd of December. She was hanged in the square, on a little gibbet that had only one arm. She had left us a year before to go into service in the house of a priest. She became pregnant, and when her child was born, she threw it into the latrine, where it was found dead. Beatrice's body was taken to the anatomy theatre, and it remained several days in the College [for a dissection]. The womb was still swollen, for the birth of the child had occurred no more than eight days before. Afterwards the hangman came to collect the pieces, wrapped them in a sheet, and hung them on a gibbet outside of town.[10]

Bodies available for dissection were those of people judged dishonorable, as were these women, but there were never enough for the medical students. They resorted to stealing corpses.

> A bachelor of medicine named Gallotus, who had married a woman from Montpellier and was passing rich, would lend us his house. He invited me, with some others, to join him in nocturnal expeditions outside the town, to dig up bodies freshly buried in the cloister cemetery, and we carried them to his

house for dissection. We had spies to tell us of the burial and to lead us by night to the graves.

Our first excursion of this kind took place on the 11th of November 1554 . . . . When we came to the monastery, we stayed to drink, quietly, until midnight. Then, in complete silence, with swords in hand, we made our way to the cemetery of the monastery of Saint-Denis. There we dug up a corpse with our hands, the earth being still loose, because the burial had taken place only that day. As soon as we had uncovered it we pulled it out with ropes, wrapped it in a cloth, and carried it on two poles as far as the gates of the town. It must then have been about three o'clock in the morning . . . . On opening the winding sheet in which the body was sewn, we found a woman with a congenital deformity of the legs, the two feet turned inwards. We did an autopsy. . . .

Encouraged by the success of this expedition, we tried again five days later. We had been informed that a student and child had been buried in the same cemetery of Saint-Denis. When night came we left the town to go to the monastery of the Augustins. In Brother Bernhard's cell we ate a chicken cooked with cabbage. We got the cabbage ourselves, from the garden and seasoned it with wine supplied by the monk. Leaving the table, we went out with our weapons drawn, for the monks of Saint-Denis had discovered that we had exhumed the woman, and they threatened us directly should we return. Myconius carried his naked sword, and the Frenchmen their rapiers. The two corpses were disinterred, wrapped in our cloaks, and carried on poles. One of us crawled inside through a hole that we discovered under the gate—for they were very negligently maintained. We passed the cadavers through the same opening, and they were pulled through from the inside. We followed in turn, pulling ourselves through on our backs; I remember that I scratched my nose as I went through.

The two subjects were carried to Gallotus's house and their coverings were removed. One was a student whom we had known. The autopsy revealed serious lesions. The lungs were decomposed and stank horribly, despite the vinegar that we sprinkled on them; we found some small stones in them. The child was a little boy, and we made a skeleton of him.[11]

Platter tries to adopt an unemotional and straightforward tone for everything he describes, whether it is how they cooked the chicken or what they found in the lungs of their student friend. Yet the drama of the scene comes through, for Platter was only eighteen at the time, and these excursions were unbelievably exciting: darkness, drawn swords, bodies wrapped in cloths, dissections by torchlight. Some details are too gruesome even for him, however. He doesn't tell us how they made the little boy into a skeleton—chemicals? boiling?—nor does he note later if this skeleton is among the various skeletons he shipped back to Basel when his studies in Montpellier were over.

Platter's medical training was rigorous, but left him time for dances, playing the lute, drinking, and an occasional trip around the area, where he began collecting plants. On one of these trips, he and his friends went to Marseilles, where they bought coral, and saw ostriches and "rams with huge curving horns." They also saw exotic humans: Turks, "galley slaves chained to their oars," and "a negro who lifted ponderous blocks of stone and let them fall on his head and his shoulders." On the way home, they stopped to visit Nostradamus, who had earlier studied medicine in Montpellier and had just published his first book of prophecies. "Several of us consulted him," Platter reports, but doesn't mention what they discovered.[12]

Platter's professional medical writings are not as lively as his journal. They were written in Latin for learned men like himself, rather than in German dialect. They have the same matter-of-fact tone, however, even when their subjects are grim or scandalous. A young woman's "husband treated her so badly," he reports, that "she often thought about killing herself. Finally she was driven to insanity and ripped her clothing off. Naked, she ripped the straw on which she was lying into tiny pieces with her fingernails." She was healed when she was bled "seven times in one week from veins in different places so that almost all of her blood was taken out," though, not surprisingly, this also made her "weak and pale." Platter not only describes her medical treatment, but adds details about her life that were also important in her cure. "Her husband died," he writes, and "she married another, with whom she lived almost forty years, healthy, though unable to bear children and with poor color."[13]

Platter views the Gonzales children through the same calm and dispassionate eyes, and with an interest in human diversity forged in the Catalan household in Montpellier. People are wrong, he says, when they think that hairy people only exist among the savages. Instead excess hairiness was possible anywhere, for "we have hair in every pore of our body." *We* have hair, he says, not *they* have hair. The Gonzales children are part of the human family, and what is interesting to Platter is why hair grows differently in various parts of the body on any human, not just them. Among non-hairy humans hair grows longer in the eyebrows than in the rest of the face, while in the Gonzales children it was the reverse, he observes.

In his medical observations, Platter does not put the Gonzales children among monsters or wonders, but among people who have unwanted hair. Their hairiness was a cosmetic, and not moral or philosophical matter. In the very next entry in *Observations*, he discusses "appearance of hairs on the forehead":

> Polonus, a certain noble soldier, in the year 1599 wished that some kind of depilatory ointment would be given to him, so that the forehead of a certain rich and snub-nosed young lady whom he had been visiting, which was covered with hair, could be freed of hair and treated so that the hair would not return. Therefore, since he wanted its effectiveness to be tested on himself first, I gave him the two following depilatories, of which one was pitch, which actually plucked out the hairs, and the other an ointment, which was able to make the hair come out on its own.
>
> To make the pitch: take the resin of the common larch tree, around four spoonfuls, and carefully add well-trodden gum from the mastic-tree.[14]

Gummy substances with which to yank out unwanted hair are still with us, and Platter's dispassionate comments on the Gonzales children reflect the calm tone that is viewed as ideal in contemporary medical diagnosis. Platter does not propose a diagnosis here, however, although he does in many of the cases recorded in his *Observations*. He makes no attempt to explain why the children are the way they are, and the only reason he brings up earlier reports of hairy wild people from around the world is to dismiss them. Aldrovandi's discussion of the family would be very different.

Cataloging and speculating: the Italian scientist

While Platter was studying medicine and collecting plants at the University of Montpellier, Ulisse Aldrovandi was doing the same at the University of Bologna in northern Italy. He did not have to arrange a place to live through the kindness of strangers, however. Aldrovandi's father was not a self-made man, but a nobleman and prosperous member of the Bologna city council. His mother was a cousin to the man who later became Pope Gregory XIII. Aldrovandi was apparently a difficult child, but one whose broad interests showed up early. As he later told the story, when he was twelve he traveled to Rome from Bologna without telling his parents "with no money, but with a daring mind." At seventeen, he went on a pilgrimage to Santiago de Compostela in the northwest corner of Spain, the furthest west one can get on the continent of Europe. Aldrovandi would never again get so far away from Bologna, but travel to find new things remained a key part of his life.

Aldrovandi's "daring mind" led him to study everything, not just medicine: philosophy, logic, mathematics, law, botany, and natural history. It also got him in trouble with the Catholic Church. At about the same time as Platter was watching French Protestants burn in Montpellier, Aldrovandi was arrested for heresy in Bologna. His crime was questioning the existence of the Trinity, the Christian doctrine that God has three parts, the Father, Son, and Holy Spirit. He quickly published a formal renunciation of his beliefs, but not quickly enough to escape several months of house arrest in Rome. Aldrovandi used the time to edit a book on ancient Roman statues, and to develop a network of friends and associates among Romans interested in botany, zoology, and geology.

The charges of heresy had little impact on Aldrovandi's scholarly career. When he returned to Bologna, he taught logic and philosophy at the university, and in 1561 became the first professor at Bologna to hold a position specifically in science, lecturing in the "natural philosophy of fossils, plants, and animals." His passion for collecting continued, and he led expeditions up into the mountains and along the coasts to find new plants, taking artists along with him to sketch them where they were growing. He eventually assembled nearly 7,000 dried plant specimens in a herbarium, each laid out neatly on a page, sometimes with an accompanying drawing.[15] Live plants were even more interesting than dead ones, and he directed the opening of a public botanical garden in Bologna, one of the first in Europe.[16] His collection included far more than plants, growing to hold 18,000 items arranged in huge display cabinets with no fewer than 4,554 drawers, as Aldrovandi reports in his 1595 description. Visitors—and there were thousands—were "stupefied . . . by so many great and wondrous things." Ever the collector, Aldrovandi kept a record of everyone who visited, organizing them into a catalog according to their social standing and geographic origins.

Among the 18,000 objects in Aldrovandi's collection were 8,000 paintings done in watercolor and tempera, a kind of paint made with egg yolk, produced by a group of artists commissioned by Aldrovandi and working under his direction. Lavinia Fontana was probably one of these, although the paintings were not signed and it is difficult to determine which of the many artists did what. Subjects of the paintings included plants, animals, rocks, and objects, often made by the artist looking at the actual thing. The collection also included many, many paintings of wondrous, weird, and exotic people and creatures, made by copying broadsheets or from reading verbal descriptions. Luther's "monk-calf" is here, painted on the same page as a pig with a man's head and a boy with disjointed hands and feet. So is a "queen from the islands of Florida," dressed in skins and with long curly hair. There are dwarves in ruffs and a bearded lady in a lace collar and satin dress. And there is a young woman with flowers in her hair, wearing a pink brocade dress and holding a piece of folded paper.

38. Tempera painting in Aldrovandi's collection by an unknown artist. The caption reads: "A hairy woman of twenty years whose head resembles a monkey, but who is not hairy on the rest of her body."

Who is this young woman? Maddalena Gonzales, the oldest Gonzales sister, would have been about twenty in the mid-1590s, and it is tempting to see this as her portrait, done from life by one of Aldrovandi's artists, just as were their paintings of plants and animals. But Maddalena had been given a house in Parma by the reigning duke in 1593, presumably on the occasion of her marriage, which makes it unlikely that she would have been in Aldrovandi's workshop in Bologna. Perhaps this simply came from the imagination of one of the artists? He or she heard Aldrovandi tell of examining a hairy girl at Mario Casali's home, and painted her from that, in the same way that an artist painted the "queen of Florida" from a traveler's story. The girl Aldrovandi examined was younger than twenty, and *did* have hair all over her body, not simply on her face, but stories often become garbled in transmission.

There may be yet another explanation. Shortly after Aldrovandi's examination of Antonietta, he received a letter from an acquaintance named Brummano:

> I know that you, Milord, may have thought that I forgot the promise I made you to send the portrait of that wild female who his Highness the Duke of Parma gave to the marchesa of Soragna and whose father, mother, and siblings are now kept, to the best of my knowledge, in the castle of Parma. My intention was to get the painting copied here in Milan by that very talented young woman, but when I arrived it had already been sent elsewhere. By investigation, I found another one in Parma, where I live, although I currently am in Milan, and this is the reason of my delay in sending it to you . . . but you will shortly enjoy the portrait of the hairy girl, which I send included here.[17]

The painting in Aldrovandi's collection might therefore be *this* painting, or a copy of it, and this painting might itself be a copy of the Lavinia Fontana painting that is on this book's cover. From his letter, Brummano originally intended to have a copy made of some painting that already existed, which suggests the original was too costly to buy or impossible to obtain. Lavinia Fontana painted Antonietta's portrait in oil paint, not tempera or watercolor, which made it expensive. But arranging for a copy of an oil painting would have been more within Brummano's price range, and he seems to have found an artist to do this, whom he describes as a "talented young woman" working in Milan. Fontana herself was certainly a talented young woman, but she was then in Bologna, not Milan. Another talented young female artist *was* in Milan at this point— Fede Galizia, the teenaged daughter of a painter already making her name doing portraits—and this may be whom the letter is referring to. By the time Brumanno had arranged for the copy, however, the oil painting had been sent somewhere else. Meanwhile, he had found yet another painting of a hairy girl, and, according to the letter, sent it to Aldrovandi. This letter and the painting itself were kept in very different parts of Aldrovandi's vast collection of stuff and documents, so we will never know for sure if these are the same.

One thing we *can* know for sure is that the oil painting by Fontana and the tempera painting in Aldrovandi's collection are related. In both, the little girl is wearing a pink brocade dress and holding a piece of paper; in both, she has flowers wound into her hair and is looking directly out at the viewer. Both of them may be products of the artist's imagination—there is no absolute proof that Lavinia Fontana painted Antonietta's portrait from life—but two artists could not have imagined the little hairy girl so similarly. The painting in Aldrovandi's collection is clearly a copy of something, and the most likely candidate is Fontana's painting.

Copying did not stop there. Also in the 1590s, the Venetian printer Giacomo Franco published in a collection of portraits an engraving of a little hairy girl, holding a carnation rather than a piece of paper, but still in the same style of dress as in the Fontana painting. The Roman printer Giovanni Orlandi lifted this for his own collection of portraits. These carried an inscription in Italian: "This is Tognina, whom you see here. She was, as a daughter of a hairy father from the Canary Islands, born completely hairy, and has a brother who is just as hairy as she is and was given to the Farnese brothers. The above Tognina lives in Parma." Antonietta has become

Tognina in this inscription, which may have been a nickname, or Franco may have simply heard the story wrong.

More important than these copies in printed portrait collections were ones ordered by Aldrovandi himself. Along with artists who used a brush, he hired engravers and woodcutters to make illustrations for what he hoped would be an encyclopedia of all of natural history. Only three volumes were published during his lifetime, but he left another eighty-five in manuscript, with so many woodcuts they filled drawer after drawer. Among them was yet another version of the girl in the brocade dress with the flowers in her hair, now holding what looks like a fly-swatter or a fan instead of a paper. Like most of Aldrovandi's woodcuts, this was never published in his lifetime, but it was decades after he died, when his successor to the chair of natural history in Bologna gathered it together with hundreds of other woodcuts of human and animal anomalies from the drawers and cabinets, along with Aldrovandi's notes on them, and published these in 1642 as *Monstrorum historia*. In contrast to the girl in the tempera painting, however, this girl is described as eight years old, so that in her age she fits with the description of Antonietta Gonzales that appears on the same page. Aldrovandi had actually examined Antonietta, and knew that she was hairy all over, so the note from the tempera painting that the girl in the brocade dress "is not hairy on the rest of her body" has also disappeared.

As the portrait was copied and recopied, and details about her body and life were changed, the images became less those of a real little girl and more those of a certain type of person—"the hairy girl." They became generic.

Several other paintings reinforce this conclusion. One is another tempera painting in Aldrovandi's collection that showed the girl in the brocade dress "whose head resembles a monkey," but in this one she is nude. Her body is hairless and her face is hairy so that she matches the description of the girl, but in her face and posture she looks nothing like her. She is even more clearly something from the artist's—or Aldrovandi's—imagination, a speculation about what the girl in the brocade dress would look like naked. A copy of this painting also appeared in the *Monstrorum historia*, but the editor

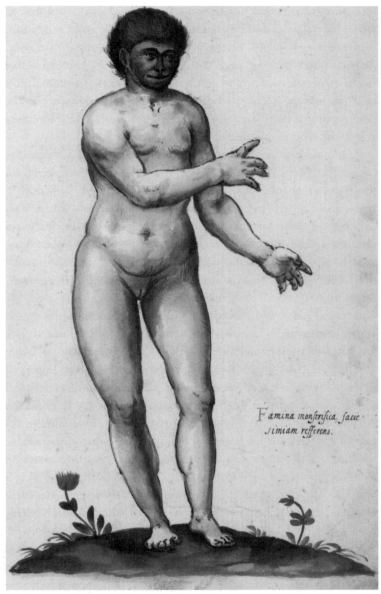

Fœmina monstrifica, facie simiam refferens.

39. Tempera painting of a girl from Aldrovandi's collection. The caption reads: "Monstrous female, whose face recalls that of a monkey." The caption includes misspelled words, suggesting that the artist who painted this was not a skilled Latinist.

recognized that it did not fit with the descriptions of Antonietta Gonzales. So instead of putting it near the woodcuts of the family, in the opening section of the book that focuses on hairy people, he put it hundreds of pages later, in a section of the book that discusses people with weird heads. Here it is stuck in with almost no commentary, and with nothing linking it to the pictures or the descriptions of the Gonzaleses. There is just a note that the picture was found in the museum, so it had to be included.

Paintings that once hung on the walls of Aldrovandi's villa also suggest that the idea of the hairy girl and her family mattered far more to him than their reality. Aldrovandi decorated his villa with emblems of objects from his natural history collection, that is, with paintings of these objects and accompanying texts. His villa was a sort of emblem book writ large, similar to Joris Hoefnagel's book and to the many emblem books that were being published at the time. The villa and all its paintings no longer exist, but the inscriptions have survived. Among the paintings of objects were six portraits: of Aldrovandi and his wife, of two Medici dukes, Francesco I and Ferdinando I, and of two hairy people, a man and a girl. Underneath the portrait of the girl was the inscription, in Latin, "Picture of hairy girl, daughter of a wild man and a European woman," with the note "A somewhat stupid peasant, on seeing a similar picture one day, said: 'I greet you, oh ape.' " Underneath the portrait of the man was the inscription "The wild man, father of the hairy girl, hairy on his whole body," with the note "The portrait shows me with a hairy face and hands, but underneath my clothing all of my bodily parts are stiff with hair." These are, of course, Petrus Gonzales and one of his daughters, although they are not identified by name. We do not know exactly when the paintings and inscriptions were made, or which Gonzales sister the painting showed. Was this Antonietta, whom Aldrovandi had examined (or would examine) in Bologna in 1594? Was it Francesca, and was perhaps this now vanished painting the model for the pencil sketch that Lavinia Fontana made? Was it Maddalena, and was this painting made before she married, when she might have been out in public more?

We cannot know for sure, but what mattered to Aldrovandi was not the identity of the girl in the painting, but her meaning. On one side of the portraits of Aldrovandi and his wife were portraits of wealthy and powerful nobles, patrons of the arts and sciences. On the other side were two hairy people, so unusual in appearance that people wondered whether they were human at all. Aldrovandi's inscription allows him both to bring up the girl's resemblance to an exotic ape, and to distance himself from this notion—yes, people think this, but only stupid peasants. Aldrovandi and his wife stand between these two ends of the human spectrum, not as elevated as dignified European nobles, but far above those connected with peasants, animals, and other exotic "wild" peoples. For the privileged visitors to his villa, the portraits did what the *Monstrorum historia* did for a wider—though still privileged, Latin-reading—group: set the Gonzales family within a framework of both hierarchy and diversity.

The Gonzales family in the *Monstrorum historia*

The *Monstrorum historia* presents the fullest discussion of the Gonzales family that exists, and they actually show up three times in the very long book. The woodcuts of the family are the first illustrations in the book, in an opening section about differences among humans around the world. The whole section reads:

> Finally hair and pelts offer us a difference; for John Mandeville describes a certain island whose inhabitants grow thick hair on their hands and face, and Pigafetta describes the men of the island Buthuan as hairy, fierce, and man-eating. Next, since we can at present disregard the wild men recounted by Pliny and in Solinus, we will consider those whom Peter Martyr discusses. He left to posterity an account that wild men are found in the province of Guacaiarina, who inhabit rough and humble caves, live on forest fruits, and never have any contact with the other inhabitants of the island; in fact, even when they are captured and treated well they are never able to become tame, since they are believed to know neither government nor laws. Likewise, on a

Spanish island subject to the British king there is an almost boundless number of wild men, who wish to enter into no kind of contact with those who live beside the sea. A certain man brought part of a wild man's pelt to the most excellent Ulisse Aldrovandi (which is still kept in the museum of the most illustrious Bolognese Senate), and brought it back to be worn as a ring for patients suffering convulsions, to their great advantage.

This wild kind of man was first seen at Bologna when the most illustrious marchesa of Soragna was received by the most illustrious man Mario Casali, for she brought with her an eight-year-old hairy girl, the daughter of a fifty-year-old wild man, born in the Canary Islands, who had not only this daughter, but had sired an older twelve-year-old girl and a twenty-year-old son; likenesses of all of these are shown here.

The girl's face was entirely hairy on the front, except for the nostrils and her lips around the mouth. The hairs on her forehead were longer and rougher in comparison with those which covered her cheeks, although these are softer to touch than the rest of her body, and she was hairy on the foremost part of her back, and bristling with yellow hair up to the beginning of her loins. The throat, chest, hands, and arms were stripped of hair. The other parts of her body were rough, and similar to the skin of an unfledged bird. No one should persuade himself that it is necessary for the whole body of the race of wild men to be covered with hair; since (as Eusebius the Jesuit has said) wild men have been seen as much in the region of the East as in the West. In the American region, they come out from their mother's womb white, fair-skinned, and light just as our infants do. If, in the course of time, hair grows out very much on some part of the body, nevertheless it must not be said that they ought to be entirely hairy.[18]

After this section, Aldrovandi continues with other hairy folk, including the wild "Cinnaminian people" who "have both a long beard and hair on their whole body" and raise dogs to guard them from "great numbers of cattle that constantly enter their

Pater annorum quadraginta, & filius annorum viginti toto corpore pilofi。

40. Woodcut of Petrus and Enrico Gonzales, from Ulisse Aldrovandi's *Monstrorum historia*, page 16. The caption reads: "The father of fifty years and the son of twenty years whose whole bodies were covered with hair." These ages matched those in Aldrovandi's text, but were not exactly right; the illustration itself as well as the caption is based on stories about the family and perhaps other paintings, not drawn from life.

homeland." Like the Gonzales family, the Cinnaminians are shown in woodcuts, although Aldrovandi provides no clue to where they and their invading cattle are to be found. Also like the Gonzales family, the appearance of the Cinnaminians is a matter of conjecture and imagination on the part of the artist.

Aldrovandi's opening discussion of the Gonzales family combines his own detailed observations of Antonietta (whom he has clearly examined without her clothes on) with descriptions of wild people from travelers' reports, including those of Sir John Mandeville (now known to be mythical) and Antonio Pigafetta, who went with Magellan. Peter Martyr in this section is Peter Martyr d'Anghiera, an Italian scholar and diplomat hired by the Spanish monarchy in the early sixteenth century to serve as a historian of the Spanish

Puella pilofa annorum duodecim .

41. Woodcut of a Gonzales sister from Ulisse Aldrovandi's *Monstrorum historia*, page 17. The caption reads: "A hairy girl of twelve years old." Aldrovandi had no doubt heard that there was another sister as well as the girl he saw, which would make this a (make-believe) portrait of Francesca.

Fœmina Cinnaminiæ gentis.

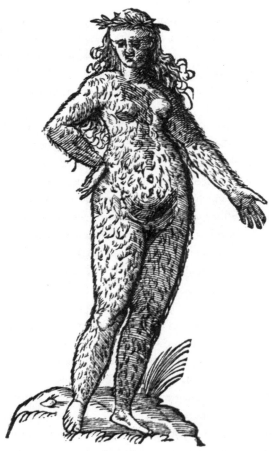

42. Woman of the Cinnaminian race, from Ulisse Aldrovandi, *Monstrorum historia*, page 20. The rock on which she stands and the crown of leaves link her with the wilderness, but her long flowing hair makes her look very much like the hairy Mary Magdalene. Her high forehead and sloping shoulders were elements in the Renaissance ideal of female beauty.

conquests. Martyr collected letters and reports from many explorers, and interviewed some personally, publishing a series of accounts of the discoveries and descriptions of various native peoples in the Americas. Aldrovandi uses these travelers' stories as an introduction to his actual examination of Antonietta, and the editor of the book adds a note that Aldrovandi's collection contained an actual skin (believed to cure convulsions) as well as the illustrations of the hairy family. Aldrovandi cautions that not all hairy people come from the west, a piece of information no doubt based on explorers' reports about the relative lack of hair among Native Americans when compared with Europeans. He then adds that not all wild people are hairy, although the fact that the hairy Cinnaminians are the very next topic in the book weakens this point.

The Gonzales family makes its next appearance in *Monstrorum historia* in a very different context—not as wild folk, but as an example of one of the many reasons why children might be born with a beard. Aldrovandi first comments that this might result from the strength of the father's "seed," which was especially powerful in shaping the fetus' head, whereas the mother's "seed" was stronger in shaping the lower parts. (Reproduction in this era was generally described as a mingling of seed, rather than as sperm fertilizing an egg.) A second cause might be the mother's, and actually also the father's, imagination:

> Sometimes the cause of this effect is to be found in the imagi-nation of the parents, on account of some fantastic vision of the parents leaving its impression; for their souls and their shared strength in forming the fetus easily cause a mark of this image on the impressionable fetus. Nor should this surprise us overly much, since if the imagination of the parents in human concep-tion is able to bring forth marks of crops and of beasts [a refer-ence to infants born with physical features that resembled plants or animals], although these differ from human nature most of all, it must all the more be able to create the likeness of a strange figure of the same species.

Finally, for some hairy children there was an easier explanation—a hairy parent:

> Even if only one of the parents should be filled with an unusual likeness, there is hardly a doubt that they will be able

to create an offspring similar to themselves; since Nature always puts forth every effort for each to bring forth something similar to itself. This happened recently at Parma in the most serene court of the Farneses, to that girl with a hairy face, who was married and bedded and gave birth to other children likewise hairy on their faces.[19]

Whom is Aldrovandi talking about here? Most likely Maddalena Gonzales, the only sister who married and had children. Although Aldrovandi had probably never seen her, he had heard about her.

The Gonzales family appears a third time, 500 pages after their first appearance in Aldrovandi's book, in a chapter on "strange deformations of the skin." Aldrovandi retells the stories of the black baby born to white parents and the hairy woman whose mother looked at the picture of John the Baptist, complete with the standard illustrations that showed up in so many books of monsters and guides to reproduction. This leads to other stories of hairy people, including more involving the maternal imagination that he takes from Conrad Lycosthenes' *Chronicle of Prodigies and Portents*:

> There was also the birth of a hairy child armed with claws like a bear, who, according to the author Lycosthenes, was born from a famous mother in the year 1282, when Pope Martinus IV was governing the Christian world. According to the pope's orders, all the images of bears that were depicted in the home of that matron were erased, due to the clear reasoning that it was from these images, received in her imagination, that the bear came into being. This hairy boy is shown here. Peucerus, too, according to Lycosthenes, seems to confirm this birth in another case, since he recorded that in the year 1549 he observed the birth of a boy covered with bear-like hairs . . . . And so beds covered with shaggy cloths must be avoided, at least those in which common women often sleep, since a view of thick hair is able to impose a similar form on the impressionable offspring.

This leads to still more reports of hairy people, drawn from his own experience and from reading the works of scholars like himself—the anatomist Realdo Columbo, the philosopher Julius Caesar Scaliger, and the naturalist Johann van den Bosch:

> Realdo Columbo claims that he saw a certain Spaniard who was covered with long hair on every part of his body except the hands and on the face. Julius Caesar Scaliger relates that he himself remembers a certain little Spanish boy who was covered with white hair, whom he said had either been brought from the Indies or [who had been] born in Spain from parents from the Indies. Likewise Henry the French king, according to Bosch, was taking care of a boy in Paris not less hairy than a dog, and having him instructed in the humanities. Even recently in the most serene court of Parma hairy people, whose images are collected in the first chapter of this History, had arrived from somewhere and were living there. So we are able to add hairy parents to the causes of hairy births already noted down, since Nature is always eager to bring forth effects not at all dissimilar to these causes; hence we understand that at Parma a hairy child of these hairy parents is living.[20]

It is not clear from this passage whether Aldrovandi understands that every one of these cases was a member of the Gonzales family, and that in Parma there were actually *three* generations of hairy people. Petrus Gonzales' childhood at the French court was a well-known part of the family's story, but Aldrovandi does not specifically link this to the people at Parma, neither here nor elsewhere in the *Monstrorum historia*. Platter does in his report of his examination of the children, but then Platter could speak with Catherine Gonzales about her children and their father. Aldrovandi sees only one little girl, Antonietta, recently given as a gift to the marchesa of Soragna and so separated from her family. What the little girl might have said to the famous scientist is unknown.

Experiment and speculation in the new science

In their discussions of the Gonzales family, Platter and Aldrovandi represent two approaches to the natural world that could be found among other scientists as well in the decades around 1600. One was focused and clinical, with a sort of "just the facts, ma'am" attitude. The other was expansive and speculative, with a lifetime's worth of learning in many subjects brought in whenever possible.

Both men—and hundreds of others—gathered objects, drawings, and descriptions into collections in part because they thought that only a complete inventory of the natural world would yield conclusions about rules and laws of nature that would be universally true. This included things that were ordinary, but also oddities and anomalies, whether these were deformed animals born locally or exotic creatures from beyond the seas. For these men of learning, monsters were not warnings from God, but facts, and only a science that included all facts would be truly comprehensive. The English philosopher and statesman Sir Francis Bacon put this succinctly in *The Advancement of Learning* (1605). He called for investigation and experiment in every field of knowledge, "of nature in course, of nature erring or varying, and of nature altered or wrought; that is, history of creatures, history of marvels, and history of arts."[21] Bacon thought that the study of "nature in course," that is, of ordinary things, had progressed well, but that the study of "nature erring and varying" (marvels) and of "nature altered or wrought" (the arts made by humans) was sorely lacking. "We are not to give up the investigation," he argued, "until the properties and qualities found in such things as may be taken for miracles of nature be reduced and comprehended under some Form or fixed Law . . . fundamental and universal."[22]

Bacon rejected earlier claims of knowledge as based on faulty reasoning, and called for natural philosophy based on what has since been called the "scientific method." (Because of this Bacon is often described in textbooks as the "father of the scientific method.") This began with the empirical observation of many similar phenomena. Those studying the phenomena would use their powers of reason to propose a generalized explanation or hypothesis for the phenomena, a process called induction. This generalization would then be tested with further empirical and inductive inquiry. Thus Aldrovandi, who compared the Gonzales family with similar cases and speculated about the reasons for their condition, followed Bacon's new "scientific method" more fully than did Platter.

The "fundamental and universal" principles underlying the cosmos could be sought in many places. The German astronomer Johannes Kepler saw a mystical harmony in the motion of the planets, guided by universal mathematical relationships: "Geometry, which before the origin of things was coeternal with the divine mind and is God himself . . . supplied God with patterns for the creation of the world."[23] Geometrical forms structured the macrocosm, according to Kepler, which meant that they must also structure the microcosm of human beings. Kepler hoped that discovering these patterns would explain how the heavenly bodies influenced human life, providing an empirical basis for one type of macrocosm/microcosm speculation, astrology.

Understanding the connections among objects and forces did not simply offer intellectual benefits, but the possibility of fabulous wealth as well. Among the ancient texts rediscovered in the fifteenth century was a body of writings attributed to Hermes Trismegistus, a god-like Egyptian sage thought to have lived at the time of Moses. These Hermetic writings—now known to have been written in the second and third centuries CE—were revered as ancient wisdom, and offered suggestions on how to exploit the hidden divine powers of minerals, plants, the planets, and other natural objects. Through processes of distillation, heating, and sublimation (cooking something to a gaseous state and then re-solidifying it), these hidden powers could be tapped to transform lead into gold or cure disease and prolong life, practices usually termed alchemy. Most scientists in the sixteenth and seventeenth centuries believed firmly in alchemy, astrology, and other bodies of knowledge now often judged to be fringe occult beliefs. They wrote treatises on "Natural Magic" as readily as those on what are now considered scientific subjects. For example, Isaac Newton spent decades trying to discover or manufacture a substance that would cause metals to grow or transform, and the members of the Royal Society of London searched through their collections in hopes of finding just such a substance.

The nineteenth-century historians of science who developed the idea of a "Scientific Revolution" often tried to ignore the alchemical and magical interests of the thinkers they championed, for they were embarrassed by them. Alchemists, however, were often the earliest to make extensive use of the "scientific method," in which a hypothesis is developed to explain a phenomenon, tested, the results recorded and measured, and the hypothesis confirmed, rejected, or modified. They invented equipment still used in laboratories, such as beakers and balance scales, and discovered new ways of producing chemical changes, such as the application of acids and alcohols. In calling for a "new learning" that would be based on observation and experimentation, Francis Bacon took his inspiration and procedures straight from alchemy.

Members of the new scientific societies that developed first in Italy and then elsewhere in Europe in the seventeenth century followed Bacon's advice. They collected and wrote about extraordinary phenomena and human anomalies, so that discussions of these in the seventeenth century are found more often in learned journals than in religious pamphlets or prophetic broadsides. The members of one learned society, the Academy of Linceans (that is, of the lynx), whose most famous member was the Italian scientist Galileo Galilei, decided to make a pictorial record of all of nature, traveling all over Europe to do so.

Collectors and their cabinets

In assembling their survey of nature, the Linceans made drawings from life, but a more important source was the materials in collections, both those assembled by private individuals and those made by the learned societies themselves. As Robert Hooke, the first curator of the collection of the Royal Society in London commented, viewing a collection offered visitors opportunity to "peruse, and turn over, and spell, and read the Book of Nature."

Every one of the paintings of any member of the Gonzales family spent most of its life in a collection, and many were made specifically for Europe's best-known collectors. The painting of Enrico with the animals in the Farnese palace garden was made for Cardinal Odoardo Farnese, who had the most important collection of classical statuary in Rome. Aldrovandi corresponded with Cardinal Farnese and his brother Ranuccio, and the cardinal visited Aldrovandi's collection in 1599. The huge paintings in Ambras castle were most likely made for the "wonder cabinet" of William V of Bavaria, and given by him to his uncle Ferdinand II of Tyrol for his even larger "wonder cabinet." Joris Hoefnagel, whose four-volume emblem book of the world's animals begins with the Gonzales family, served as court painter to William V and later to Emperor Rudolf II, whose collection was the most costly in Europe. Rudolf purchased Hoefnagel's emblem book for his collection. The painting of the Gonzales family in it served as a model for the painting of the whole family together probably made by Joris Hoefnagel's son Jacob. This was the first image in a volume of paintings based on the contents of Rudolf II's actual collection, a volume that later acquired the title "The Museum of Rudolf II."

Lavinia Fontana's painting of Antonietta, probably made at the order of the marchesa of Soragna, who owned the little girl, may have been given to the Gonzaga family, the rulers of the Italian city of Mantua. A 1627 inventory of their collection mentions a picture of a "hairy girl." Vincenzo Gonzaga, the reigning duke in the decades around 1600, was a patron of the arts and sciences, and an avid collector of art, music, scientific objects, and the people who made these. He hired the Flemish painter Peter Paul Rubens and the composer Claudio Monteverdi to make works for him, and offered Galileo a position. Vincenzo's uncle Ludovico Gonzaga was the same person who had been a little boy at the French court of Henry II when Petrus Gonzales was also there as a child. Petrus Gonzales and Ludovico Gonzaga were almost exactly the same age, and both were taught Latin by humanist tutors at the French court. It is hard to imagine how Ludovico could not have known about Petrus, although whether he later told his nephew about the little

43. Anton Mozart, *The Presentation of the Pomeranian Art Cabinet to Duke Philipp II of Pomerania, c.* 1615. The artist captures the splendor of the inlaid "cabinet of curiosities," with its doors and drawers both hiding and displaying the collection, as well as the solemnity of the occasion, with the duke and duchess surveying the contents. This cabinet was made in Augsburg, and survived until the Second World War.

hairy boy is not known. The Gonzagas' collection included nature as well as art, and Aldrovandi sought permission to have his painters depict the objects in it for his own collection.

Thus the final world we can see through the story of the Gonzales family, and the one in which they "lived" the longest, was that of collectors, many of whom were directly connected with one another. In the letter accompanying the portrait of Antonietta that Brummano sent to Aldrovandi, he also mentioned "a weird and bizarre snake, as big as a pigeon from Pisa . . . with extravagant colors . . . I believe it has four feet and pinioned wings. In sum, I think I have never seen anything similar. It was killed by a farmer with a shovel four years ago in Naviglio, three miles away from Milan, and then a priest kept it and gave it to the Count Antonio della Somaglia, my magnificent lord, who keeps it among his most precious memories in his studio." Knowing Aldrovandi's interests in the unusual, Brummano tells him, "I think I will send you shortly a portrait of it."[24] The portrait of Antonietta, and actually Antonietta herself, was no different than this portrait of the unusual snake, all of them objects to be possessed, displayed, and exchanged.

Collecting was not a new activity in the sixteenth century. The largest medieval collections were those of religious relics, objects associated with holy figures from the Bible or the saints. Most churches had a few relics, such as bones, articles of clothing, or even the dust from a saint's tomb, which were understood to contain the power of the saints to perform miracles. Wealthy nobles and rulers assembled vast numbers of objects, buying them from dealers, who often disassembled or cut apart existing relics to offer ever more objects. In the late fifteenth century, collectors were increasingly interested in more fantastic relics: a saint's tears or saliva, milk from the Virgin Mary, wood from Noah's ark, and even the foreskin of the baby Jesus, taken when he was circumcised. (There were quite a few of those around Europe.) Their collections became places of pilgrimage, providing both entertainment and spiritual benefit to those who saw the sacred objects. Sometimes the relics were taken on the road, with broadsheets advertising them posted in advance.

The supernatural powers of religious relics were not lost in sixteenth- and seventeenth-century collections. Indeed, many of these collections included religious relics, stuck in among the dried plants, animals in jars, fossils, and music boxes. Other objects were thought to have special powers as well, including unicorns' horns (generally the tusk of a narwhal, an animal unknown in Europe until the seventeenth century), which could prolong life, and bezoars (stones that formed in the intestines of animals, similar to kidney stones), regarded as a universal antidote against poison. Many middle-class collectors were physicians or apothecaries, and their objects contained lots of substances thought to have curative or therapeutic powers.

Not only were the objects themselves thought to have special power, but the relations and connections among them were as well. Collectors organized their items according to resemblances or analogies they saw between one kind of object and another, hoping through this to emphasize the fundamental unity of all creation and the links between the macrocosm and the microcosm. This unity and the macrocosm/microcosm relationship were not simply a matter of natural forces, however, but had supernatural and mystical overtones. As the German Jesuit Athanasius Kircher put it in a phrase painted on the ceiling of his huge cabinet of curiosities in Rome: "Whosoever perceives the *chain* that binds the world below to the world above will know the mysteries of nature and achieve miracles."[25] This chain was not visible to everyone: only to those with enough knowledge to grasp it. Thus collectors often reserved certain parts of their collections to learned visitors, men like themselves who would approach these with the proper spirit and not just gawk.

Objects that crossed or mixed categories appeared to offer particular insight into the links of that chain, which accounted for their popularity in collections. These objects had to be real, however. It was fine to be astonished at how much a tree root looked like a sculpture or a painting fooled the eye, but the astonishment came because visitors knew what these things really were. Two-headed calves created by sewing on an extra head, or dragons created by stitching wings on lizards were not acceptable. Such things were for the vulgar common people to stare at in marketplaces, and were not fit for scholarly musuems or princely palaces.

The portraits of the Gonzales family, copied, recopied, given as gifts, and reworked into new portraits, were ideal for every type of collector. They stood between animal and human, wild and civilized, perfect examples of something that crossed and blended categories. Scholarly authorities such as Scaliger and Aldrovandi vouched for their authenticity, that they were not people wearing bear suits or the product of an artist's imagination. As portraits, they did not have medicinal properties, but they were linked with objects that did. As the *Monstrorum historia* tells it, Aldrovandi's collection also included "part of a wild man's pelt" that could be "worn as a ring for patients suffering convulsions, to their great advantage." That piece of fur, and the tempera paintings of the hairy-headed girl, were transferred to the natural history museum of the city of Bologna after Aldrovandi's death, where the paintings can still be found.

The portraits and descriptions were enough for collectors, and the real family was no longer necessary. Although live human oddities remained standard features of court life, the Gonzales family left the courtly world. In 1602—about the same time that Jacob Hoefnagel was painting the family group for Rudolf II and someone was painting Petrus and one of his daughters for Aldrovandi's villa— Enrico Gonzales, the oldest brother, moved from the Farnese palace in Rome to the tiny village of Capodimonte, not too far from that city. By 1606, Maddalena Gonzales, the oldest sister, and her husband were in Capodimonte as well, for their daughter was confirmed in the church there. In 1608, Petrus, Catherine, Francesca, and Orazio joined them. Orazio occasionally went to Rome, where he held the same minor position at the Farnese court that Enrico had held earlier, but he spent most of his time in Capodimonte. The two brothers married local girls in the village, Enrico four times. Their wives had children, some of whom inherited their fathers' condition, and almost all of whom died young. The brothers never lost their status as oddities and were labeled in legal records, letters, and other documents as "the hairy ones" until their death, the younger brother Orazio dying in 1628 and the older brother Enrico in 1656.

Of the sisters, there is a death record for Francesca, who died the year after her younger brother in Capodimonte. She had never married, and most likely lived in the household of her parents until they died, Petrus in about 1618, Catherine in 1623. After their deaths, she probably lived with one of her brothers, as it was highly unusual for a single woman to live alone in Italy during that era. Her older sister Maddalena's death is not recorded, nor is that of her younger sister Antonietta. In fact, there is no further trace of Antonietta after her visit to Mario Casali's house. Aldrovandi's description of the little girl he saw in 1594 with the cheeks "softer to touch than the rest of her body" and "skin similar to that of an unfledged bird," and Lavinia Fontana's portrait of the same girl from about the same time, are the first and last we hear of her. Her portrait was still being copied a decade later, but the marvelous hairy girl the pictures showed was probably long since dead.

44. Lavinia Fontana, *Portrait of a Gonzales Sister*. Of all of the portraits of the Gonzales sisters, this tiny pencil sketch is the most mysterious. Whom it portrays, when it was made, and why it was done are all unknown, and it is not absolutely certain that the artist was Lavinia Fontana. Despite this uncertainty, it seems to portray a real girl, not a generalized idea.

Afterword

THE MANY STORIES OF THE GONZALES SISTERS

During their lifetime, the Gonzales sisters were fit into many different stories—warnings about God's judgment on the world, tales of monstrous females, praise of the creative powers of nature, legends about wild folk, accounts of exotic wonders in far-away lands, narratives about dangerous beasts and beasts within, fantasies about a mother's imagination, anecdotes about people with odd heads, descriptions of savage peoples in lands newly conquered.

After their deaths, they slipped from view for a while. Most of the cabinets of curiosities and chambers of art and wonders were broken apart in the eighteenth century. The objects in them that were considered high art, especially paintings and sculptures, became the core of the new art museums that were opening in many cities. The natural specimens and scientific instruments were moved to natural history museums. The oddities that had so fascinated people in the sixteenth and seventeenth centuries were now seen as evidence of the lack of sophistication of people of earlier times, their weird "baroque" sensibility now being replaced by an "enlightened" rationality. Many of the oddities were sold, sometimes to traveling shows in which their owners still exhibited them, but now to crowds of ordinary people at markets and fairs who paid a tiny admission fee, rather than to aristocratic guests or visiting scientists. The paintings of the Gonzales family gathered dust, just as the family itself slipped into obscurity, their genetic condition no longer handed down as children died young or became less hairy as the generations passed.

In the late nineteenth century, the family came back into the limelight, but now as examples of terrible skin conditions afflicting humans. Emperor Franz Joseph I ordered copies made of the Ambras paintings in 1872 and gave them to the imperial skin clinic in Vienna, where they hung for many years in a large examination room. German dermatologists wrote scholarly articles about the family, giving their condition the medical terminology we still use to talk about it—*hypertrichosis universalis*—and debating whether it occured in various forms of this. At the same time, German historians were creating what would become modern professional history, using methods they saw as scientific, such as intensive research in archives. These historians were totally uninterested in people like the Gonzales family, however, for "history" was about great men and their ideas, or great leaders and their armies. History was certainly not about hairy people, and even less about hairy *women*. In fact, history was not about any women at all.

In the late twentieth century, the Gonzales family came back into history again. Now they were not simply part of natural history as they had been to scholars like Aldrovandi, but part of many different branches of history: art history, the history of science and medicine, the history of ideas, the history of popular culture and folklore, the history of marginalized groups, the history of human oddities. Their re-emergence is linked with the expansion of history itself, from a largely political and military story to one that explores every aspect of human experience and every type of person: poor and rich, lowly and powerful, female and male. Their story can be, and has been, linked with many things that scholars and readers (or viewers) of history find interesting: freaks and monsters, human–animal relationships, people's search for "identities," or encounters with those who seem different, whether inhabitants of the New World or space aliens. Theories have been developed to help us think about these issues, many of which I have used in this book: feminist theory, post-colonial theory, queer theory, disability theory, and yes, even monster theory.

What this means is that just like people who lived in their own times, we continue to use the Gonzales sisters as a lens to view other things, a way to help us understand the world around us as it was and is. Is this fair? Are we treating them simply as objects, just as the marchesa of Soragna appears to have treated Antonietta? Perhaps. But I have tried as much as possible (and probably more than I should, as a historian and not a novelist) to include some speculations about what they themselves might have thought, how they might have understood the worlds in which they lived. That is as far as we can go, for not one shred of evidence survives from any female member of the family. In that, they are like most girls of humanity's past. But they are more visible than most, and we can do one thing that no one who wrote about them in their own day thought important to do. We can remember them not simply as marvelous hairy girls, but as individuals with names: Maddalena, Francesca, and Antonietta Gonzales.

Notes

Preface: The Gonzales sisters and their worlds

1. Ulissa Aldrovandi, *Monstrorum historia* (Bologna: Typic Nicolai Tebaldini, 1642; repr. Paris: Belles lettres, 2002), p. 18.
2. Matteo Bandello, *Novelle*, cited in James V. Mirollo, "The Aesthetics of the Marvelous: The Wondrous Work of Art in a Wondrous World," in Peter G. Platt, ed., *Wonders, Marvels, and Monsters in Early Modern Culture* (Newark, NJ: University of Delaware Press, 1999), p. 26.

Chapter 1: Wonders, beasts, and wild folk

1. Martin Luther and Philipp Melanchthon, *Deuttung der czwo grewlichen Figuren, Bapstesels czu Rom und Munchkalbs zu Freijberg ijnn Meijsszen funden* (Wittenberg, 1523). My translation.
2. Hans Zimmermann, pamphlets reprinted in Walter L. Strauss, *The German Single Leaf Woodcut 1550–1600*, vol. 3 (New York: Abaris Books, 1975), pp. 1206 and 1207. My translation.
3. Augustine, *City of God*, Book 21, Chapter 8, trans. Gerald G. Walsh, SJ and Daniel J. Honan (Washington, DC: Catholic University Press, 1954), p. 362.
4. Pliny, *Natural History*, trans. H. Rackham. Loeb Classical Library (Cambridge, Mass.: Harvard University Press, 1938), vol. 2, pp. 513, 515, 521, 523.
5. Cited and translated in Zakiha Hanafi, *The Monster in the Machine: Magic, Medicine, and the Marvelous in the Time of the Scientific Revolution* (Durham, NC: Duke University Press, 2000), p. 80.
6. Gerald of Wales, *Topographie Hibernie*, Preface, p. 119, quoted in Lorraine Daston and Katherine Park, *Wonders and the Order of Nature, 1150–1750* (New York: Zone Books, 1998), pp. 25–6.
7. Ranulph Higden, *Polychronicon*, 1.34, quoted in Daston and Park, *Wonders*, p. 25.

8. The 1601 English translation of Pliny made by Philemon Holland is available at: http://penelope.uchicago.edu/holland/index.html
9. *The Travels of Sir John Mandeville*, trans. C.W.R.D. Moseley (London: Penguin Books, 2004), p. 117.
10. Amerigo Vespucci, Account of his First Voyage (1497), at: http://www.fordham.edu/halsall/mod/1497vespucci-america.html
11. Jean de Léry, *History of a Voyage to the Land of Brazil, Otherwise Called America*, trans. Janet Whatley (Berkeley: University of California Press, 1990), p. lxi.
12. Sir Walter Raleigh, *The Discoverie of the large and bewtiful Empire of Guiana*, ed. V.T. Halrow (1596; London: Argonaut Press, 1928), pp. 56–7.
13. Quoted in Léry, *History*, p. xlix.
14. Cited in Anthony Pagden, *The Fall of Natural Man: The American Indians and the Origins of Comparative Ethnology* (Cambridge: Cambridge University Press, 1986), p. 42.
15. Papal bull Sublimus Dei, at http://en.wikisource.org/wiki/Sublimus_Dei
16. The National Library of Medicine website has a digital copy of Gesner's *Historiae animalium* that incorporates the "Turning the Pages" feature by which every page can be seen just as it appears in the book: http://archive.nlm.nih.gov/proj/ttp/books.html
17. Edward Topsell, *Historie of Foure-Footed Beastes* (London, 1607) reprinted in M. St. Clare Byrne, ed. *The Elizabethan Zoo* (Boston: Nonpareil Books, 1979), pp. 101, 104–5.
18. Augustine, *City of God*, Book 16, Chapter 8, trans. Walsh and Honan, p. 502.
19. Bernal Díaz del Castillo, *Historia verdadera de la conquista de la Nueva España*, 1607, quoted in Roger Bartra, *Wild Men in the Looking Glass: The Mythic Origins of European Otherness*, trans. Carl T. Berrisford (Ann Arbor: University of Michigan Press, 1994), pp. 1–2.
20. *Travels of Sir John Mandeville*, trans. Moseley, pp. 137 and 181.
21. Antonio Pigafetta, *The First Voyage around the World*, ed. Theodore J. Cachey, Jr. (New York: Marsilio, 1995), p. 81.
22. Bolzani's work appeared in an anonymous English translation, ascribed to one "Johan Valerian, a great clerke of Italy," as *A Treatise which is Intitled in Latin Pro Sacredotum Barbis* (London, 1533). The quotations are from f. 10r and ff. 17ᵛ–18ʳ.
23. John Bulwer, *Anthropometamorphosis* (London, 1654), pp. 208, 198.
24. More, *A Dialogue of Sir Thomas More, Knight*, quoted in Mark Albert Johnston, "Bearded Women in Early Modern England," *Studies in English Literature* 47 (Winter 2007), p. 18.
25. Pierre d'Ailly, *Imago mundi*, trans. Edwin F. Keever (Wilmington, NC: privately published, 1948), p. 42.
26. Gerald of Wales, *The Journey through Wales/The Description of Wales* (New York: Penguin, 1988), p. 116.
27. *Democrates secundus*, trans. and cited in Pagden, *Fall of Natural Man*, p. 117.
28. Aristotle, *Generation of Animals*, trans. A. L. Peck, Loeb Classics (Cambridge, Mass.: Harvard University Press, 1943), Book IV, vi, p. 460.
29. Valeriano, *Treatise*, f. 10ʳ.
30. Bulwer, *Anthropometamorphosis*, p. 215.

Chapter 2: Myths and histories

1. Avvisi di Roma, in the Biblioteca apostolica vaticana, Urb. Lat., 1063, *c.* 419^r, cited in Roberto Zapperi, "Ein Haarmensch auf einem Gemälde von Agostino Carracci," in Michael Hagner, ed., *Der falsche Körper: Beiträge zur Geschichte der Monstrositäten* (Göttingen: Wallstein Verlag, 1995), p. 45. My translation.
2. Alonso de Espinosa, *The Guanches of Tenerife*, trans. Sir Clements Markham (London: Hakluyt Society, 1907), p. 32.
3. Extract from Columbus' journal, October 1492, at: http://www.fordham.edu/halsall/source/columbus1.html
4. Pliny, *Natural History*, trans. H. Rackham. Loeb Classical Library (Cambridge, Mass.: Harvard University Press, 1938), pp. 2:223.
5. "Periplus of Hanno", in B. H. Warmington, *Carthage* (London: Penguin, 1964), p. 76.
6. Ulisse Aldrovandi, *Monstrorum historia* (Bologna, 1642), p. 16.
7. Pierre d'Ailly, *Imago mundi*, pp. 41, 42.
8. Espinosa, *Guanches*, pp. 33, 39.
9. Quoted in John Mercer, *The Canary Islands: Their Prehistory, Conquest and Survival* (London: Rex Collins, 1980), p. 228.
10. Quoted in ibid., p. 232.
11. See http://www.pbs.org/wgbh/pages/frontline/shows/secret/famous/medici.html

Chapter 3: Massacring beasts, monstrous women, and educated gentlemen

1. Alvarotto's dispatch is in the state archives in Modena, and is reprinted in Roberto Zapperi, *Der wilde Mann von Tenerifa: Die wundersame Geschichte des Pedro Gonzalez und seiner Kinder* (Munich: C.H. Beck, 2004), p. 189. My translation.
2. Ulisse Aldrovandi, *Monstrorum historia* (Bologna, 1642), p. 580.
3. Text of the letter at: http://www.nostradamus-repository.org/letter.html
4. Translated in Mack Holt, *The French Wars of Religion, 1562–1629* (Cambridge: Cambridge University Press, 1995), p. 19.
5. A. Du Val, *Mirouer des Calvinists* (1559), quoted in Luc Racaut, *Hatred in Print: Catholic Propaganda and Protestant Identity during the French Wars of Religion* (Aldershot: Ashgate, 2002), p. 60.
6. Pamphlet, 1564, translated in Holt, *French Wars*, p. 62.
7. Quoted in Barbara Diefendorf, *Beneath the Cross: Catholics and Huguenots in Sixteenth-century Paris* (New York: Oxford University Press, 1991), p. 153.
8. Hotman, *Lettre adressée au Tiger de la France*, in Racaut, *Hatred in Print* p. 73.
9. G. Witzel, *Discourse des moeurs* (1567), quoted in Racaut, *Hatred in Print* p. 91.
10. Translated in David Teasley, "Legends of the Last Valois: A New Look at Propaganda attacking the French Monarchs during the Wars of Religion 1559–1589" (Dissertation, Georgetown University, 1985), p. 104.

11. Protestant martyrology, quoted in Diefendorf, *Beneath the Cross*, p. 101.
12. The quotations are all taken from *The History of the Life of Katharine de Medici, Queen Mother and Regent of France* (London, 1693).
13. http://www.swrb.ab.ca/newslett/actualNLs/firblast.html
14. Anonymous 1636 pamphlet published in London, referring to the royal dwarf Jeffrey Hudson, cited in James Knowles, " 'Can ye not tell a man from a marmoset?': Apes and Others on the Early Modern Stage," in Erica Fudge, ed., *Renaissance Beasts: Of Animals, Humans, and Other Wonderful Creatures* (Urbana: Universtity of Illinois Press, 2004), p. 158.
15. Henry II's entry into Rouen has been analysed in Michael Wintroub, *A Savage Mirror: Power, Identity, and Knowledge in Early Modern France* (Stanford: Stanford University Press, 2006).
16. Abel Jouan, *Recueil et discours du voyage de Charles IX* (Paris, 1566), reprinted in Victor E. Graham and W. McAllister Johnson, *The Royal Tour of France by Charles IX and Catherine de' Medici: Festivals and Entries 1564–6* (Toronto: University of Toronto Press, 1979), pp. 281–2.
17. Thomas More, *Utopia*, trans. Paul Turner (London: Penguin, 1965), pp. 75, 78–9.
18. Ibid., pp. 90, 94.
19. *Ample discours de l'arrivee de la Royne catholique . . .* (Paris, 1565), in Graham and Johnson, *Royal Tour*, p. 304.
20. Jouan, *Recueil*, p. 119.
21. Louise Labé, quoted and translated by Jeanne Prine, in Katharina Wilson, ed., *Women Writers of the Renaissance and Reformation* (Athens: University of Georgia Press, 1987), p. 149.

Chapter 4: The sanctity of marriage, the marvel of birth

1. Copy of a letter from William V to Archduchess Maria, April 3, 1583, Bavarian State Archives, Munich, Geheimes Hausarchiv, Korrespondenzakten 606 V, fol. 212v, reproduced in Roberto Zapperi, *Der wilde Mann von Teneriffa: Der wundersame Geschichte des Pedro Gonzales und seiner Kinder* (Munich: C.H. Beck, 2004), pp. 194–5. My translation.
2. *D. Martin Luthers Werke: Kritische Gesamtausgabe. Tischreden* (Weimar: 1883—), vol. 4, no. 4474, p. 332.
3. Ambroise Paré, *On Monsters and Marvels*, trans. Janis L. Pallister (Chicago: University of Chicago Press, 1982), p. 43.
4. *Luther's Works*, vol. 5, ed. Jaroslav Pelikan (St. Louis, MO: Concordia, 1968), p. 382.
5. Ibid., p. 38.
6. Martin Luther, Lectures on Genesis, in *Luther's Works* (Concordia edn.), vol. 5, p. 381.
7. *"Mother and Child Were Saved": The Memoirs (1693–1740) of the Frisian Midwife Catharine Schrader*, trans. and annotated by Hilary Marland (Amsterdam: Rodopi, 1987), pp. 62–3, 76.
8. John Maubray, *The Female Physician* (London, 1724), pp. 62–3.
9. Quillet's poem was first published after his death in a French translation, *La Callipedie ou l'art d'avoir de beaux enfans* (Paris, 1655), and only later in its Latin original. This translation comes from the 1749 French edition, as

cited in Jacques Gélis, *History of Childbirth: Fertility, Pregnancy and Birth in Early Modern Europe*, trans. Rosemary Morris (Boston: Northeastern University Press, 1991), p. 54.

10. Ibid., p. 38.

11. Montaigne, *The Complete Essays of Montaigne*, trans. Donald M. Frame (Stanford: Stanford University Press, 1958), Book I, Essay 21: "Of the Power of Imagination."

12. See Mary Fissell, "Hairy Women and Naked Truths: Gender and the Politics of Knowledge in *Aristotle's Masterpiece*," *William and Mary Quarterly* 60/1 (January 2003).

13. Pierre Boaistuau, *Histoires prodigieuses*, trans. and cited in Marie–Hélène Huet, *Monstrous Imagination* (Cambridge, Mass.: Harvard University Press, 1993), p. 21.

14. Memmingen Stadtarchiv, Hebammen, 406, no. 22 (1625).

15. Munich Stadtarchiv, Zimilien, no. 41 (Eidbuch 1488).

16. Frankfurt Stadtarchiv, Eidbuch, vol. 2, no. 240 (1509).

17. *Statuts et Reglements ordonnez pour toutes les Matronnes, ou Sage femmes de la Ville, Fauxbourgs, Prevosté, et Vicomté de Paris* (Paris, n.d.), pp. 3,8, 9, trans. and quoted in Wendy Perkins, *Midwifery and Medicine in Early Modern France: Louise Bourgeois* (Exeter: University of Exeter Press, 1996), pp. 3, 4, 5.

18. Memmingen Stadtarchiv, Hebammen, 406, no. 1.

19. Strasbourg Archives municipales, Statuten, vol. 7, fol. 19 and vol. 33, no. 75.

20. Nuremberg, Germanisches Nationalmuseum, "Schuld und Rechnungsbuch Dr. Christoph Scheurl," fol. 10. My translation.

21. Louise Bourgeois, *Observations divers* (Paris, 1609, 1617, 1626), vol. 2, pp. 225–6, 233 trans. and quoted in Perkins, *Midwifery and Medicine*, pp. 56, 57.

22. Bourgeois, *Observations divers*, vol. 1, 97, cited in Perkins, *Midwifery and Medicine,* p. 57.

23. Bourgeois, *Observations divers*, vol. 2, 233, cited in Perkins, *Midwifery and Medicine*, p. 62.

24. Ulisse Aldrovandi, *Monstrorum historia* (Bologna, 1642), p. 473.

Chapter 5: God's miraculous creation

1. Hoefnagel's Bible quotations are all in Latin, and most come from the Vulgate, the official Catholic Bible in his day. I have used the Douay-Rheims translations, made by English Catholics, the Old Testament of which was first published in 1609. Chapter and verse citations given are those in the Vulgate; they sometimes differ slightly from those in modern Bible translations.

2. Edward Topsell, *Historie of Foure-Footed Beastes* (London, 1607), in M. St. Clare Byrne, ed., *The Elizabethan Zoo* (London: F. Etchells & H. McDonald, 1926), pp. 88, 89–90.

3. Cited in David Cressy, *Agnes Bowker's Cat: Travesties and Transgressions in Tudor and Stuart England* (New York: Oxford University Press, 2000), p. 40.

4. Luca Landucci, *A Florentine Diary from 1450 to 1516 by Luca Landucci, Continued by an Anonymous Writer till 1542 with Notes by Iodoco Del Badia*, trans. Alice de Rosen Jervis (New York: E.P. Dutton, 1927), cited in

Lorraine Daston and Katherine Park, *Wonders and the Order of Nature, 1150–1750* (New York: Zone Books, 1998), p. 177.

5. Johannes Multivallis Tornacensis' continuation of the chronicle of Eusebius of Caesarea, in *Eusebii Caesarensis episcopi chronicon* (Paris: Henri Estienne, 1512), fol. 175ʳ⁻ᵛ, cited in Daston and Park, *Wonders*, p. 182.

6. Conrad Lycosthenes, *Prodigiorum ac ostentorum chronicon* (Basel: H. Petri, 1557), dedicatory epistle, in Daston and Park, *Wonders*, p. 183.

7. Edward Fenton, *Certaine Secrete Wonders of Nature, containing a description of sundry strange things, seeming monstrous . . .* (London, 1569) (translation of Pierre Boaistuau, *Histoires prodigieuses . . .*) cited in Dudley Wilson, *Signs and Portents: Monstrous Births from the Middle Ages to the Enlightenment* (London: Routledge, 1993), p. 53.

8. Printed in Joseph Lilly, ed., *A Collection of 79 Black Letters, Ballads and Broadsides, Printed in the Reign of Queen Elizabeth, between the Years 1559 and 1597* (London: Lilly, 1867), p. 203.

9. Jennifer Spinks, "Monstrous Births and Counter-Reformation Visual Polemics: Johann Nass and the 1569 *Ecclesia Militans*," *Sixteenth Century Journal*, forthcoming.

10. Montaigne, *The Complete Essays of Montaigne*, trans. Donald M. Frame (Stanford: Stanford University Press, 1958), Book II, Essay 30, p. 539.

11. Cited in Erica Fudge, *Brutal Reasoning: Animals, Rationality, and Humanity in Early Modern England* (Ithaca, NY: Cornell University Press, 2006), p. 2.

12. John Woolton, *A Newe Anatomie of the Whole Man . . .* (London: Thomas Purfoote, 1576), cited in Fudge, *Brutal Reasoning*, p. 12. Emphasis in the original.

13. [Thomas Rogers], *A philosophicall discourse*, sig. 162ʳ cited in Fudge, *Brutal Reasoning*, p. 15.

14. Vicary, *A Profitable Treatise of the Anatomie of Mans Body* (London, 1548, repr. Henry Bamforde, 1577), sig. M4ʳ⁻ᵛ, cited in Fudge, *Brutal Reasoning*, p. 43.

15. [Thomas Wright], *The Passions of the Mind* (London, 1601), p. 12, cited in Fudge, *Brutal Reasoning*, p. 47.

16. John Moore, *A Mappe of Mans Mortalitie* (London, 1617), p. 43.

17. George Gascoigne, *A Delicate Diet, for Daintie Mouthde Droonkardes* (London, 1576), iv, cited in Fudge, *Brutal Reasoning*, p. 62.

18. Thomas Young, *Englands Bane: Or, The Description of Drunkennesse* (London: William Jones, 1617), sig. F2ᵛ⁻ʳ, cited in Fudge, *Brutal Reasoning*, pp. 63–4.

19. Juan Luis Vives, *The Passions of the Soul*, trans. Carlos G. Noreña (Lampeter: Edwin Mellen, 1990), p. 92.

20. Claude Prieur, *Dialogue de la lyncanthropie* (Paris, 1596), cited in Nicole Jacques-Lefèvre, "Such an Impure, Cruel, and Savage Beast: Images of the Werewolf in Demonological Texts," in Kathryn A. Edwards, ed., *Werewolves, Witches, and Wandering Spirits: Traditional Belief and Folklore in Early Modern Europe* (Kirksville, MO: Truman State University Press, 2002), p. 197.

21. Augustine, *City of God*, trans. Henry Bettenson (Harmondsworth, Middx: Penguin, 1972), Book XIV, 16, p. 577.

22. Thomas Aquinas, *Summa Theologica*, trans. the English Dominican Fathers (New York: Benzigen Brothers, 1947), Q. 28, 2, pp. 493–4.

23. Martin Luther, *Sermon on Genesis*, 1527, trans. in Susan C. Karant-Nunn and Merry E. Wiesner-Hanks, *Luther on Women: A Sourcebook* (Cambridge: Cambridge University Press, 2003), pp. 18, 19.

24. Martin Luther, Lectures on Genesis, in *Luther's Works*, ed. Jaroslav Pelikan (St Louis: Concordia, 1958), vol. 1, p. 71.
25. Dorothy Leigh, *The Mother's Blessing* (London, 1637), pp. 38–9 and 44.
26. Translated in Teasley, "Legends of the Last Valois", pp. 132–3.
27. Quoted in Cressy, *Agnes Bowker's Cat*, p. 40.
28. Quoted in Wilson, *Signs and Portents*, p. 56.
29. Martin Luther, wedding sermon from 1531, trans. in Karant-Nunn and Wiesner-Hanks, *Luther on Women*, p. 153.
30. Aristotle, *The Politics*, at: http://www.constitution.org/ari/polit_01.html
31. Luther, Lectures on Genesis, in *Luther's Works*, ed. Pelikan, vol. 1, pp. 115, 151.
32. Martin Luther, Tabletalk, trans. in Karant-Nunn and Wiesner-Hanks, *Luther on Women*, pp. 28–9.
33. Church of England, *The Two Books of Homilies* (Oxford, 1859), p. 505.
34. The best survey of this controversy is in Manfred P. Fleischer, " 'Are Women Human?' The Debate of 1595 between Valens Acidalius and Simon Geddicus," *Sixteenth Century Journal* 12/2 (Summer 1981): 107–20.

Chapter 6: Medical marvels and cabinets of curiosities

1. Felix Platter, *Observationum Felicis Plateri . . . libri tres* (Basilea 1680), Lib. III, p. 572.
2. Ulisse Aldrovandi, *Monstrorum historia* (Bologna, 1642), p. 16.
3. *Beloved Son Felix: The Journal of Felix Platter, a Medical Student in Montpellier in the Sixteenth Century*, trans. Seán Jennett (London: Frederick Muller, 1961), p. 50.
4. Ibid., p. 53.
5. Ibid., p. 56.
6. Ibid., p. 59.
7. Ibid., p. 70.
8. Ibid., p. 50.
9. Ibid., p. 88.
10. Ibid., p.126.
11. Ibid., pp. 89–90.
12. Ibid., pp. 106–7.
13. Felix Platter, *Observationes: Krankheitsbeobachtungen in drei Bücher*, translated from Latin into German by Günther Goldschmidt (Bern and Stuttgart: Hans Huber, 1963), p. 78. My translation.
14. Platter, *Observationum*, p. 572.
15. Digital versions of each page in his herbarium can be seen at: http://www.sma.unibo.it/erbario/erbarioaldrovandi.html
16. http://www.sma.unibo.it/ortobotanico/
17. University Library of Bologna, Aldrovandi Foundation, Ms 136, Tomo XVI, cc. 271ᵛ–272ᵛ, reprinted in Attilio Zanca, "In teme di *hypertrichosis universalis congenita*: contributo storico-medico," *Physis* 25 (1983), pp. 65–6. My translation.
18. Aldrovandi, *Monstrorum historia*, pp. 16–18.
19. Ibid., p. 473.
20. Ibid., p. 580.
21. Cited in Daston and Park, *Wonders and the Order of Nature*, p. 222.

22. Cited in ibid., p. 228.
23. Johannes Kepler, *The Harmony of the World* (1619), trans. E.J. Aiton, A.M. Duncan, and J.V. Field, *Memoirs of the American Philosophical Society*, vol. 209 (Philadelphia: American Philosophical Society, 1997), p. 304.
24. University Library of Bologna, Aldrovandi Foundation, Ms 136, Tomo XVI, cc. 271ᵛ–272ᵛ, reprinted in Attilio Zanca, "In teme di *hypertrichosis universalis congenita*," pp. 65–6.
25. Cited in Patrick Mauriès, *Cabinets of Curiosities* (London: Thames and Hudson, 2002), p. 34.

Acknowledgments and Further Reading

The Gonzales family crossed many borders, both geographic and theoretical, so writing about them meant venturing into new territories for me as well. For their help on this adventure I would first like to thank my editor at Yale, Heather McCallum, who initially suggested I write a book like this, and to the anonymous readers for Yale, who offered valuable advice at several stages. Joy Reeber, Stella Lineri, Carlos Galvão–Sobrinho, Martha Carlin, Peter Matheson and Kay Edwards provided assistance with translations and suggestions for reading in the fields in which they are far more knowledgable than I am. My deepest thanks go to my colleagues and friends Mary Delgado and Jeffrey Merrick, who read every word of the text, sometimes more than once, and helped me with everything from conceptual framework to word choice.

The Gonzales family and their portraits have been examined in scholarly articles in art history, medical history, anthropology, the history of freaks and marvels, folklore, the history of science, genetics, and ethnography. They show up in popular books about freaks, and on websites and blogs about art, human abnormalities, hair, and other topics. A painting of a Gonzales sister has been featured on the covers of several recent books, including Lorraine Daston and Katherine Park, *Wonders and the Order of Nature, 1150–1750* (New York: Zone Books, 1998) and the hardcover version of Armand Leroi, *Mutants:*

On Genetic Variety and the Human Body (New York: Viking, 2003). In both of these books and many of the articles and websites, however, the discussion of the Gonzales family is slight. The only extended discussion of the family is Roberto Zapperi, *Il selvaggio gentiluomo: l'incredibile storia di Pedro Gonzales e dei suoi figli* (Rome: Donzelli, 2004), which has been translated into German and Spanish, but not English. The suggestions for further reading below include only materials in English, but the scholarly studies mentioned can guide you to materials in other languages.

Chapter 1   Wonders, beasts, and wild folk

There are many recent studies of ideas about wonders and marvels in the Renaissance and early modern period. Daston and Park's *Wonders and the Order of Nature* is the best place to begin for a broad and deep overview. Peter G. Platt, ed., *Wonders, Marvels, and Monsters in Early Modern Culture* (Newark: University of Delaware Press, 1999), Timothy S. Jones and David A. Sprunger, eds., *Marvels, Monsters, and Miracles: Studies in the Medieval and Early Modern Imaginations* (Kalamazoo, Mich.: Medieval Institute, 2002), and Laura Lunger Knoppers and Joan B. Landes, eds., *Monstrous Bodies/Political Monstrosities in Early Modern Europe* (Ithaca, NY: Cornell University Press, 2004) all contain articles by scholars in a range of fields. Ottavia Niccoli, *Prophecy and People in Renaissance Italy* (Princeton, NJ: Princeton University Press, 1990) and William E. Burns, *An Age of Wonders: Prodigies, Politics and Providence in England 1657–1727* (Manchester: Manchester University Press, 2002) offer specialized examinations of specific countries. For ideas about how to think about the monstrous, see Jeffrey Jerome Cohen, ed., *Monster Theory: Reading Culture* (Minneapolis: University of Minnesota Press, 1996).

Richard Bernheimer, *Wild Men in the Middle Ages: A Study in Art, Sentiment, and Demonology* (Cambridge, Mass.: Harvard University Press, 1952), Edward Dudley and Maximillian E. Novak, *The Wild Man Within: An Image in Western Thought from the Renaissance to Romanticism* (Pittsburgh: University of Pittsburgh Press, 1973), and

Roger Bartra, *Wild Men in the Looking Glass: The Mythic Origins of European Otherness*, trans. Carl T. Berrisford (Ann Arbor: University of Michigan Press, 1994) provide extensive information about European ideas about wild folk. Charlotte F. Otten, ed., *Werewolves in Western Culture: A Lycanthropy Reader* (Syracuse, NY: Syracuse University Press, 1986) has excellent original sources on werewolves, and the best discussion of their role in European culture.

For issues surrounding gender and hair in the Renaissance, see Will Fisher, "The Renaissance Beard: Masculinity in Early Modern England," *Renaissance Quarterly* 54 (Spring 2001): 155–87 and the chapter on beards in his *Materializing Gender in Early Modern English Literature and Culture* (Cambridge: Cambridge University Press, 2006). On hairy women, see: Carole Levin, "St Fridiswide and St Uncumber: Changing Images of Female Saints in Renaissance England," in Mary E. Burke, et al., eds., *Women, Writing, and the Reproduction of Culture in Tudor and Stuart Britain* (Syracuse, NY: Syracuse University Press, 2000), pp. 223–37; Mary Fissell, "Hairy Women and Naked Truths: Gender and the Politics of Knowledge in *Aristotle's Masterpiece*," *William and Mary Quarterly* 60/1 (January 2003): 43–74; and Mark Albert Johnston, "Bearded Women in Early Modern England," *Studies in English Literature*, 47 (Winter 2007): 1–28.

Chapter 2 Myths and histories

Over the last several decades, scholars in many fields have written on contacts between Europeans and peoples elsewhere in the world in the era surrounding the voyages of Columbus. These are often conceptualized as "encounters with the other." On this, see Urs Bitterli, *Cultures in Conflict: Encounters between European and Non-European Cultures, 1492–1800*, trans. Ritchie Robertson (New York: Polity Press, 1989); Jerry Bentley, *Old World Encounters: Cross-Cultural Contacts and Exchanges in Pre-Modern Times* (New York: Oxford University Press, 1993); O. R. Dathorne, *Imagining the World: Mythical Belief versus Reality in Global Encounters* (Westport, CT: Bergin and Garvey, 1994); and Stuart Schwarz, ed., *Implicit Understandings: Observing, Reporting and Reflecting on the Encounters between Europeans and Other Peoples in the Early Modern Era* (Cambridge: Cambridge University Press, 1994).

Two fine surveys of European exploration and colonization are Felipe Fernández-Armesto, *Before Columbus: Exploration and Colonization from the Mediterranean to the Atlantic, 1229–1492* (London: Macmillan Education, 1987) and Geoffrey Vaughn Scammell, *The First Imperial Age: European Overseas Expansion, c. 1400–1715* (London: Unwin Hyman, 1989). On the Canary Islands specifically, see John Mercer, *The Canary Islands: Their Prehistory, Conquest and Survival* (London: Rex Collins, 1980) and Felipe Fernández-Armesto, *The Canary Islands after the Conquest: The Making of a Colonial Society in the Early Sixteenth Century* (Oxford: Clarendon Press, 1982).

Voyages to the Americas had a particularly strong impact on Europeans' sense of their history and their place in the world relative to others. For discussions of New World voyages from the point of view of literary critics, see Stephen Greenblatt, *Marvelous Possessions: The Wonder of the New World* (Chicago: University of Chicago Press, 1991) and Anthony Pagden, *European Encounters with the New World: From Renaissance to Romanticism* (New Haven: Yale University Press, 1993). From the point of view of historians, see J.H. Elliott, *The Old World and the New, 1492–1650* (Cambridge: Cambridge University Press, 1972) and Roger Schlesinger, *In the Wake of Columbus: The Impact of the New World on Europe, 1492–1650* (Wheeling, Ill.: Harlan Davidson, 1996). From the point of view of art historians, see John F. Moffitt and Santiago Sebastián, *O Brave New People: The European Invention of the American Indian* (Albuquerque: University of New Mexico Press, 1996).

Stephen Greenblatt's *Renaissance Self-Fashioning: From More to Shakespeare* (Chicago: University of Chicago Press, 1980) has been the most influential analysis of the way people in the Renaissance fashioned new identities for themselves. His focus of study was learned men, but Natalie Zemon Davis has broadened this. In her *Fiction in the Archives: Pardon Tales and their Tellers in Sixteenth-Century France* (Stanford, Calif.: Stanford University Press, 1987), she provides examples of the way people accused of serious crimes fashioned stories about themselves and their actions to gain pardons from the king, and in *The Return of Martin Guerre* (Cambridge, Mass: Harvard University Press, 1984), she examines the life of the most famous impostor of the sixteenth century.

For the perspectives of artists who painted the Gonzales family, see Barry Wind, *"A Foul and Pestilent Congregation": Images of "Freaks" in Baroque Art* (Aldershot: Ashgate, 1998), Christiane Hertel, "Hairy Issues: Portraits of Petrus Gonsalus and his Family in Archduke Ferdinand II's *Kunstkammer* and their Contexts," *Journal of the History of Collections* 13 (2001): 1–22 and Caroline P. Murphy, *Lavinia Fontana: A Painter and her Patrons in Sixteenth-century Bologna* (New Haven:Yale University Press, 2003). These studies are based on older scholarship about the Gonzales family, however, and include some details about their lives that are most likely not accurate. Louise Hawes, *The Vanishing Point* (Boston: Houghton Mifflin, 2004) is a fictionalized biography of Lavinia Fontana designed for young adults.

Chapter 3 Massacring beasts, monstrous women, and educated gentlemen

Mack Holt, *The French Wars of Religion, 1562–1629* (Cambridge: Cambridge University Press, 1995) is a thorough and insightful analysis of the political, religious, and social issues involved in this bloody episode in French history. Barbara Diefendorf, *Beneath the Cross: Catholics and Huguenots in Sixteenth-century Paris* (New York: Oxford University Press, 1991) provides a close look at religious conflicts in the French capital, and Luc Racaut, *Hatred in Print: Catholic Propaganda and Protestant Identity during the French Wars of Religion* (Aldershot:Ashgate, 2002) offers a more detailed study of the venom that fueled those conflicts. Robert M. Kingdon, *Myths about the St. Bartholomew's Day Massacres, 1572–1576* (Cambridge, Mass.: Harvard University Press, 1988) examines the way in which stories told and written about the massacre further fueled religious hatred.

Two good recent biographies of Catherine de Medici are R.J. Knecht, *Catherine de' Medici* (London: Longman, 1998) and Leonie Frieda, *Catherine de' Medici: Renaissance Queen of France* (New York: HarperCollins, 2003).

Lisa Hopkins, *Women Who Would Be Kings: Female Rulers of the Sixteenth Century* (London: St Martin's Press, 1991) and Sharon L. Jansen, *The Monstrous Regiment of Women: Female Rulers in Early Modern Europe* (New York: Palgrave, 2002) analyse the debate about female rulers. Amanda Shephard, *Gender and Authority in Sixteenth-century England: The Knox Debate* (Keele: Keele University Press, 1994) provides a closer look at the best-known part of that debate.

John Adamson, ed., *The Princely Courts of Europe: Ritual, Politics and Culture Under the Ancien Régime 1500–1750* (London: Weidenfeld & Nicolson, 1999) provides fascinating studies of various courts, with many illustrations, and Regina Schulte, ed., *The Body of the Queen: Gender and Rule in the Courtly World from the 15th to the 20th Century* (New York: Berghahn, 2005) includes essays that discuss gender in many of those courts. Victor E. Graham and W. McAllister Johnson, *The Royal Tour of France by Charles IX and Catherine de' Medici: Festivals and Entries 1564–6* (Toronto: University of Toronto Press, 1979) examines the most extensive royal tour of the sixteenth century. Charles G. Nauert, Jr., *Humanism and the Culture of Renaissance Europe* (Cambridge: Cambridge University Press, 1995) provides a thorough introduction to humanism, and Margaret King, *Women of the Renaissance* (Chicago: University of Chicago Press, 1991) a thought-provoking analysis of the position of humanist women.

Chapter 4 The sanctity of marriage, the marvel of birth

Michael Mitterauer and Reinhard Sieder, *The European Family: Patriarchy and Partnership from the Middle Ages to the Present*, trans. Karla Oosterveen and Manfred Horzinger (Chicago: University of Chicago Press, 1982) and Beatrice Gottlieb, *The Family in the Western World: From the Black Death to the Industrial Age* (New York: Oxford University Press, 1993) present useful introductions to family life in Europe over broad time periods. Both of these books cover the debate about whether families were unfeeling and cold or supportive and warm. Linda Pollock, *Forgotten Children: Parent–Child Relations from 1500 to 1900* (Cambridge: Cambridge University

Press, 1983) includes many examples of parents who cared deeply about their children. The essays in André Buguière, et al., eds., *A History of the Family*, 2 vols (Cambridge, Mass.: Harvard University Press, 1996) provide insight into Renaissance and early modern families in different parts of Europe. Martha C. Howell, *The Marriage Exchange: Property, Social Place, and Gender in the Cities of the Low Countries, 1300–1500* (Chicago: University of Chicago Press, 1998) explores the social and economic aspects of marriage.

Jacques Gélis, *History of Childbirth: Fertility, Pregnancy and Birth in Early Modern Europe*, trans. Rosemary Morris (Boston: Northeastern University Press, 1991) examines beliefs as well as practices regarding pregnancy and birth, while Jacqueline Marie Musacchio, *The Art and Ritual of Childbirth in Renaissance Italy* (New Haven: Yale University Press, 1999) looks at visual representations of childbirth. Hilary Marland, ed., *The Art of Midwifery: Early Modern Midwives in Europe* (London: Routledge, 1993) includes essays focusing on different areas of Europe. Wendy Perkins, *Midwifery and Medicine in Early Modern France: Louise Bourgeois* (Exeter: University of Exeter Press, 1996) presents a thorough study of the life and works of the best-known sixteenth-century French midwife.

The maternal imagination and the monstrous births that could result from it have been examined in Dudley Wilson, *Signs and Portents: Monstrous Births from the Middle Ages to the Enlightenment* (London: Routledge, 1993); Marie-Hélène Huet, *Monstrous Imagination* (Cambridge, Mass.: Harvard University Press, 1993); A.W. Bates, *Emblematic Monsters: Unnatural Conceptions and Deformed Births in Early Modern Europe* (Amsterdam: Editions Rodopi, 2005); and Julie Crawford, *Marvelous Protestantism: Monstrous Births in Post-Reformation England* (Baltimore, MD: Johns Hopkins University Press, 2005).

Chapter 5   God's miraculous creation

Joris Hoefnagel's emblem book has been studied in Marjorie Lee Hendrix, "Elementa depicta: Joris Hoefnagels' *The Four Elements*," *FMR: The Magazine of Franco Maria Ricci* 9 (1985): 77–92 and Lee Hendrix, "Of Hirsutes and Insects: Joris Hoefnagel and the Art of the Wondrous," *Word & Image* 11 (1995): 373–90. For emblem books more generally, see Daniel Russell, *Emblematic Structures in Renaissance French Culture* (Toronto: University of Toronto Press, 1995).

For ideas about the macrocosm/ microcosm in the Renaissance, see Paul Oskar Kristeller, *Renaissance Thought and its Sources* (New York: Columbia University Press, 1979) and the old, but still useful, George Perrigo Conger, *Theories of Macrocosms and Microcosms in the History of Philosophy* (New York: Columbia University Press, 1922).

Peter Limm, *The Dutch Revolt 1559–1648* (London: Longman, 1989) provides a brief introduction to the Dutch religious wars, and Geoffrey Parker, *The Dutch Revolt* (London: Penguin, revised edition 1990) is a more detailed analysis. There are no histories of Bavaria or its Wittelsbach rulers in this period available in English, but Ulrike Strasser, *State of Virginity: Politics, Religion, and Gender in a German Catholic Polity* (Ann Arbor: University of Michigan Press, 2004) includes discussion of the religious policies of the fervently Catholic dukes. Good general surveys of the Catholic Reformation include Michael A. Mullett, *The Catholic Reformation* (London: Routledge, 1999), and R. Po-chia Hsia, *The World of Catholic Renewal, 1540–1770* (Cambridge: Cambridge University Press, 1998).

On ideas about animals in the Renaissance, the work of Erica Fudge has been especially important, including Erica Fudge, ed., *Renaissance Beasts: Of Animals, Humans, and Other Wonderful Creatures* (Urbana: University of Illinois Press, 2004) and Erica Fudge, *Brutal Reasoning: Animals, Rationality, and Humanity in Early Modern England* (Ithaca, NY: Cornell University Press, 2006). Joyce E. Salisbury, *The Beast Within: Animals in the Middle Ages* (New York: Routledge, 1994) provides an excellent discussion of an earlier period. For ideas about women, see Merry E. Wiesner-Hanks, *Women and Gender in Early Modern Europe* (Cambridge: Cambridge University Press, 3rd edition 2009).

Chapter 6 Medical marvels and cabinets of curiosities

Patrick Mauriès, *Cabinets of Curiosities* (London: Thames and Hudson, 2002) and Oliver Impey and Arthur MacGregor, eds., *The*

Origins of Museums: The Cabinet of Curiosities in Sixteenth and Seventeeth-century Europe (Oxford: Clarendon Press, 1985) discuss collections and collectors, and have fabulous color illustrations. Paula Findlen, *Possessing Nature: Museums, Collecting, and Scientific Culture in Early Modern Italy* (Berkeley: University of California Press, 1994) and David Freedberg, *The Eye of the Lynx: Galileo, his Friends, and the Beginnings of Modern Natural History* (Chicago: University of Chicago Press, 2003) investigate the role of collection in the early development of science.

There are many studies of science and natural history in this era. Peter Dear's *Revolutionizing the Sciences: European Knowledge and its Ambitions, 1500–1700* (Princeton, NJ: Princeton University Press, 2001) is a good place to start. Charles Webster, *From Paracelsus to Newton: Magic and the Making of Modern Science* (Cambridge: Cambridge University Press, 1982), Mary Baine Campbell, *Wonder and Science: Imagining Worlds in Early Modern Europe* (Ithaca, NY: Cornell University Press, 1999), and Zakiha Hanafi, *The Monster in the Machine: Magic, Medicine, and the Marvelous in the Time of the Scientific Revolution* (Durham, NC: Duke University Press, 2000) pay particular attention to the role of magic and wonder in early modern science. Brian W. Ogilvie, *The Science of Describing: Natural History in Renaissance Europe* (Chicago: University of Chicago Press, 2006) examines the way that descriptions gradually became ways of classifying knowledge and understanding the world. The essays in Pamela H. Smith and Paula Findlen, eds., *Merchants and Marvels: Commerce, Science, and Art in Early Modern Europe* (New York: Routledge, 2002) focus on the economic and social context of art and science, and the close relations between art and science.

Index